Life of Edward H. Rollins; a political biography

James Otis Lyford

LIFE OF EDWARD H. ROLLINS

LIFE OF
EDWARD H. ROLLINS

A Political Biography

BY

JAMES O. LYFORD

BOSTON
DANA ESTES & COMPANY
PUBLISHERS

Copyright, 1906

BY DANA ESTES & COMPANY

———

Colonial Press
Electrotyped and Printed by C. H. Simonds & Co.
Boston, U. S. A.

PREFACE

———◆———

For nearly seventy-five years after the government was founded, the principal gateway of political preferment was through training at the bar. When in the fifties slavery agitation broke the solidarity of old political parties, it brought to the front new leaders. It was not the men of the legal profession, trained as they were to respect precedent, who were first moved, as a rule, to break away from party ties and embark in a movement which promised neither political emolument nor honor. Therefore, it occurred that voices hitherto silent and men unaccustomed to lead came or were forced to the front to give utterance and direction to the crusade against slavery. They stepped from all walks of life. They were tribunes of the people. They spoke as they were moved to speak by the intensity of their feelings, and they began the organization of their scattered forces into an aggressive army which they led through successive defeats to final victory.

Coöperating with Lincoln, Seward, Chase, Sumner, and Hale, intellectual giants trained for the bar, there were, from other callings, such men as Henry Wilson, Nathaniel P. Banks, Zachariah Chandler, Justin S.

v

Morrill, Simon Cameron, and Edward H. Rollins;
men who in their respective States did the great work
of detail so essential to the success of any onward
movement. If they were not leaders in enunciating
principles and debating constitutional questions, they
were great lieutenants in mobilizing and marshalling
the people for the contest. They directed the political campaigns of their States, and they were advisers
whose counsel was sought in national contests. It was
such men as these who were drawn to the support of
Lincoln in preference to Seward at the National Republican Convention of 1860, who sustained the President during the trying war period, who represented
the business interests of the country, who assisted in
shaping national platforms, and whose help was vitally
essential in those days of peril.

With the triumph of the Republican party, these
men came to share in political honors, and many of
them sooner or later were sent to represent the people
in the national House or Senate. Their services were
useful and patriotic, and their judgment important
to the cause they had at heart. They were practical
men and men of affairs. They helped to shape legislation. They kept in touch with the public pulse.
They were active both at Washington and at home.
They were indefatigable workers. They inspired war
meetings. They looked after the comfort of the
soldiers. They reconciled differences in the party, and
they were serviceable in many unrecorded ways.

As history is now written, it does not focus wholly

on the central stars of any era, but is distributed over all the people. The initiative and execution of able lieutenants and the thoughts and responses of those in the ranks are often essential to the correct understanding of the period under consideration.

To tell of one having a political career beginning at the birth of the Republican party, identified for a generation with the victories of that party in New Hampshire, for years managing its political campaigns, possessing the confidence of Lincoln, Stanton, and other great leaders of that epoch, rising by the force of his own personality to the highest political honors of his State, successively Speaker of the New Hampshire legislature, member of Congress for three terms, and United States Senator, is to summarize the political history of the State for a most interesting period.

The life of Edward H. Rollins is written, therefore, along the line of his activities. Consequently, the political campaigns from 1855 to 1883, of which he was a prominent factor, have been given in brief outline. This helps to a proper understanding of his career, besides affording opportunity for collecting and preserving facts connected with the political history of New Hampshire for this period which, except for a work of this kind, are not likely to be gathered together. So far as the scope of this work would permit, a side-light is thrown upon Rollins's contemporaries, both Republicans and Democrats. In doing this, opinion has been more freely expressed about those whose life-work, like his own, is completed. If Rollins appears as the central figure, it is because it is his biography that is being written, and not the history of the Republican party of New Hampshire. It has not been the purpose to accord him a position beyond his deserts or to minimize the part of others in the politics of the State during a very eventful period of our history.

Edward H. Rollins was the architect of his own career. For the most part he was self-instructed. The best of his years were spent in the public service. The State of New Hampshire was his pride, and to her interests he devoted a large part of his life.

It was the privilege of the writer to be intimately associated with Senator Rollins during the later years of his activity both in New Hampshire and at the capital of the nation, and through early interest and participation in the political affairs of the Granite State to have met personally most of his contemporaries. This intimacy extended as well to the Rollins's family life. It is gratifying to find that the impression formed of him as a public man and a citizen during those earlier years is confirmed by this later review of the period in which he lived. It is largely from appreciation of his services to the State which gave him birth that this biography is undertaken. There has been no attempt to eulogize him, but rather to present to the reader the story of an eventful epoch in New Hampshire, with the conviction that the recital of Senator Rollins's part therein will prove to be the strongest tribute that can be paid to him.

CONTENTS

LIST OF ILLUSTRATIONS

LIFE OF EDWARD H. ROLLINS

—◆—

CHAPTER I.

THE TIMES AND THE LEADER

FEW of the generation now active in politics have
nowledge of the important position occupied by New
Jampshire in the political contests of the country for
early a quarter of a century succeeding the birth of
he Republican party. Her elections were annual until
878. Occurring the second Tuesday of March, they
vere the first in the year, and therefore regarded as
n index of popular feeling. During all this period
he State was closely contested by the Republican and
Democratic parties. The result being in doubt until
he votes were counted, the eyes of the whole country
vere fixed upon New Hampshire, and almost every
lection of the State became national in its character.
State affairs were incidentally discussed by local
peakers and by the press, but the all-absorbing issues
vere made by the national administration at Wash-
ngton. During the Civil War, when the approval of

11

the people of the conduct of the war meant so much to Lincoln and Stanton, those great men watched with intense interest the progress of New Hampshire campaigns. The national committees of both parties aided in the canvass. Men of national reputation on both sides, leaders prominent in other States, distinguished members of Congress, took part in the campaigns, speaking upon the stump. The State was visited by correspondents of leading metropolitan newspapers, who gave to their readers thrilling accounts of the campaigns, forecasting the result. The individual voter was scheduled in every town by school districts, and returns made to the party headquarters at Concord. So accurate was the Republican canvass that its State committee dared to publish in advance its figures, sure that they would be verified by the returns.

The intensity and the excitement of these campaigns have never been exceeded in any State. The voter who was not willing to make his vocation or business subsidiary to politics was regarded as unpatriotic. Men gave freely of their time and money to carry elections. Absent voters were brought home, and they were numerous. Young men who went beyond the State limits to begin life did not abandon the parental home until they were married, and trace of them was kept, not only by the town committees, but in many instances by the State committee itself. Boston, the metropolis of New England, drew many of the young men from New Hampshire. The preponderance of Republicanism in Massachusetts had its influence upon not a few f the young Democrats who drifted there. Their hange of views was often known at Republican headquarters at the capital, even before the intelligence eached the town where they voted. Then the local Republican committee was advised to send for the voter, and he appeared in town the morning of election, returning on a Republican voter's certificate, to he surprise of the local Democrats. It has been frequently said that the absent voters carried the State Republican in many a close election. This is undoubtedly true, and it was owing to the superior organization of the Republican party, with its better knowledge of individual voters and its systematic ffort to have every vote count. The importance of ne vote was emphasized in almost every letter or ircular sent out by the Republican State committee. f the election of Marcus Morton as Governor of Massachusetts by one majority was cited once by the Republican leaders and newspapers, it was a thousand imes, to point to the importance of individual action.

The campaigns, until 1878, occurred in midwinter, he conventions being held in December or January. Travelling by rail and in the highways was frequently blocked by snow-storms, mails were delayed and communication cut off for several days with some sections f the State. No inclemency of the weather, however, lampened the ardor. Many towns in those days had o be reached by long rides in stages, or by private eams. It was before the time of telephones, and the elegraph was but little used. Correspondence was conducted without the service of stenographers or typewriters, yet all the minutiæ of town politics was under advice from State headquarters. No locality was so unimportant as to be omitted from the care of the State committee.

Then there was the stump speaking. Every one in the State on both sides who could enlighten an audience was drafted into service, while the best oratorical talent was drawn from the country at large. Toward the close of the campaign, the announcements of meetings for the week filled several columns of the newspapers. So great was the interest that halls were not large enough to hold the gatherings. In one campaign in the sixties, the late Senator Daniel W. Voorhees, of Indiana, was advertised to speak at Loudon. The largest hall was the church, and not half of the people congregating could gain admittance. A window of the church was taken out, a temporary platform laid across the window-sill, and, standing in the window, Senator Voorhees addressed both the crowd inside and outside the church. Such experiences were not uncommon. In those days the people of New Hampshire had the pleasure of listening to the great leaders on both sides. In the published lists of stump speakers in various campaigns will be found such names as Abraham Lincoln, Stephen A. Douglas, Hannibal Hamlin, Thomas A. Hendricks, Henry Wilson, Frank P. Blair, Salmon P. Chase, Zachariah Chandler, Montgomery Blair, Anson S. Burlingame, Thomas Ewing, Jr., Andrew G. Curtin, James R. Doolittle, Nathaniel P. Banks, John

. Gordon, Lucius Q. C. Lamar, Galusha A. Grow,
ohn A. Andrew, William B. Allison, Joseph R. Haw-
y, Daniel E. Sickles, Horace Maynard, Daniel W.
oorhees, James G. Blaine, Eugene Hale, William P.
rye, Benjamin F. Butler, Henry L. Dawes, Richard
)'Gorman, James A. Garfield, James W. Nye, Lot M.
[orrill, John A. Bingham, William W. Eaton, Patrick
.. Collins, John Covode, George G. Gorham, Frederick
)ouglass, Julius C. Burrows, Edward F. Noyes, and
lichard Oglesby.

In addition to conducting such a speaking campaign,
1e State committees prepared the ballots and sent them
) each town. This was no easy task when care had
) be taken that they did not fall into the hands of the
nemy in season to counterfeit and distribute on elec-
ion day, to the confusion of the voter. It was no in-
requent occurrence for local leaders to call attention
) spurious ballots at the opening of town meeting,
allots which had the insignia of one party at their
ead and perhaps the names of some of its candidates,
ut with the names of opposing candidates interjected
ere and there on the ticket.

The Republicans always made their fight for the con-
ol of the legislature, or, more particularly speaking,
or a majority of the House of Representatives. It
ok a majority vote to elect State Senators, Council-
rs, and governors. If there was no choice by the
eople in Senatorial or Councillor districts or of gov-
rnor, the majority in the legislature filled the vacan-
ies thus arising. The meeting opened in each town or

ward with the ballot for moderator, and this became the test vote. The party electing its moderator usually carried with it the representative and the town officers. Before the towns of Gilmanton, Sanbornton, and Gilford, for example, were divided, seven or eight hundred voters gathered in each town to contest the election. So firm was the alignment, and so close the issue, that in these and other towns of the State the voters often balloted all day for the choice of moderator, frequently having a tie vote. Here again the importance of the one vote was brought home. The one vote in the town might elect the moderator and the representative, and the one representative might control the legislature.

The State committee, and in such matters the committee meant its chairman or guiding spirit, had to reconcile differences in towns arising out of the conflicting ambition of men to go to the legislature. It was these personal appeals from headquarters for harmony, for the burial of animosities, with promise to interfere next time in behalf of the disappointed, that contributed largely to saving the day in an important campaign.

Well-nigh perfect as was the Republican organization in those years, it was almost equalled in effectiveness by the cohesion and discipline of the Democratic party, led by Harry and George A. Bingham, John G. Sinclair, John H. George, John M. Hill, John W. Sanborn, Frank Jones, and other strong, energetic, and adroit men, some of whom, like Henry O. Kent, were originally Republicans. The Democratic party was a dangerous antagonist. Successive defeats never chilled its efforts or abated its zeal. Its leaders were alert, trappy, sagacious, and ready to seize upon a mistake and count it to their advantage. They were aided by a vigilant newspaper press which had its readers in every hamlet. Every act of the legislature, every appointment of the governor, was closely analyzed, and the vote of every member of the legislature scrutinized, especially if he were a new member and a candidate for reëlection, as was the custom. "To die a yearling," as it was called, — that is, to fail of reëlection, — was a political disgrace, and the care of the party managers extended even to a supervision of every member of the legislature. Politics permeated everything year in and year out. The close election whetted the appetite of the minority and increased their efforts in the next campaign.

It is still a marvel how year after year, with the two exceptions of 1871 and 1874, the Republican party held control of the State by the narrowest of margins. There were seasons when it seemed as if victory must perch on the Democratic banner. There were critical times in the Civil War period when successive Union defeats in the field gave Democratic victories all over the country except in New Hampshire. There were years of the Grant administrations when dishonesty of federal officials, mistakes of Republican Congresses, and party quarrels overturned doubtful and strong Republican States, but New Hampshire stood true through it all to the Republican cause. There were unfortunate nominations made by New Hampshire Republicans which at the outset threatened the loss of the State. At such times Democratic activity would be doubled. Its hurrah was the loudest, its meetings the largest, the vigor of its newspapers the most pronounced. Yet, somehow, by the hardest kind of work the Republicans would rally, stand closer together, become aggressors, turn the flank or break the centre of the enemy, and the election would be won. The voter who has just come of age has no conception of the political campaigning which occurred in New Hampshire from 1856 to within a decade of the present century. It has not its counterpart in any State during the entire history of the country. The nearest approach to it has been in the State of Indiana, but in that State there have been no victories like those won in New Hampshire largely through the superiority of party organization and the tactful skill of the chairman or directing spirit of the State committee.

The Republican organization of New Hampshire was created by Edward H. Rollins, who was the first chairman of its State committee, and during the early life of the party the work of organizing it and conducting its campaigns was largely done by him, aided by Sylvester Dana and William E. Chandler as secretaries. The headquarters for several years was in the back room of Rollins's drug store on Main Street, in Concord, on the site of what is now the New Hampshire Savings Bank Building.

The work of creating a new political party is at all

nes one calling for the largest executive ability. The
ation must be from the ground up. Even with sla-
ry as a momentum, in the fifties, an immense amount
laborious detail was necessary to bring the deserters
om the two old parties together. The old line Whig
d the Democrat of years' standing, with antago-
sms of a lifetime, did not readily coalesce and work
harmony. Recruits were welcome, but individuals
equently overrated their own importance to the new
urty. There were conflicting ambitions, jealousies,
fferences as to methods, all of which had to be ad-
isted by some directing force. Without such direc-
on, individual enthusiasm and effort frequently go
, waste. As essential as the orator and the writer,
ho announce, define, and advocate great principles,
. the practical man of affairs, — he who has knowledge
f men, who effectively organizes them into a working
ody, who is a good judge of public opinion, and who
iobilizes the supporters of an idea into a successful
orce. It was here that the service of Edward H. Rol-
ins to the Republican party of New Hampshire was
reatest. He builded an organization which in service
utlived his own time. New issues and new leaders
ame, but the fruit of his work continued in the chan-
iels into which he had directed it. In the eighties
here came from Maine and other States Republicans
vho sought the secret of Republican organization in
New Hampshire, an organization which had so continuously under adverse circumstances won victories over
a most vigilant and aggressive foe.

Recalling these exciting political campaigns in New Hampshire and Rollins's part therein, Senator Eugene Hale, of Maine, says:

" I think my earliest acquaintance with the late Senator Rollins was somewhere in the seventies, when New Hampshire held her annual elections in March, and when all the available stump speakers were sent there by the National Committee to talk for the Republican cause. I have spent weeks there in these campaigns, driving out from the railroad towns to the smaller country centres, with the snow so deep that the tops of the fences could not be seen. Mr. Rollins managed these campaigns with great ability, and his figures and predictions on the night before the election sometimes came out within one hundred votes of the actual result. He was an ardent Republican, a fine manager and organizer, and if the last vote was not got out in New Hampshire it was no fault of his."

The life of Edward H. Rollins was a prominent part of the political history of New Hampshire from the time of the birth of the Republican party, in 1856, until his retirement from the United States Senate, in 1883. There were but few of the important political campaigns of that period of which he was not the guiding spirit of the Republican party. He lost no political battle when he directed the Republican forces, and nearly all of these contests were struggles for party ascendency in a State with forces very evenly matched. There were times during the Civil War, and in the reconstruction period which followed, when the loss of

ew Hampshire by the Republicans would have fore-
ıadowed national disaster to that party.

As a leader of men, it was natural that Rollins
ıould aspire to political honors. These came to him
ɔt without a struggle. His success crossed the ambi-
ons of other able men. Except his first reëlection
, the National House of Representatives, he attained
ɔ public position without a contest. The State could
ɂ held by the Republican party only by distributing
nong the party leaders the posts of honor. Rotation
ı office was a constant cry. It was the shibboleth of
ollins and others when they aspired to office. His
ıblic service was creditable to himself, and of ad-
ıntage to his State. The story of his life, therefore,
ust be written as a part of the political campaigns of
ew Hampshire for almost a generation.

CHAPTER II.

ANCESTRY AND EARLY LIFE [1]

James Rawlins, from whom Edward H. Rollins was descended, landed in America in 1632, and went to Ipswich, Massachusetts. No less than ten families by the name of Rawlins came to this country between 1630 and 1680. Some settled in Maryland, some in Virginia, and their descendants remained in those States or migrated to sections of the South or to the West. Others, however, came North and settled in New England. The families in the South continued to write the name as it was originally spelled: Rawlins. The New England families, however, even prior to the Revolutionary War, generally changed it to Rollins.

The history of James Rawlins before he came to this country is not clear. The Rawlins family in England is very ancient. The name has been a fixed surname for more than five hundred years. It is an old family in Cornwall, and more ancient in Hertfordshire. The name Rawlins is supposed to be derived from Rawle, and Rawle from Ralph, which was contracted from

[1] Prepared by the late John F. Rollins, youngest brother of Edward H. Rollins.

22

adolph or Rudolph, and Rudolph is the same as the French Raone. The name Raone is derived from, or the same as, Rollo, originating with Rollo, the Scandinavian, conqueror of the North of France about A. D. 11, who became Duke of Normandy. The conclusion of antiquaries is that Rawlins was originally Scandinavian, then French, then English.

In tracing the family in England, it is noticeable that its members seemed to lean strongly toward the Church, for no less than twenty-five of the name were prominently identified with various parishes. One was Bishop of St. David's; another, Prioress of Bromehall Priory; and one was an ardent follower of Luther in the Reformation. The family also contributed to the liberal arts, to the science of letters, and numbered some musicians of note.

The genealogist of the family says: " The American family, while contributing a fair proportion to marine, mercantile, mechanical, and professional pursuits, has been mainly engaged in agriculture. A large proportion of the New England men were above the ordinary stature, many of them possessing unusual strength, and in the earlier generations seemed remarkable for longevity."

From Ipswich, James Rawlins soon moved to Newbury, Massachusetts, but, in 1644, he appears at Dover, New Hampshire. On July 10th of that year, he received a grant of land from the town. This land lies on the banks of the Piscataqua about four miles up the river from Portsmouth. The only knowledge to be gleaned of him is that obtained from the town records, and these record only his offences against the province laws, or what were deemed offences at that time. In 1634, he was fined five shillings for paying one of his servants more than the statutory price of labor. In 1656, he was fined two shillings six pence for not going to church, and in 1659 he was admonished by the governor, by order of the Court, for entertaining "Ye Quakers." He may be judged leniently for not going to church when it is known that he was ordered to attend at Dover, a distance of several miles by trails exposed to attacks by Indians. His other offences seem to have been of like character, which to-day would commend him for his spirit of independence. To sum him up, he was probably one of the hardy pioneers of the period, a plain, sturdy farmer, possessed of good common sense and practical ideas. He probably spent his life as quietly and contentedly as his savage foes would permit, cultivating his farm, and rearing a family which was subsequently to do its part in carrying out the undertaking of founding a new State. At a ripe old age his spirit was gathered to his fathers, and his ashes, the first of his name in the new world, were mingled with the virgin soil which he aided in clearing from the "forest primeval."

He left seven children, six boys and one girl. This girl was captured, and afterward rescued from the Indians in 1677, according to Belknap's history. James Rawlins's wife, Hannah, survived him. Unfortunately, there is not even a side-light to be thrown upon the woman who shared the experiences of pioneer life with her husband. All record of her maiden name and character is probably forever lost. These early settlers had little aptitude, and no leisure, for writing history, nor did they realize that they were making history, and that to their descendants a record of their lives, their trials, their joys, their failures, and their successes would have been priceless. All that can be done is to build upon the fragmentary foundation of scattered records the superstructure of their lives, in which the imagination must paint most of the picture.

It is a remarkable fact that the original Rawlins place still remains in the hands of the direct descendants of James Rawlins, never having been deeded at all. It has come down from father to son or daughter, by will or direct inheritance, ever since the death of its first owner, in 1685. As early as 1697 the house now standing on this place was built, and it has not been materially changed since its erection. It is of the old square colonial order with great central chimney and yawning fireplace. It stands on an eminence from which the land slopes gradually to the river. The shade-trees, probably planted by the early members of the family, are now among the grandest in New England. The king of them all, however, known as "the Rollins elm," was blown down a few years ago. This tree measured at its smallest circumference twenty-one feet six inches, and its spread was more than one hundred feet.

Ichabod, the eldest son of James Rawlins, following

the English custom, came into possession of the farm. He married Mary Tibbets, daughter of the constable of Dover, who resided at Dover Neck. She lived only a short time, leaving one son, Jeremiah. Ichabod married again, this time, Elizabeth — surname not known — by whom he had one daughter named Hannah, born July 16, 1706. Ichabod was killed by the Indians, soon after his daughter's birth, as he was driving a team, presumably an ox team, from Lieutenant Field's garrison to James Bunker's. The scene of his death lay between Dover and Durham.

Ichabod's brother Thomas lived near Exeter, and was one of Edward Gove's company who were found in arms endeavoring to incite an insurrection for the overthrow of the arbitrary government of Edward Cranfield. Thomas, with the others, was arrested and tried for treason; but all were pardoned, except Gove, who was imprisoned for three years.

Ichabod's son, Jeremiah, seems to have left the paternal acres, probably to his sister Hannah, and settled in what is now Somersworth, then a part of Dover. He was one of the petitioners, in 1729, to incorporate Somersworth as a separate parish. In his will, dated December 7, 1752, he bequeathed to his wife, while unmarried, one-half the homestead, a negro servant, and lands in Rochester; to his son, Ichabod, the homestead, land in Canterbury, and a part of a sawmill. The remaining property he left to his other children. Jeremiah's wife, born in 1681, by whom he had a large family, was Elizabeth Ham, granddaughter of William Ham, of Exeter and Portsmouth, who emigrated from England.

Jeremiah left most of his estate to his eldest son Ichabod, who settled in that part of Dover which was afterward named Rollinsford in his honor. He was a man of great prominence in the community, the first one of the name to take any great part in public affairs. He was a member of the Revolutionary conventions at Exeter in April, May, and December, 1775, taking a prominent part. On June 20th, he was sent in company with Timothy Walker, of Concord, to ascertain the losses at Bunker Hill, and to make the men compensation. He was a member of the convention when it resolved itself into an independent State government, a delegate to the legislature in 1776, and the first Judge of Probate under the State government. He was also a member of the Executive Council in 1789.

Judge Ichabod Rollins — the name now has the New England spelling — was a slaveholder. His first wife was Abigail, daughter of Capt. Benjamin Wentworth. His second wife was Margaret Frost. He died in 1800. His daughter Elizabeth married Jonathan Chadbourne, of Berwick, Maine, and Chadbourne's daughter Abigail married George W. Wallingford, of Kennebunk, only son of Samuel Wallingford, who served with great distinction under John Paul Jones, and who was killed on the *Ranger* in the action with the *Drake*. Sarah Orne Jewett has clothed the family with the mantle of romance in her " Tory Lover."

James, son of Judge Rollins, lived in Somersworth, but there seems to be small record of him except that he raised a family of thirteen children by his two wives. The first wife was Hannah Carr, daughter of Dr. Moses Carr, of Newbury, Massachusetts. The second wife was Lucy Gerrish, of Dover.

Daniel Rollins, the father of Edward H. Rollins, was the son of James Rollins by his second wife, Lucy Gerrish. He was born May 30, 1797, and resided on his farm in Rollinsford. He married, November 20, 1823, Mary Plumer, daughter of Ebenezer Plumer, of Rollinsford, a near relative of Governor William Plumer, of New Hampshire. They had the following children, Edward H., James G., William A., Lucy G., John F., and Elizabeth W.

Edward Henry Rollins, eldest son of Daniel and Mary Plumer Rollins, was born in the homestead of his grandfather, James Rollins, in Rollinsford, October 3, 1824. When he was three years old, his father removed from the old house to a new one built on the opposite side of the road, which Edward afterward owned and used as a summer residence.

Daniel Rollins was a farmer. Until Edward was seventeen years of age, his life was spent upon his father's farm. His boyhood did not differ from that of the average farmer's son of New England in the early part of the nineteenth century. The farms of those days produced most of the household needs, and the boys were made serviceable as soon as their years admitted of their performing any work. They attended

DANIEL ROLLINS
(FATHER OF EDWARD H. ROLLINS)

school summer and winter until they were old enough to help in the hay-field, when their schooling was limited to the winter term. As the eldest of the family, Edward's services were called into requisition by his father at an early age, and he had put upon him the usual responsibility of an eldest son. This responsibility gave him confidence in himself, and taught him that self-reliance which contributed so much to his success in after-life. He entered upon his tasks with a cheerful spirit, and acquired those habits of application and industry which are the foundation of prosperity in manhood. His boyhood days were to him always a pleasant recollection, and no place had nearer and dearer associations than this old farm at Rollinsford.

While Edward inherited from his father many strong qualities, — the Rollins family for generations being a race of earnest, upright, and prominent citizens, — he also owed a great deal to his mother. Her family, the Plumers, were people of note in the State, furnishing a governor, a United States Senator, and other prominent officials for the public service. Edward's mother, who outlived him and died at the ripe age of ninety-two, was a remarkable woman, one of the strong characters of our early New England life. She was an untiring example of industry. To the last days of her life her mind was clear and her faculties exceptionally keen. Small of stature, she was a woman of indomitable courage, facing emergencies with the hardihood of a man. She brought up a large family of children with an eye single to their moral and spiritual welfare.

The Bible was her guide, and her faith in it never wavered. Reading it constantly, knowing many of its passages by heart, she actually lived up to both the letter and spirit of her religious convictions.

For his mother, Edward had the greatest love and reverence. To the close of his life, her slightest wish was to him a command, and he carefully avoided in her presence everything which would offend her views of right and wrong. She was the only person whom he seemed to fear. In later life, when her home was with him on the farm at Rollinsford, it was almost ludicrous to see the expedients to which he resorted to escape her reprimands. She had strong prejudices against any form of work on the Sabbath. It sometimes happened that a large amount of hay would be left in the field on Saturday night. Like all good farmers, Mr. Rollins disliked to have his hay wet by a shower. Therefore, when the clouds threatened rain on Sunday, his manœuvrings to get a yoke of oxen and a hay-rack out of the barn without his mother knowing it reminded one of a boy in his teens rather than the head of a family. If perchance she discovered him, she firmly forbade the work, and it is needless to say that her orders were obeyed.

During Mr. Rollins's last illness, when a shock of apoplexy had temporarily clouded his mind, he imagined that he was away from home, and no assurance could persuade him that he was at Rollinsford. Finally he was asked if his mother should come to his bedside and assure him that he was at home, would he believe it. "Yes," he replied most emphatically, "mother never told a lie."

Many incidents are related of the resolute character of Edward's mother. One or two will illustrate her forcefulness. When the farm buildings at Rollinsford were burned, she was recovering from a broken hip. The fire occurred on a cold winter night. Although nearly eighty years of age, she made her way out of the house without assistance, and immediately started to help in putting out the fire. The neighbors formed a line from the pump to the house to pass buckets of water to throw upon the flames. She insisted upon pumping the water until forcibly removed. The next day she was up at the usual hour apparently unaffected by the excitement and her exertions.

Her determination is illustrated by an experience upon the farm with her grandson, Frank W. Rollins, when a boy of nine years of age. In the stable was a balky and tricky horse named Beauty, whose characteristics were thoroughly known to the grandmother. Frank, in the absence of the men in the hay-field, was sent to harness the animal. The moment he came near the stall, Beauty began to kick vigorously. After trying in vain to get near her, Frank returned to the house and reported the situation to his grandmother. Going to the stable, the old lady took the horsewhip and administered a vigorous and evidently wholesome punishment to the high-strung beast. Then standing by, whip in hand, she directed Frank to go into the stall and lead out the animal. Beauty backed out with circumspection, her ears laid over, but with an eye on Mrs. Rollins, fully recognizing that a master hand was in control.

Such was the mother of Edward H. Rollins, an earnest, strong, and commanding woman, faithful to her convictions and resolute in her purpose. If her training of her children partook somewhat of the old Puritan sternness, it nevertheless inspired affection and made a lasting impression upon her sons and daughters.

Edward's education was begun at the red schoolhouse near his father's residence. He was a studious boy, quick of apprehension, and stood well in his classes. Such leisure hours as were afforded he devoted to poring over the few books that were the possessions of the family. These he read again and again, committing to memory some of their pages. Mastering the branches taught in the district school, he began preparations for a collegiate course. He attended Franklin Academy at Dover and the academy at Berwick, Maine, for a few terms, making commendable progress. One of his teachers was John G. Pike, under whose instruction he studied Latin and Greek. This instructor entertained a very high opinion of Edward's scholarship, as well as of his original talent.

George A. Gordon, at one time recording secretary of the New England Historical Genealogical Society, was a fellow pupil with Edward at the Franklin Academy. The majority of the boys who attended this academy were farmers' sons from the neighboring towns. Most of them went for only a term or two, the exception being those who entered the course with a view to fitting for college. Gordon says that " Edward was a quiet and studious boy in the school, accurate in recitation, and never in trouble on account of his deportment. A leader in sports and games, his enthusiasm was contagious. He excelled as a runner, leaper, and wrestler. Naturally taking command, he decided contested points among the boys, pacified their contentions, and marshalled their forces with a skill never questioned and ever satisfactory. He was a lad of handsome presence, robust and sturdy, though not large, with a luxuriance of spirit, fervor, and animation which gave him the power of producing positive results."

One of his associates at Berwick Academy was James Wingate Rollins. This institution was four miles from Edward's home, and he walked to and from it daily while a student there. Wingate Rollins says of him that he " took high rank among his school fellows for ability and thoroughness in his studies. He was especially good in mathematics, in which he was surpassed by few if any. He was very popular. Frank, outspoken, and full of pluck, he was liked by all and soon became a leader of the school."

Edward's first disappointment in life came when it was apparent that his father's lack of means would prevent his completing an academic course and entering Dartmouth College. He, however, accepted the situation in a brave and cheerful spirit. He entered upon the activities of life with a firm determination to educate himself, as many others of preceding generations had done when the family resources failed to provide a college education. His studious habits did not cease upon leaving school. He was an omnivorous reader, and his reading took a wide range. He advanced in the higher mathematics without instructors, and it was his delight in later life to supervise the study of his children in this branch of learning. He read translations of the classics and all the standard authors, Shakespeare being his favorite. He bought books as his means allowed, and his library in its selection showed a scholarly taste. If the deprivation of a college training was to him a deep regret, he nevertheless became by self-education a well-read and cultured man.

When Edward left the academy, he went to Concord to begin life in the drug store of John McDaniel. Here he remained for three years, going home only for an occasional visit. At the end of that time, thinking he could better himself, he left the employment of McDaniel and returned to Rollinsford. While waiting for employment, he assisted in the work upon the farm and taught school in the red schoolhouse where he had been a pupil. He was a successful teacher, excelling in mathematics. Not only the scholars but their parents took delight in sending him difficult problems to solve. Mathematics was the test in those days of a teacher's proficiency. Subsequently he taught school in South Berwick. Thomas J. Goodwin of that town writes of this school:

" I was one of Mr. Rollins's scholars in District Number 2, in the winter of 1845-6. I was about thirteen years of age and have a very vivid recollection of the school that he kept. He boarded with William H. Peters, who resided opposite my home. Mr. Rollins's salary was four dollars and a half per week and board. He kept a model school. I have recently spoken to others who attended that school with me, although the majority of the boys and girls have passed away, and they as well as I have most pleasant recollections of this term. It seemed all too short."

In 1846, Rollins obtained a clerkship in the wholesale drug store of Seth W. Fowle & Co., on Washington Street, Boston, where he remained nearly two years, at a salary of from three hundred to four hundred dollars per year. His most intimate friends were his fellow clerks, among whom were Mr. Weeks, the founder of the Weeks & Potter Co., druggists, and Samuel Blake. The clerks boarded with Mr. Weeks's father on Fort Hill. Mr. Weeks says that Rollins was even then as ardent a politician as he became in later life, and that he and Blake, being on opposite sides, were debating politics whenever they had an opportunity, much to the annoyance of their friends. After leaving Mr. Fowle's store, Rollins was for a brief time employed at Quincy, Massachusetts. He then returned home and arranged for the purchase of a drug store in Dover, with his cousin, Charles Rollins, as a partner. The fathers of these young men were to advance the money, but, when they came to close the trade, the proprietor repudiated the bargain. Late in the fall of 1847, Mr. Rollins went to Concord and bought the drug business of R. C. Osgood, whose store was on the east side of Main Street nearly opposite the State House. R. C. Osgood was the successor of the drug firm of Osgood & Rand. The newspaper advertisements of the time show that Rollins took possession of this store December 3, 1847. The purchase price was one thousand dollars, which Rollins obtained on a note endorsed by his father and William W. Rollins. Within a year he paid the note. In Rollins's advertisement in the local newspapers of 1848 it appears that he kept " a choice assortment of family groceries." Later, he started his brother, John F. Rollins, in the drug business at Penacook, a suburb of Concord. In October, 1859, the business of the two brothers was united under the firm name of Rollins & Company, and so it continued until Feb. 4, 1861, when Edward retired from the firm.

In 1851, Rollins's store was destroyed by fire. He continued the business in a store on Main Street, a little north of his own, until he completed Rollins's Block on the site of the Osgood & Rand store. In this block Rollins carried on the drug business until he disposed of his interest therein. It was in the back room of this store that many political conferences were held. In this room all the earlier State canvasses were made by Rollins as chairman of the Republican State Committee.

When Mr. Rollins came to Concord, he went to board

with Mrs. Nancy M. West, the widow of John West, who resided in what was known for many years as the West-Rollins homestead situated on the west side of Main Street opposite the New Hampshire Historical Society Building. Here he became acquainted with Ellen Elizabeth West, daughter of Mrs. West, whom he married February 13, 1849. This house continued to be his home during his long and eventful life, and in it all his children were born. These children were Edward Warren, born November 25, 1850; Helen Mary, born September 4, 1853; Charles Montgomery,[1] born February 27, 1856; Frank West, born February 24, 1860; and Montgomery, born August 25, 1867. All are now living except Charles, who died when about five years of age.

[1] Died June 25, 1861

CHAPTER III.

WHEN Edward H. Rollins settled in Concord, the various stores of the town were places of evening resort, where men gathered to discuss local affairs and politics. It was not long before his drug store became a rendezvous for local politicians, and later, as he became more prominent, for State politicians visiting the capital. Rollins was originally a Webster Whig, and he was very soon actively identified with the Whig party in New Hampshire. In 1850, he was a member of its State committee, and had as his associate, from Concord, Lyman D. Stevens, who later became mayor of the city, member of the legislature, State Senator and Councillor. In 1851, Rollins, with other members of the State committee, signed the call for the State convention of that party. This convention nominated a candidate for governor and delegates to the national convention to be held the next year. The nomination of Winfield Scott for President by that convention disappointed many New Hampshire Whigs who favored the nomination of Daniel Webster. It is very probable that Rollins was among this number. Although he was a delegate to a Whig State convention held in Septem-

38

ber, 1852, to nominate a candidate for governor for the campaign of 1853, he ceased to be a member of the State committee.

As a national party, the Whig party expired with the Presidential campaign of 1852. As an organization, it continued to exist in New Hampshire for four years longer, but its strength dwindled from 17,590 votes in March, 1853, to 2,360 votes in March, 1856. In the State elections of 1853 and 1854, carried by the Democrats on the popular vote, the opposition was divided between Whigs and Free-soilers.

Before the election of 1855, by secret organization, the American or Know Nothing movement was suddenly developed, upsetting the calculations of the leaders of the old parties. Opposition to slavery extension was the impetus which led many in New Hampshire to join this new American party or, remaining outside its secret councils, to support its ticket at the polls. The cause which led to the organization of the Know Nothing party in other States, opposition to the participation and influence of naturalized citizens in our politics, played but a small part in the formation of the Know Nothing councils of New Hampshire or in the legislative work of that party after it came into control of the State government. From the first, the views of its members in New Hampshire on the slavery question were pronounced, and the Know Nothing organization was used by the opponents of slavery extension as a means of defeating the Democratic party. The new movement was the stepping-stone to the forma-

tion of the Republican party in the State, but the
merging of its forces into the Republican organization
between the spring and fall campaigns of 1856 was so
quietly brought about that it is difficult to fix the precise moment of transition.

Rollins was an intense opponent of slavery, and to
one of his capacity for organization the Know Nothing
councils appealed with especial force as an effective
means of opposing slavery extension and defeating the
dominant party in the State. Men were rapidly join-
ing the Know Nothing lodges, and it was at once apparent that the movement would have an important
bearing upon the politics of the State. There is no
doubt that the leaders of both of the old parties hoped
to control and use the order. Indeed, not a few conspicuous Democrats became members of Know Nothing
lodges, who withdrew when they found that Democratic
ascendency in the State was threatened by it. The
greater number, however, drifted from it into the
Republican party for the same purpose that they
originally joined it, — to circumscribe or overthrow
slavery.

The acceptance of the city charter by the voters of
Concord occurred at the spring election of 1853. The
city was divided into seven wards. Rollins's residence
was in Ward 4, a ward famous for its political contests and the number of its residents who have attained
important State and national positions. Probably no
town or ward of the State has been the home of so
many men who have been prominent in public life.

At one time, about 1888-9, a good share of the State government resided in this ward. The following is a list of its residents who have held national and State offices at the time of their residence there:

U. S. Senators, Franklin Pierce, George G. Fogg, Edward H. Rollins, and Jacob H. Gallinger.

U. S. Representatives, Edward H. Rollins and Jacob H. Gallinger.

Minister to Switzerland, George G. Fogg.

U. S. District Attorney, John H. George.

U. S. Marshal, Joab N. Patterson.

Naval Officer of Customs, Boston, James O. Lyford.

Second Auditor of the Treasury, Joab N. Patterson.

U. S. Pension Agents, George Minot and John George.

Governors, Onslow Stearns and Frank W. Rollins.

Secretaries of State, Philip Carrigan and Ai B. Thompson.

President of Constitutional Convention of 1902, Frank S. Streeter.

Railroad Commissioners, Granville P. Conn and John M. Mitchell.

Insurance Commissioner, Oliver Pillsbury.

Bank Commissioner, James O. Lyford.

Forestry Commissioner, George H. Moses.

Adjutant General, Augustus D. Ayling.

State Historians, Nathaniel Bouton and Isaac W. Hammond.

Presidents of the Senate, Onslow Stearns, Jacob H. Gallinger, and Frank W. Rollins.

Speakers of the House, Edward H. Rollins and Samuel C. Eastman.

Supreme Court Judges, Ira Perley, Asa Fowler, William L. Foster, and Alonzo P. Carpenter.

For fifty years Ward 4 has been a battle-ground, no election ever going by default. It was won from the Democratic party by the Whig-Free-soil coalition in 1854, held by an alliance that centred around the American party in 1855 and '56, and carried by the Republican party ever after, but never in all the years without a contest. The Democratic leaders of the ward have always been aggressive, and they have marshalled the minority with a skill which has often taxed the energies of the Republicans to overcome. It was in this political centre that Rollins began his political career. The Republican canvasses of the ward in the early years were made by Charles H. Herbert under Rollins's personal supervision. Herbert, who is still living, thus speaks of these local campaigns:

"No town or ward of the State has witnessed more intense political contests than Ward 4. The Democrats under the leadership of John H. George fought to the finish, or until the last vote was counted and declared. No Republican victory ever had any effect upon the next contest. No matter how badly the Democrats were beaten, they came up just as confident the next time. The Republicans, however, left nothing to chance. We knew how every voter stood and what influence surrounded him. I used to make the canvasses of the ward, and then we would meet at Rollins's house to go over them. Politics lasted the year round. In those early years we were at Rollins's house discussing the political situation almost as much as we were at home. His home was political headquarters not only for the ward but for the entire city. The Republican party of New Hampshire was cradled in that old house and in the back room of his drug store. He looked after every detail. Nothing in politics, with him, was too small to be unimportant. If he started in to accomplish anything, he never let up until he brought it about. He never forgot a political promise, and he never failed to keep one.

" In 1855, Edward H. Rollins and William Ballard were the candidates for representatives to the legislature. We had the advantage of the Democrats in that they did not know who of their men had joined the Know Nothing councils, as the members were pledged not to divulge their membership. Therefore, our canvass was more accurate, but the Democrats were determined and confident. For several weeks before election we met almost every night at Rollins's house to listen to reports on the situation. Every absent voter who would support our ticket was brought home regardless of expense, and we had committees to see that every voter was brought to the polls. Our organization was well-nigh perfect, and every man under Rollins's direction knew what his duties would be on election day. When we made up our final canvass the night before election, Rollins said, with a confidence that gave us courage, ' We shall carry the ward to-morrow.'

Carry it we did, to the surprise and chagrin of the Democrats. The same painstaking methods established by Rollins for taking the poll of the ward continued all the years that I was active in politics."

The State ticket of the Know Nothing party in this campaign of 1855, and its candidates for Congress, were nominated at a mass convention held at Manchester. Their candidates were, for governor, Ralph Metcalf, a former Democrat; for Congress, James Pike, of South Newmarket, Mason W. Tappan, of Bradford, and Aaron H. Cragin, of Lebanon.

On the committee to notify Metcalf of his nomination was Ruel Durkee, of Croydon, who had secured Metcalf's assent to becoming the candidate of the party, and who was afterward prominently identified with the Republican party from its birth until his death. Durkee was a quaint and original character whose large and ungainly figure attracted attention at all political gatherings on account of his dress and general appearance. He wore a swallow-tail coat and double waistcoat summer and winter, with a silk hat of antique brand, and trousers that were built on the Turkish plan, full and flowing. Even on the hottest day his waistcoat was buttoned up to his chin. He was neither handsome nor prepossessing. He was plain and rough of speech, with a variety of odd characteristics. There was neither charm in his conversation nor magnetism in his personality. Yet he wielded for many years a great influence in Republican councils, made and unmade public men of the State, and was credited by such astute politicians as Rollins and Chandler with controlling appointments and shaping nominations for office. Although uneducated, he possessed a large fund of common sense, and his judgment of men and measures was remarkably accurate. His homely and laconic comment often nipped in the bud the aspirations of ambitious men. By leading men of the party he was feared and courted. He aspired to no office except that of chairman of the Board of Selectmen of Croydon, which he held for upwards of thirty years. He attended all legislative sessions, seeking but not imparting information. In all important controversies before the legislature, especially railroad contests, Durkee was invariably the retained agent of one of the parties. His favorite maxim was, "Don't write, send word." He literally followed this maxim through life. If he contributed to the support of the federal government, it was not through the Post Office department. Durkee's interests in politics were almost always antagonistic to Rollins's ambition.

The campaign which followed the nominations was intense and the result a surprise to the Democrats. Metcalf was elected by the people; the Know Nothing majority in the legislature was overwhelming, and all three candidates for Congress had good majorities.

The American party, made up of men who had long been in political antagonism, was without recognized leadership. Its ranks were full of ambitious men. Its danger was that personal disappointment at not securing recognition would outweigh the principles for which the party stood, and that it would break into factions with its first taste of power. Elected to this legislature were a number of able men who afterward were honored by high positions in the Republican party. Among Rollins's contemporaries in the legislature were Daniel M. Christie, of Dover, Daniel Clark, of Manchester, Jacob Benton, of Lancaster, James W. Emery, of Portsmouth, Thomas M. Edwards, of Keene, Mason W. Tappan, of Bradford, Bainbridge Wadleigh, of Milford, Joel Eastman, of Conway, John J. Prentiss, of Claremont, Thomas L. Tullock, of Portsmouth, Paul R. George, of Hopkinton, Jonathan Kittredge, of Canaan, William M. Weed, of Sandwich, and William H. Gove, of Weare, representing the majority, and Samuel Herbert, of Rumney, and John G. Sinclair, of Bethlehem, representing the minority.

The legislative caucus of the American party developed several candidates for Speaker, but only one ballot was necessary to nominate. This ballot was as follows: Jacob Benton, 2; Daniel Clark, 2; Thomas M. Edwards, 4; Jonathan Kittredge, 7; Joel Eastman, 23; Edward H. Rollins, 39; John J. Prentiss, 108.

In the make-up of the committees Rollins was put on the judiciary committee, of which Christie was the chairman, while Edwards, Emery, Benton, Herbert, and Sinclair were among his associates. Clark was chairman of the committee on banks, Wadleigh of manufactures, Gove of agriculture, George of mili-

tary affairs, Kittredge of incorporations, Tappan of
railroads, and Eastman of elections, but none of them
was a member of the judiciary committee, although
five were lawyers.   Either there were too many
lawyers in the House for the membership of that committee, or, what is more probable, the chairmanship of
a committee was considered a greater recognition than
membership of the judiciary committee.   Yet Clark
was a formidable candidate for United States Senator
at that session, there being two vacancies to fill, and
Christie, Edwards, and Eastman were voted for in the
American legislative caucus.   Edmund Burke, of Newport, and Gilman Marston, of Exeter, also received
votes at this caucus.

Edmund Burke was intellectually one of the strongest men of his time in New Hampshire, a man of extensive reading and wide information.   He was lacking
in the attributes of the orator, and was rather prosaic
as a public speaker, but he wielded a ready pen, which
he employed through life both in attack and defence.
He was a Democratic member of Congress from New
Hampshire for three terms from 1839 to 1845, and
Commissioner of Pensions under Polk.   With the
possible exception of Pierce, he had the largest acquaintance with public men in the country of any man
in New Hampshire at the time of Pierce's nomination
for the Presidency.   He headed the delegation from the
State to the Democratic National Convention in 1852,
and played a large part in shaping that convention in
favor of Pierce.   Both he and his friends expected that

he would be a member of Pierce's cabinet, but the latter ignored him. For this slight and ingratitude Burke was determined to overthrow Pierce's supremacy in New Hampshire, and for this purpose allied himself with the American party, being one of its active members. His affiliation was short-lived, however, and he returned to the Democratic party to become one of its extreme advocates. He was appointed Commissioner of Patents by President Buchanan, and later wrote a defence of Buchanan's administration. He did not afterward hold public office, but he was prominent in Democratic councils until the time of his death.

Of the members of this legislature four were afterward elected to Congress, Tappan, Edwards, Benton, and Rollins: three became United States Senators, Clark, Rollins, and Wadleigh: Kittredge was made Chief Justice of the Superior Court, and William Haile, of the State Senate, became governor.

Rollins appears from the reports made by him at this session of the legislature to have done his share of committee work. Two of these were adverse reports on legislation affecting the property rights of married women. If he were opposed at that time to enlarging the property rights of women, he outgrew his opposition, for his will left almost all his property to his wife to dispose of as in her judgment seemed best.

In initiating legislation Rollins's efforts were confined to securing charters for banks and insurance companies and amendments to existing charters. He had

charge of the bill amending the charter of the city of
Concord, taking prominent . . . .
amendments. The . . . .
cal legislation, the legi . . . .
considerable number of De . . . .
districting the State in Sen . . . .
direction of this legislation Rollins . . . . . . and
rapidly developing, at this time, those qualities as a
party manager which afterward . . . .
gnished. In the name of the Speaker he was . . .
Speaker pro tem . . .

The next . . . .
party while the . . . . A . . .
meeting, of which Rollins was . . . . . . at Concord, in July. It was . . . .
Senators, John P. H . . . . . . J . . . . . . In the campaign of 1856 the De . . . . to
regain control of the St . . . The M . . . .
sides its importance in . . . the New State . . . . .
of the Presidential . . . .
prospects of President Pi . . . .
tion at the hands of his party. The . . . .
influence that Administration . . . Washington . . . exert
was used to spur the De . . . of New Hampshire
to activity. The attention of the whole country was
riveted upon the State. The American party as
it was soon to be called, the Republican party now
thoroughly organized, Rollins becoming its recognized
manager.

The campaign was conducted with great energy on

both sides. The chairman of the Democratic State committee was Francis B. Peabody, of Concord. He enriched the canvass by securing the presence, as speakers, of these distinguished Democrats, Howell Cobb, of Georgia, James L. Orr, of South Carolina, Joseph Lane, of Oregon, and John B. Weller, of California. In no place was the contest fiercer than in Concord, the home of President Pierce, and in no ward of that city was the struggle greater than in Ward 4. The *Statesman* described the Ward 4 contest as " the hardest fought battle that ever took place within the boundaries of ' ancient Penacook.' " It " beat all sanguinary contests in a city notorious for the energy with which political contests have been waged," and " when the vote was declared toward evening, showing the reëlection of Rollins and Ballard to the legislature, the old town hall shook with a volume of applause like that of olden times. There has rarely been manifested deeper disappointment than that of the Democrats of Ward 4 at this result."

The returns from the State showed a considerable gain for the Democrats on the popular vote, a gain sufficient to prevent an election of governor by the people. The American party carried the legislature, but by a greatly reduced majority. There had been close elections in a number of wards and towns, Rollins being reëlected by only seven majority.

As soon as the result of the election was known, Rollins announced his candidacy for Speaker of the

House. Prentiss, who was Speaker in the previous legislature, was reëlected to the House, and again a candidate for the position of presiding officer. According to precedent he was entitled to a renomination. He had made a model presiding officer and was personally popular. Rollins, however, asserted that Prentiss had made an agreement not to be a candidate for reelection to the Speakership. A third candidate appeared in the field, Aaron F. Stevens, of Nashua, who continued a rival of Rollins for party honors until both retired from active political life. When the legislature met, indications pointed to the renomination of Prentiss. It was then that Rollins decided upon a bold move, the success of which launched him upon an extended political career. Had he failed, his defeat in the circumstances might have brought his political ambitions to an untimely end. He attended the legislative caucus and demanded to be heard before the vote was taken. He recited the agreement with Prentiss, and requested the caucus to observe it if Prentiss did not. The lights and shadows of that gathering have disappeared, and it lives mostly in tradition as an aggressive contest on Rollins's part fraught with danger to his future.

The vote in caucus was as follows: First ballot: David Cross, of Manchester, 1; James N. Lovering, of Exeter, 1; Aaron F. Stevens, of Nashua, 21; John J. Prentiss, of Keene, 50; Edward H. Rollins, of Concord, 72.

Second Ballot: William Haile, of Hinsdale, 1;

John J. Prentiss, of Keene, 30; Aaron F. Stevens, of Nashua, 36; Edward H. Rollins, of Concord, 80.

None of the newspapers of the American party referred to the incidents of the caucus. The *Union Democrat,* of Manchester, made the caucus the subject of a spicy editorial, attacking personally both Rollins and Prentiss, and sneering at the new party. The *New Hampshire Patriot* gives the Democratic version of the caucus as follows:

" THE HINDOO NOMINATION

" E. H. Rollins, of Concord, was nominated for Speaker by the Hindoo caucus. This was a very remarkable result, and we have the facts from which a very interesting chapter might be written upon the subject, but we must defer it to a more convenient season. The result shows the power Rollins possesses to control his party. Against all precedents and against the real wishes of four-fifths of the members he received the nomination. Prentiss had been Speaker but one year, made a very good one, was very generally acceptable to his party, desired and labored for a renomination, to which he was entitled by precedent, and which a large majority of the members really wished to confer upon him, yet he received but fifty votes out of nearly one hundred and fifty cast in the caucus. Such a result must have been very humiliating to him, as it is very discreditable to his party. The fact is they were driven, frightened into the abandonment of Prentiss and the nomination of Rollins by the loud boasts and threats of certain friends of the latter, who represented that some twenty or thirty members had pledged themselves to stick to Rollins in the House. This secured his nomination.

" The caucus was a secret one, but we learned that there was a long and acrimonious discussion in regard to the Speakership, in the course of which it came out that before the State election Rollins had been promised the office by many of the leading men of the party, and that Prentiss had pledged himself that he would not be a candidate for renomination and to vote for Rollins. Yet within twenty-four hours of his election in March Prentiss began to fugle and trade for a renomination. After these developments and certain pretty plain hints that trouble would follow the violation of this contract with Rollins, the ballot was taken, when Rollins had 72, Prentiss 50, and Stevens, of Nashua, 21. Prentiss then withdrew, and Rollins was nominated on the next ballot, having 80 votes to 67 for others. Prentiss then moved that the nomination be made unanimous, and made a speech promising his cordial support of it. The nomination was a very bitter pill to a large portion of the members, but they regarded it as a medicine to be taken for the good of the system, and so swallowed it. As Rollins is in the medicine trade, it was just in his line to administer such doses, and he did it very successfully."

That there are exaggeration and misstatement in the *Patriot* article is apparent to all who knew Rollins, for never was there a more loyal party man. However strongly he might feel that he deserved recognition, nothing could induce him to pursue a course that would hazard the unity of the party organization. Although defeated several times in after years in his ambition to be United States Senator, there is never a word in his correspondence with his most intimate friends, before or after the contests, that can be tortured into a menace or threat such as is indicated in this article. There is little doubt that an understanding was reached among the leaders of the American party prior to election that Rollins should be Speaker in event of success. That Prentiss was a party to this understanding is most probable, but such arrangements are never reduced to writing, or generally disseminated at the time. There is always a difficulty in enforcing them if a change of circumstances leads either party to ignore the arrangement. Rollins regarded all his political promises as sacred. Moreover, he was always pronounced in his condemnation of those who failed to keep their political obligations. Therefore, when Prentiss ignored the understanding, Rollins determined to face him in the caucus, and to appeal to that body to observe it if Prentiss did not. His course provoked criticism from members of his own party at the time, and the incident was kept alive by the Democrats for several years, much to Rollins's annoyance. In a letter to William H. Gove, of Weare, dated October 22, 1858, he said:

"I desire a correct version of the story told you by

Col. John H. George in regard to the organization of the House, etc., in 1856. I have heard various reports of the conversation and wish a correct one. You will, of course, be as willing to communicate the facts in the case to me as to any other individual. Having labored most untiringly and most devotedly to promote the welfare and prosperity of the Republican party from the day of its organization to the present time, having never in a single instance done or said anything inconsistent with perfect integrity, having toiled in season and out of season, devoting the best energies of my life, and having incurred a large expense in aid of the cause, I feel, as you would under similar circumstances, indignant that a slander of that character should be started even by a political opponent, and sorry that it could be reported or believed by a Republican. If I can get the yarn in some tangible shape, I propose to probe it to the bottom. You will oblige me by giving me the desired information at your earliest convenience."

Nothing appears to have come of this appeal to Gove, and the presumption is that the exaggeration of the *Patriot* story grew out of the intensity of partisan feeling at the time. As chairman of the Republican State committee, Rollins was to the close of his political career the subject of Democratic misrepresentation, to most of which he gave little or no attention.

Rollins was now thirty-one years of age. Ahead of him was the task of showing the public that he had qualifications for the Speakership. What made the task more difficult was that he had supplanted a most popular presiding officer with whose administration of the office his own would surely be compared. His only experience in presiding had been in Masonic bodies, and the few occasions he had occupied the chair at the previous session of the legislature. His speech to the House upon taking the chair indicated that he fully realized the embarrassments of his undertaking. He said:

"Gentlemen: I accept the office to which you have elected me by your kind partiality, feeling truly grateful for the honor thus conferred upon me, only regretting that I cannot bring to your service an amount of ability and experience commensurate with its duties and responsibilities. I promise you, however, that my most earnest efforts will be directed to the discharge of the duties of presiding officer in a faithful and impartial manner, and thus, if possible, make apparent to you what language would fail to do, my appreciation of this mark of your confidence and esteem. Relying upon your kindness and forbearance, I shall look to you for wise counsel and a generous and cordial support. I shall expect the hearty coöperation of the many here who are so well qualified by their large legislative experience to give good counsel, assuring them that their advice will ever be most kindly received. Allow me, gentlemen, to express the hope that we may commence at once the business of the session and pursue it with so much diligence that we shall in a brief space of time accomplish all needful reforms, pass all salutary laws required of us by the people of New Hampshire, and be in readiness to separate for our several homes, having done nothing to impair the kindly feelings we now entertain for each other, or to lessen the confidence reposed in us by our constituents."

Rollins surpassed all expectations as a presiding officer. He showed remarkable aptitude for the position, and was regarded in the legislature, and later in the national House and Senate, as a most competent occupant of the chair.

The Presidential campaign was under consideration before the legislature assembled, in fact even before the March election. George G. Fogg, the editor of the *Independent Democrat,* published at Concord, was a delegate to a national convention held at Pittsburg, February 22, 1856. This convention was made up of men of various parties who were opposed to slavery extension. It was the forerunner of the Philadelphia convention held June 17, 1856, which nominated Fremont and Dayton for President and Vice-President. Fogg was a member of the national committee appointed by the Pittsburg convention which, on March 26, 1856, issued the call for the convention at Philadelphia. This call invited "the people of the United States, without regard to past political differences or divisions, who are opposed to the repeal of the Missouri Compromise, to the policy of the present administration, to the extension of slavery in Territories, in favor of the admission of Kansas as a free State, and of restoring the action of the federal government to the principles of Washington and of Jefferson, to send three delegates from each Congressional district, and six delegates at large to this convention."

This call was published in both Fogg's paper and in the *Statesman*. In the latter paper it is referred to as "the call for the Republican convention." In response to it a State call was issued May 10, 1856, for a mass-meeting, June 10th, at Concord, of all those who could act together on the principles set forth in the national call for the Philadelphia convention. At this mass-meeting the following delegates were elected to the Philadelphia convention:

State: Amos Tuck, of Exeter, William M. Weed, of Sandwich, Daniel Clark, of Manchester, Benjamin Pettingill, of Salisbury, Levi Chamberlain, of Keene, and Daniel Blaisdell, of Hanover.

District Number 1: Henry A. Spear, of Laconia, James W. Emery, of Portsmouth, George P. Folsom, of Dover.

District Number 2: George G. Fogg, of Concord, Austin F. Pike, of Franklin, and John H. Gage, of Nashua.

District Number 3: John H. White, of Lancaster, Alvah Smith, of Lempster, and Greenleaf Cummings, of Lisbon.

Fremont was nominated June 19th, and that evening, at Concord, Fremont Club Number 1, of New Hampshire, was organized at Depot Hall. The New Hampshire delegates at Philadelphia at a meeting that morning voted " that this delegation unanimously recommend and urge the immediate formation of Fremont Clubs in every town in the State, to be numbered in the order of their formation." It does not appear that information of this vote was sent by telegraph to Concord on that day; thus the probability is that the call for the Depot Hall meeting was issued without knowledge of the action of the New Hampshire delegates at Philadelphia. The officers of this club were: President, E. H. Rollins; recording secretary, William E. Chandler, corresponding secretary, James Peverly; treasurer, Sylvester Dana; vice-presidents, Albert H. Drown, Cyrus Robinson, Moses Humphrey, Hamilton E. Perkins, John Y. Mugridge, Peter Sanborn, Benjamin Green; executive committee, James Peverly, A. B. Holt, J. L. Jackson, L. D. Brown, William Ballard.

This meeting was attended by Jacob Benton, of Lancaster, George W. Everett, of New London, Aaron F. Stevens, of Nashua, Bainbridge Wadleigh, of Milford, George W. Nesmith, of Franklin, and other American members of the legislature then in session, who participated in the proceedings, making the action taken by the Concord supporters of Fremont the basis of action for other towns. The meeting voted "that all friends of liberty in this State be invited to form Fremont Clubs in the several towns, and to correspond with this club," thus making the Concord club the nucleus of a party organization for the State. It was around this club that the Republican party of New Hampshire had its beginning, although the name Republican had not yet common acceptance with all who became members of Fremont Clubs in New Hampshire.

"For several months," says William E. Chandler, "the straight name 'Republican' was carefully avoided by the leaders to offend no sensibility of the recruits. All were Fremonters in that they supported Fremont for President, and were opposed to slavery extension, but they had been drawn from the Democratic, the Whig, the Free-soil, and American parties with more or less attachments to old associations and some suspicion of the new." The term "Republican" was applied to the new party by the Democratic newspapers of the State, who soon enlarged it into "Black Republican." It is only occasionally in the campaign that the *Statesman* and the *Independent Democrat* made use of the former term. The Fremont Clubs were the rallying-point; through them the Republican organization was perfected.

A State committee was appointed for the campaign, with Rollins as chairman, and Sylvester Dana, of Concord, as secretary. Dana is one of the few of the old guard still living. He identified himself with the Free-soil party on attaining his majority, and held to that organization until the Republican party was formed out of the forces hostile to the extension of slavery. Earnest and active in politics during all the crucial years of slavery agitation, his interest in public affairs has never abated. For many years, and until retired by age limitations, he was judge of the police court of

Concord. He was closely associated with the leaders of the Republican party in its formation and development.

There is no reference in the newspapers to a State committee during this campaign. Dana, however, gives it as his recollection that the committee was appointed after the legislature adjourned in July, and that it was the work of leading American members of the legislature and others who were brought into conference with them. It was at this conference, made up of Know Nothings, Whigs, and Free-soilers, that an agreement was reached as to the officers of this committee, and on motion of Amos Tuck, of Exeter, Rollins and Dana were elected to the positions of chairman and secretary.

Besides his work as chairman of the State com. '+-tee, Rollins took part in the speaking of this campaign. It was not his first appearance on the stump. In the spring campaign of 1856 he made one or more speeches. His maiden effort was at Chichester. He had as associate speakers at the meeting John Y. Mugridge and others, of Concord. According to a report of the meeting which appeared in Fogg's newspaper, the speakers had a baptism of fire through an attempt of the Democrats to break up the meeting. Mugridge, who was the first speaker, had a number of interruptions, but, when Rollins took the floor, the demonstrations were decidedly hostile. The newspaper account of the meeting says: " The evident intention was to prevent Rollins from speaking, but he was not a man to be bluffed in that way. He waited coolly until the storm had in a good measure spent itself, and then proceeded to show, and did show, to every unprejudiced mind that the American party now occupies the same ground on the question of slavery extension that the Democratic party occupied under Jefferson, and even to the time when the infamous Fugitive Slave Law was enacted. Mr. Rollins stated as a fact, which made quite an impression on the minds of the audience, that of the five who had come from Concord to have a friendly discussion with the people of Chichester, four had always been with the Democratic party." The other speakers were also interrupted, and two Democrats insisted upon addressing the meeting. When they had finished, Rollins again took the floor and replied to their charges against the preceding legislature. In the fall campaign of 1856 Rollins again spoke at Chichester, and this time with Mugridge and Chandler. The meeting was orderly throughout.

The *Independent Democrat* of October 30, 1856, says: "We learn that the returns by the Fremont State committee, the result of an actual canvass of nearly every town of the State, indicate more than six thousand majority for Fremont over Buchanan." This was one of the first, if not the first, of Rollins's State canvasses which for accuracy have never been surpassed, and which gave him a reputation all over the country as a sagacious political manager. Fremont's actual majority over Buchanan was 5,556.

John H. George, of Concord, was chairman of the Democratic State committee during the Presidential campaign as well as during the succeeding spring campaign of 1857. Strong personality showed itself in his positive convictions and in his fearlessness in expressing them. The only offices he ever held were in line with his profession, those of county solicitor of Merrimack County and United States District Attorney, both by appointment. He was a candidate of his party several times for Congress, and stumped the district. Had George ever been elected, no rules or traditions of the national House of Representatives would have prevented him from impressing himself upon that body. All his political movements were frontal attacks made without regard to consequence to himself. He neither conciliated enemies nor flattered friends. On the stump he spoke his mind and courted joint discussion of political issues. Had his lot been cast earlier in the century, when his party was in power in the State, nothing could have prevented his attaining its highest gifts. He was an antagonist to be feared at the bar or in the forum, being thoroughly equipped and ready for any emergency. A long life as a minority leader neither dampened his ardor nor affected his genial disposition.

George and Rollins were neighbors, and their social relations were never disturbed by their antagonism in politics. In fact, each held the other in the highest personal esteem, being drawn together by certain attributes which were common to both men. Intense in their convictions, each believed in direct methods. Both were positive and aggressive men, yet neither cherished resentment after conflict. An incident occurred on the night of Rollins's first reëlection to Congress which shows their mutual regard. George was Rollins's opponent at this election. The contest had been particularly close, and the early reports so far indicated George's election that the Democrats of Concord began to celebrate. Later and more complete returns showed Rollins's election beyond a doubt. Leaving his political friends, George hastened to Rollins's house, announced his own defeat, and congratulated his opponent. Of the large company assembled at the Rollins's home that night to felicitate its owner, none entered more heartily into the spirit of the occasion and none was more sincerely earnest in his congratulations than George, although his own ambition to go to Congress had been particularly acute at the time.

CHAPTER IV.

POLITICAL ALLIANCES

THE Democrats of New Hampshire made the spring campaign of 1857 a continuation of the Presidential campaign of 1856. At their convention September 4, 1856, to nominate Presidential electors, they selected their candidate for governor for the March election of 1857. John S. Wells, of Exeter, was renominated. Their candidates for Congress who were nominated much later were George W. Kittredge, of Newmarket, George W. Morrison, of Manchester, and William P. Wheeler, of Keene. John H. George continued as chairman of the Democratic State committee. After the November election of 1856 had shown Buchanan to have a majority of the electoral votes, the Democratic State committee at one of its meetings did the surprising thing of voting to recommend Wells for a position in Buchanan's cabinet, thereby admitting the probability of his defeat at the polls. The general trend of the newspaper discussion of the campaign of 1857 indicated that Democratic hopes were centred on carrying the legislature, with the possibility of electing one or more of their candidates for Congress.

The incoming of a new Democratic national administration was a stimulus to their efforts.

The party in power in New Hampshire met in convention January 8, 1857, in response to a call of its State central committee. The committee had not yet formally adopted the name " Republican " for their party. The call was as follows:

" A State convention of all the people of New Hampshire who are opposed to the policy of the present sectional, proslavery, anti-American administration, which repealed the Missouri Compromise and forced slavery upon Kansas by fear and border ruffian violence, of all who are in favor of restoring freedom to Kansas, and reëstablishing constitutional principles that slavery shall not be extended over territory now free, and all who supported Fremont and Dayton at the late Presidential election, will be held at Concord on Thursday, January 8, 1857, at eleven o'clock in the forenoon for the purpose of nominating candidates for governor, railroad commissioner, and three Representatives to Congress to be supported at the coming State election."

The convention was called to order by Rollins as chairman of the State central committee, who presided until an organization was effected. A committee was appointed to report permanent officers for the convention, and the same committee was authorized to report a State central committee. Amos Tuck, of Exeter, was made president of the convention. A committee on resolutions reported the platform, and then the convention proceeded to ballot for governor. A large number of candidates were voted for, but the contest was between Ichabod Goodwin, of Portsmouth, and William Haile, of Hinsdale. Goodwin had been the candidate of the Whig party at the previous spring election, receiving 2,360 votes. There was a strong sentiment in the convention in favor of his nomination, but the leaders favored the selection of one less closely identified with the old Whig organization. An informal ballot for governor resulted as follows:

Ichabod Goodwin, of Portsmouth, 181, William Haile, of Hinsdale, 130, with 136 complimentary votes given to seventeen leading members of the party. Haile was nominated on the third ballot, and his nomination was made unanimous.

The State committee selected by the convention was as follows:

Rockingham County — James M. Lovering, of Exeter, Thomas L. Tullock, of Portsmouth, Amos Tuck, of Exeter, Joseph P. Morse, of Portsmouth, Amos C. Clement, of Plaistow.

Strafford County — George M. Herring, of Farmington, M. C. Burleigh, of Somersworth, Richard N. Ross, of Dover, George C. Peavey, of Strafford.

Belknap County — H. A. Spear, of Laconia, J. P. Morrison, of Gilford, C. K. Kelley, of Sanbornton, George W. Morrison, of Gilmanton.

Carroll County — William M. Weed, of Sandwich, Larkin D. Mason, of Tamworth, Luther D. Sawyer, of Ossipee, Elijah Wadleigh, of Wakefield.

Merrimack County — Edward H. Rollins, of Concord, George W. Everett, of New London, Austin F. Pike, of Franklin, Sylvester Dana, of Concord, William E. Chandler, of Concord, Nehemiah G. Ordway, of Warner.

Hillsborough County — Charles P. Danforth, of Nashua, Frederick Smyth, of Manchester, Charles H. Campbell, of Amherst, Hosea Eaton, of New Ipswich, Daniel McCaine, of Francestown.

Cheshire County — F. A. Faulkner, of Keene, Amasa May, of Gilsum, Milan Harris, of Nelson, Charles J. Amidon, of Hinsdale.

Sullivan County — John J. Prentiss, of Claremont, Ruel Durkee, of Croydon, Alvah Comings, of Cornish, Levi W. Barton, of Newport.

Grafton County — John H. Thompson, of Holderness, George S. Towle, of Lebanon, Greenleaf Cummings, of Lisbon, Jacob C. Bean, of Enfield, Joseph Chamberlain, of Warren.

Coos County — Aurin Chase, of Whitefield, Frederic G. Messer, of Colebrook, Barker Burbank, of Shelburne, James S. Brackett, of Lancaster.

The foregoing comprise the first State committee of the Republican party of New Hampshire. The names are almost identical with those appended to the call for the convention. There were seven changes and five additions. Of the names which appear in the committee but do not appear in the call the best known are those of William E. Chandler, Nehemiah G. Ordway, Charles J. Amidon, and Levi W. Barton.

Chandler did not become of age until December 28, 1856.

The committee organized with the choice of Edward H. Rollins as chairman and Sylvester Dana as secretary, they having been chairman and secretary of the committee in the Presidential campaign of 1856.

The work of the State committee in making the canvass of the State and mapping out the campaign was done by Rollins, assisted by Secretary Dana and William E. Chandler, the latter being especially active in the preparation of circulars and other political literature. Following so closely the strenuous Presidential canvass of 1856, this campaign was lacking in public demonstration, though no less earnestly conducted by the Republicans. As an indication of the frankness with which political methods were discussed by the newspapers at this time, the following extract from an editorial in the *Statesman*, addressed to " Republican Office-holders," is given. After referring to the activity of the Democratic federal office-holders in the previous Presidential campaign, the *Statesman* makes this appeal to the Republican State officials:

" There are now a good many men holding office in New Hampshire whose tenure depends entirely upon the continuance of the Republican party in power. They have, therefore, an important stake in the approaching election, and, as the men within New Hampshire who will hold positions under the government [federal] are at work to overthrow the Republicans it is the duty of office-holders under the State government to do all in their power to thwart them. The enemy is quietly but diligently at work. The inmates of the custom-houses at Boston and Portsmouth are, we are informed, entertaining strong hope that New Hampshire is about to go over to the black Democracy. A year ago, Hopkinton, in this county, and other towns were carried by emissaries and money from the Boston custom-house. . . . Probably these United States government office-holders will soon be prowling over the State attending to the closely balanced towns. It is, therefore, right that the Republican office-holders should meet them in their own mode of warfare."

The total vote at the election of 1857 fell off some six thousand from the Presidential vote of 1856, but it was concentrated on the two candidates for governor of the Republican and Democratic parties, there being less than five hundred third party or scattering votes. The Republican candidate for governor had three thousand plurality, and over twenty-five hundred majority.

When the legislature of 1857 met, Rollins was renominated for Speaker by acclamation on motion of Aaron F. Stevens, of Nashua. The principal committee appointments included the leading men of the legislature. Napoleon B. Bryant, of Concord, was chairman of the committee of elections; Henry A. Bellows, of Concord, of judiciary; James M. Lovering, of Exeter, of banks; Jacob H. Ela, of Rochester, of retrenchment and reform, William H. Y. Hackett, of Portsmouth, of railroads; Frederick Smyth, of Manchester, of incorporations. On the judiciary committee were Stevens, of Nashua, Lewis W. Clark, of Manchester, George W. Stevens, of Laconia, and William C. Patten, of Kingston. Ezekiel A. Straw, of Manchester, and James F. Briggs, of Hillsboro, were also members of this legislature. Briggs, who later became a Republican, was at that time a Democrat. He was a rival of Rollins for the Senatorship at the time the latter was defeated for reëlection, in 1883. Stevens, of Nashua, and Ela became members of Congress. Smyth and Straw became governors of the State, and Clark was appointed, twenty years later, to the Supreme Court of the State.

Upon this legislature devolved the duty of filling the vacancy in the United States Senate occasioned by the death of Senator James Bell, May 26, 1857. The Republican legislative caucus to nominate a candidate was held soon after the legislature was organized. Only one ballot was necessary, and this was as follows:

George W. Nesmith, of Franklin, 1; Amos Tuck, of Exeter, 8; Ichabod Goodwin, of Portsmouth, 23; Thomas M. Edwards, of Keene, 44; Daniel Clark, of Manchester, 110.

The choice of Daniel Clark, who had been a prominent candidate for Senator in 1855, when Hale and Bell were chosen, was commended in the highest terms by the Republican newspapers of the State. At the conclusion of his term, he was reëlected for a full term of six years, serving in all ten years in the Senate. He became one of the leaders of that body, and was chosen president *pro tem* in 1864. The office at that

time was more important than now, as it carried with
it the succession to the presidency. Clark was a man
of great ability, attaining national distinction. His
defeat for reëlection, in 1866, for which he himself
was in part responsible, was a distinct loss to the State.
After the choice of his successor, he resigned to take an
appointment as United States district judge for New
Hampshire, a position he held until his death. In
1876, he was elected to the Constitutional Convention
of the State and chosen to preside over its delibera-
tion, a fitting and, as it proved to be, the best selection
that could have been made. No one who saw him as
he presided over this convention or took part in the debates of that body but felt the influence of his commanding presence and impressive speech.

Amos Tuck was one of the early Free-soilers of New
Hampshire. He was elected to Congress in 1847, and
twice reëlected. Hostility to slavery extension kept
him in opposition to the Democratic party, and he was
a leading spirit in the founding of the Republican
party. The designation " Republican " was a name
that he early suggested for the new party, and he continued prominent in its councils for many years. He
became acquainted with Abraham Lincoln while both
were members of Congress, and he was one of the three
men considered by Lincoln for appointment as Secretary of the Navy in his first administration. Tuck
was appointed naval officer of customs at Boston in
1861, and reappointed by Lincoln in 1865. With the
other officials of that port he was removed by President

Johnson, who desired to make Hannibal Hamlin, of Maine, collector of Boston, and who, at that time, was attempting, through federal appointments, to secure support for his policy of reconstruction of the South in antagonism to that of the Republican majority in Congress. While naval officer at Boston, Tuck had strong support in the Republican caucus of 1864 as a candidate for the United States Senate. His interest in politics continued until his death some years later, but he was not again a candidate for office.

Thomas M. Edwards was at this time a prominent leader of the new party. He had taken a conspicuous part in the legislatures of 1855 and 1856, being chairman of the judiciary committee in the latter year. In both legislatures he had borne a leading part in debates upon political questions. He was recognized as a man of character and ability, and worthy of promotion. In 1859, he was elected to Congress, where he served two terms.

At the close of the legislative session of 1857, Nehemiah G. Ordway was appointed high sheriff of Merrimack County, in place of William H. Rixford, removed by address of the legislature. Ordway had been made doorkeeper of the House of Representatives of the State in 1855, when the Know Nothing party attained power, and he was now coming to the front as an active party worker. He was a strong, courageous, and aggressive personality, indefatigable in his labors. His untiring industry and aggressive Republicanism soon brought him into leadership. Inspiring his deputies with his own zeal, by their aid he became an active force in political campaigns. Later, he was city marshal of Concord, and in 1863, after Rollins was sent to Congress, he was made sergeant-at-arms of the National House of Representatives, a position he held until his election to the New Hampshire legislature, in 1875. Subsequently Ordway was appointed Governor of the Territory of Dakota, largely through Rollins's influence.

From about the time of Ordway's appointment as sheriff dates the political copartnership of Rollins, Chandler, and Ordway, an association which secured for the party a strong and able leadership, and for the State of New Hampshire exceptional recognition at Washington during Lincoln's administration. They formed, as it were, the Republican machine in the eyes of both party associates and political enemies. Few men in public life have been more bitterly or unjustly assailed. Campaigns were fought around their personality. Their success provoked jealousy. At times it was doubtful who were more hostile to them, the Democrats who assailed them in partisan warfare, or Republicans who were envious of their leadership.

For a period of four years, from 1868 to 1872, the hostility to the "firm," as Rollins, Chandler, and Ordway were called, threatened the overthrow of the Republican party of New Hampshire. So wrought up was this feeling of jealousy that some Republicans would have almost welcomed Democratic success in the State if it had brought with it the downfall of the triumvirate. Yet looking over the literature of the time, one reaches the conclusion that the jealousy they provoked in the Republican party arose almost wholly from rival ambitions and disappointed hopes natural in a State producing a large number of able men as candidates for the few high positions which it had to bestow. Rollins bore with remarkable patience these personal attacks from within and without the party, but Chandler and Ordway fought them to the finish, especially the attacks from party associates. Their different attitudes under fire were due first to their different personalities, and second to their official relations at the time to the party. Rollins, as chairman of the State committee, was charged with the responsibility of Republican success in the State, while Chandler was holding no official position except that of secretary of the National Committee, and Ordway was absent from the State most of the time because of his official duties in Washington. Then again, the attacks were oftentimes more severely personal on Chandler and Ordway than on Rollins. Furthermore, Rollins did not lose sight of his ambition to go to the United States Senate, which could not be realized if the Republican party was defeated in New Hampshire by personal quarrels. Thus it was that for several years a great part of the history of the Republican party of New Hampshire was identified with the personal and political association of these three men.

The Democrats, following their custom, opened the campaign of 1858 early in the summer. Their State convention met June 10, 1857, while the legislature was in session. Asa P. Cate, of Northfield, was nominated for governor, and John M. Hill, of Concord, was made chairman of the Democratic State committee. Hill was a son of former governor and United States Senator Isaac Hill. He was a man of strong convictions and strong party feelings, but a most estimable citizen. He was associated for a time with William Butterfield in the publication of the *New Hampshire Patriot,* a paper founded by his father. While not aspiring to office, he was an active leader and counsellor in the Democratic party for many years. In 1884, he was a nominee of his party for governor, polling the full party strength. In later life his partisan feelings softened, and in 1896, with thousands of other Democrats of New Hampshire, he refused to endorse the national platform and candidates of the Democratic party. He had intimate business relations for many years with Rollins, each holding the other in high esteem.

As soon as the legislature of 1857 adjourned, the Democratic newspapers began an attack upon the Republican State administration and this was continued throughout the campaign. The Democratic party of the country was dividing on the policy which Buchanan's administration was pursuing toward Kansas, and, therefore, New Hampshire Democrats were disposed to avoid national issues.

The call for the Republican State convention was signed by the entire State committee. The convention met at Concord, January 7, 1858. Anthony Colby was chosen president, and Governor Haile was renominated by acclamation. The platform was reported by Amos Tuck, and the issue of the campaign was outlined in this plank:

" While we stand ready to defend on all proper occasions the measures of the government of this State since it has been under the control of the party now in power, and challenge the severest scrutiny of our enemies, we yet refuse to be drawn away from the great national questions whose merits are more than all else at issue in the canvass which we this day inaugurate."

The convention was a very enthusiastic one, and was addressed during the proceedings by James W. Nye, of New York, afterward United States Senator from Nevada. Rollins was reëlected chairman of the State committee, and William E. Chandler was made secretary. The *Statesman* compliments Rollins for his zeal in having secured the organization of the Republican clubs in the various towns of the State before the meeting of the convention. Democratic attacks on the State administration were met and answered, but the issues brought home to the people by the Republican State committee and the Republican press were those of national import.

This was a speaking campaign, although there were no speakers from outside the State on the Democratic side, and but few on the Republican. The principal speakers for the Democrats were John H. George, Walter Harriman (then a Democrat), John S. Wells,

George W. Morrison, Lewis W. Clark, George W. Stevens, George A. Bingham, William T. Norris, and John M. Shirley. The Republican State committee appears to have drawn upon nearly all its local speakers for service in this campaign, and in addition they had the assistance of Thomas Russell and Charles C. Woodman, of Massachusetts, and the Rev. E. Nute, a negro from Kansas. The activity of the Republicans in this canvass may be judged by the fact that more than seventy-five Republican meetings were scheduled for one of the closing weeks of the campaign.

Rollins, in addition to his duties as chairman of the State committee, spoke a number of times in this campaign. His experience was enriched by an unexpected joint debate at Warner. Napoleon B. Bryant had been advertised to speak there, but, being unable to fill the engagement, Rollins took his place. At the close of his speech one of the local leaders undertook to answer Rollins on the spot. Such occurrences were not uncommon in those days. Only meagre accounts of the discussion survive in the newspapers of the day. The Democratic newspapers do not refer to it, but both the *Independent Democrat* and the *Statesman* credit Rollins with having the best of the debate.

The election resulted in a great victory for the Republicans. It was a straight contest between the Republican and Democratic parties, no third party appearing in the field, and the scattering vote being surprisingly small. The election returns show the following result: Haile, 36,326; Cate, 31,679; scattering, 72.

At the close of this campaign Rollins made a visit to Washington, probably his first, in company with George G. Fogg. The latter, in his editorial correspondence from the capital to the *Independent Democrat,* refers to their visit and the courtesy shown them by Senator John P. Hale in extending to them the privileges of the floor of the United States Senate. Eighteen years of active political strife were to intervene before Rollins was to enter that body as a member. Fogg, in this correspondence, takes occasion to say that the recent political victory in New Hampshire was largely due to the "indefatigable labor" of Rollins as chairman of the State committee.

The campaigns of both political parties of New Hampshire at this time were conducted in the simplest and most economical manner. The rank and file were enthusiastic in the cause. They did the work assigned to them without compensation for time or expenses. They devoted days and nights to making canvasses. They rode miles in all kinds of winter weather to get information, attend conventions and rallies, and to get voters home. If they employed help, they gave the preference to voters of their own political faith. The headquarters in each town was usually a country store, and in many localities there were a Republican and a Democratic store. Custom at these stores was usually along party lines, the Republicans patronizing the Republican store, and the Democrats the merchant who voted their ticket. The country store and the tavern, if there was one, were places frequented by the active politicians, and the winter evenings were spent in political discussion, the local talkers displaying their acumen in puncturing the weak points of their opponents' arguments. The newspapers were intensely partisan, publishing nothing that reflected upon their side, unless it was a garbled quotation to be branded as false or shown up as inconsistent. Only the leaders read the newspapers of the opposition. The subscription lists of the party organs were made up almost wholly from devotees of the cause they represented. The "lying sheet" of the other side was banished from a majority of households. The political worker during the closing days of a campaign was excused by his employer from his daily toil without loss of wages if he could be of service to the party. The boys, too, were early inducted into politics, being taken to political rallies and assigned to work which their elders could safely entrust to them. Even the women were imbued with the spirit of their husbands, fathers, and brothers, and entered with enthusiasm into campaigns, preparing many a supper with which to close a political rally.

The records of the secretary of the Republican State committee for the years 1858, 1859, and 1860, fortunately preserved, give authentic information of the manner of conducting the campaigns of those early days, the expenses of the committees, and how the funds were raised. As at present, the legitimate expense of the campaign had to be provided for by the

State committee, and was incurred in getting voters home, circulating literature, employing outside speakers, conducting correspondence, providing for State conventions and for mass-meetings at central points when these were held. These expenses were not so large as they are at the present day, but the committee appears to have had equal difficulty in providing for them. The funds were almost wholly raised from assessments of office-holders and candidates for elective offices. The federal patronage prior to March 4, 1861, was in Democratic hands, and the Republicans had to depend upon the generosity of the State and county officials and their candidates for office.

The salaries of State and county officials were very meagre. The governor received $1,000 a year, the secretary of state, $800, the deputy secretary of state, $200, while the fees of the office were divided between them, probably not enhancing their compensation to more than $1,200 and $500 respectively. The State treasurer received $600, the attorney-general, $1,800, the adjutant-general, $400, the chief justice of the supreme judicial court, $2,000, his associates, $1,800 each, while the chief justice of the court of common pleas had a salary of $1,600 and his two associates, $1,500 each. The county solicitors received from thirty to fifty dollars annually, according to the size of the county, while the judges of probate had compensation ranging from $150 to $425 annually, the latter being the compensation of David Cross, judge of probate of Hillsboro County. Amos Hadley, who was

State printer June 30, 1859, received from the State
$5,863.04 for the public printing. Members of Congress and United States Senators were at that time receiving a salary of $3,000 a year. From the foregoing it will be seen how difficult it was to raise from $1,500 to $2,000, which the Republican State committee required for use in those campaigns.

William E. Chandler was secretary of the State committee in the campaigns of 1858 and 1859, and Benjamin F. Prescott began his long career as secretary in 1860. It is from the records of these three years that extracts are taken. At the organization of the State committee January 7, 1858, the chairman and secretary were instructed to give to Charles C. Woodman a written testimonial of their appreciation of his services upon the stump in the last two campaigns. After making arrangements for speakers and for a thorough canvass of the State by the first day of February, the committee voted:

" That the list of uncollected assessments upon officeholders be forwarded to the county committees for collection.

" That the New Hampshire delegation in Congress be assessed the sum of $500 toward the expenses of the campaign, reserving to the committee the right to call upon the delegation for $500 additional if needed.

" To pay General James W. Nye fifty dollars for services and expenses to address the State convention."

The delegation in Congress at that time consisted of Senators John P. Hale and Daniel Clark and Representatives James Pike, Mason W. Tappan, and Aaron H. Cragin. They were required to pay $100 apiece into the campaign fund, with the contingency that each might be asked to duplicate this sum. Small as was the amount called for, some of the delegation appear to have been delinquent in its payment. That they sent only fifty dollars apiece is shown at the next meeting, February 10, 1858, when the committee voted:

" That the secretary be requested to instruct the members of the House of Representatives in Congress to forward fifty dollars each to the treasurer of the committee, being the amount still unpaid of their assessment voted January 7, 1858."

This second demand of the committee was not honored, for, at a meeting of the committee in November, 1858, it was voted:

" That the Congressmen (Senators already elected, and Representatives hereafter to be elected) be assessed $200 each.

" That a request be made for fifty dollars each from the Representatives in Congress, being the balance of assessment heretofore ordered."

The campaign of March, 1858, was simply a State election, the members of Congress being elected in the spring of 1857. The latter may have felt that the off year did not directly concern them, and that the assessment of the State committee was out of proportion to their interest in the campaign. It is possible also that they contributed to individual appeals outside of the

State committee, for, at a meeting of the committee, January 3, 1860, it was voted:

"That no money shall be credited to our members of Congress unless the same shall first be sent to the State central committee."

At this same meeting, on motion of Anthony Colby, it was voted:

"That Mason W. Tappan pay $100 due from him on his assessment."

Tappan undoubtedly had as an offset to this assessment his contributions to some localities hard pressed for funds, as he was always responsive to such calls.

At a meeting of the State committee January 20, 1859, a finance committee, consisting of Edward H. Rollins, Joseph P. Morse, of Portsmouth, Nehemiah G. Ordway, of Concord, Banbridge Wadleigh, of Milford, Greenleaf Cummings, of Lisbon, and George W. Gilman, of Meredith, was appointed. At an adjourned meeting, they made a report which was accepted. The report proposed "a basis of assessment for State and county officers not elected by the people, excepting the governor, judges, attorney-general, and past and present members of Congress and candidates for the same." It was voted "to assess the Senators in Congress each $150, and the present Representatives in Congress each $100, and the candidates for the same each $200." It was also voted "that the secretary be authorized and instructed to write the Republican members of the bench and request fifty dollars each, also to write Governor Haile and Attorney-General John Sullivan for aid, without naming the amount."

It was voted "that the matter of assessing the State liquor agent at Boston be left to the discretion of the officers of the committee."

Voted "that the matter of campaign newspapers be referred to county committees with instructions to subscribe for as many as they see fit and to raise and pay to newspapers all they can."

"Voted that fifty dollars be appropriatd to the *Winnepisseogee Gazette.*"

At the meeting of the State committee in February, 1859, it was voted to give the town of Meredith an order for the assessment of Samuel W. Rollins. The latter at that time was solicitor for Belknap County, with an annual salary of thirty dollars. It is probable that his assessment was five dollars.

At another meeting of the committee the same year, on motion of Henry O. Kent, of Lancaster, it was voted "that the assessment of officers be the same as last year, with the exception of Ethan Colby, of Colebrook, and that the sum of ten dollars be placed after his name, instead of five dollars, and that the secretary inform the various officers of the amount assessed."

In preparing for the spring campaign of 1860, it was voted "to assess each member of Congress $200, and that the treasurer draw from them the sum of $500 for this spring's campaign."

The allotment of funds to the towns is shown at one of the meetings of the committee, when it was voted

" to allow ten dollars to Atkinson, ten dollars to New-ton, and twenty dollars to Newmarket, if there be funds." Twenty dollars was allotted to Brookfield, and it was voted to allow William M. Weed twenty-five dollars for money expended by him at Ossipee. Twenty-five dollars was allowed Austin F. Pike for Sanbornton. At that time Sanbornton was one of the large towns of the State, and included the present town of Tilton in its boundaries. It was closely contested, and the allotment made to it indicates the measure of help the State committee gave to the towns.

The judges of the court appear to have responded to their assessment, with the exception of Chief Justice Ira Perley. He wrote a vigorous protest to the call made upon the court for political contributions, but commended the work of the committee, and expressed his deep interest in the cause. Whether he protested to enforce a principle, and then quietly handed in a contribution through some third party, as a later chief justice of the New Hampshire court was accustomed to do, is unknown.

The practice of having the State committee prepare a list of officers for a coming State convention to be submitted to the convention for its ratification orig-inated at a meeting of the committee held April 25, 1860, to arrange for the State convention which was to elect delegates to the Chicago National Convention. On motion of Henry O. Kent, of Lancaster, it was voted " that one from each county be selected to report permanent officers for the convention to choose delegates to the Chicago Convention." The report of this committee was accepted, and then it was voted " that the list of officers proposed by the committee be proposed to the convention by the chairman of the State committee." The object of this innovation was to save the time of the convention in perfecting an organization, and to give opportunity to the presiding officer to prepare an address, and to the committee on resolutions to prepare a platform. This precedent has been followed ever since, though in later years it devolved upon the chairman of the State committee and the executive committee to select some time in advance the presiding officer and committee on resolutions. Once, at least, in 1898, the practice was called in question, but the party representatives by a large majority decided to continue it.

The meetings of the committee in these early years were held at one of the hotels in Concord, and appear to have been almost wholly executive sessions from which the public was excluded. The entire records of the secretaries for the years 1858, 1859, and 1860 are contained in a blank book of some forty pages.

CHAPTER V.

A CANDIDATE FOR CONGRESS

The call for the Republican State Convention of 1859 was signed, as heretofore, by the full State committee. There was no contest for the nomination for governor, as the Republican leaders now considered their party compact enough to present that sterling representative of the old Whig party, Ichabod Goodwin, of Portsmouth, who had been a candidate two years before. At the time James Pike, Mason W. Tappan, and Aaron H. Cragin were renominated for Congress, in 1857, it was expected that they would step aside at the close of their two terms for new candidates. The theory of rotation in office was generally accepted by the new party as a governing principle in nominations, the governor and most of the members of the legislature receiving but two nominations. But, when the legislature of 1858 met, it had to choose a successor to United States Senator John P. Hale. He had been elected in 1855 to fill out a vacancy occasioned by the death of Charles G. Atherton. Hale had served one full term from 1847 to 1853, and, with this part of a term, had had ten years in the Senate. To give him another term would accord to him greater length of service in the Senate than any of his prede-

88

cessors in New Hampshire. The question of rotation, therefore, was at once raised by other candidates and their friends. It was discussed in the press, but the standing of Hale before the country and the pressure from outside the State for his return, together with his home support, gave him an easy victory.

Hale had been in public life since 1834, when he was appointed United States District Attorney for New Hampshire by President Jackson. In 1843 he was elected to Congress as a Democrat. Opposing his party on the slavery question, he incurred its hostility when a candidate for reëlection. This break with the Democratic leaders resulted in his election to the United States Senate, in 1847, by a coalition legislature opposed to the Democratic party. For several years he stood almost alone in the Senate in opposition to slavery. He was nominated for the Presidency in 1852 by the Liberty party. In 1865, at the expiration of his last term in the Senate, he was appointed minister to Spain. In 1859, he was one of the most prominent Republicans of the country. A ready and eloquent speaker, he was a formidable antagonist in debate. His joint discussion on the slavery question with Franklin Pierce, in the Old North Meeting-house of Concord, just after his break with the Democratic party, was an inspiration to the friends of liberty throughout the State, and gave him national prominence. In the Republican legislative caucus of 1859, he was nominated by a very large majority, the vote being as follows: William Haile, 1; George W.

Nesmith, 4; Anthony Colby, 7; Amos Tuck, 26; Thomas M. Edwards, 30; John P. Hale, 127.

The *Statesman* editorially expressed the belief that Hale's reëlection was a dangerous precedent for the Republican party to set, and intimated that this action of the legislature would justify Tappan and Cragin in asking for a third term in Congress.

Soon after the legislature adjourned the canvass for delegates to the three Republican Congressional conventions began. Pike was not a candidate for renomination in the First District, but both Tappan and Cragin sought renominations in the other two districts. Rollins was a candidate in the Second District. His candidacy was only well under way when the *New Hampshire Patriot* opened upon him with a revival of its old charge made in the Speakership fight that he had coerced the party into retiring Prentiss for himself, coupled with the statement that he and his friends had made overtures to John S. Wells, the Democratic candidate for governor in 1856, to elect Wells governor in return for Democratic support of Rollins for Speaker. That paper also intimated that Rollins had no sympathy with the Republican party. The *Independent Democrat,* Fogg's paper, made immediate reply, as follows:

" The *Patriot* of this week contains a mean and dastardly article written by John H. George charging Edward H. Rollins, of this city, with having conspired with the Hunkers, in 1856, to make John S. Wells governor. The charge is as false as the coon skin source, whence it originated, is base and dastardly. This much we say without consulting with Mr. Rollins, who is now out of the city, but who on his return will, we venture to promise, brand the lie as it deserves."

The *Patriot* returned to the charge in its next issue, exonerating George of any connection with the article, but declining to give a bill of particulars on Fogg's simple denial. To this renewed attack Fogg replied:

"The *Patriot* sticks to its whole-cloth lie that E. H. Rollins conspired with the Hunkers, in 1856, to elect John S. Wells governor. Let it stick to it. It may as well lie about that as anything else. The efficient service which Mr. Rollins has always rendered the Republican cause in this State has stirred up Hunker malignity to its lowest and foulest depths. Hence this lying charge of the *Patriot*. Mr. Rollins has served long enough and faithfully enough in the Republican party to render his political integrity secure from question. We herewith publish the remarks of the *Manchester American* upon this matter."

The *American,* after reciting the charges of the *Patriot,* says: "We are authorized to deny this insinuation *in toto.* It is without the shadow of foundation. Mr. Rollins never proposed such a bargain, nor was a party to it, nor was there any such thing. We deem it proper to say thus much in relation to this matter because it has been brought before the public. We say it in justice to Mr. Rollins and to the Republicans who were in the legislature at the time, and to the Republican party."

Referring to the *Patriot's* insinuation that Rollins was not at heart a Republican, the *American* said: "There is one thing we desire to say with the utmost distinctness, and that is that after a man has for a series of years manifested his attachment for the party and its principles, as has Mr. Rollins, his fidelity is not to be questioned. Mr. Rollins has since the year 1855 acted in good faith with the present dominant party, and he is entitled to the fullest confidence and respect of the party. The Republican party of this State arose from the ruins of the old parties, and is composed of men from them all. It was called into existence by a new and remarkable crisis in public affairs. Its history is brief. Now, who is to be considered only a true Republican? Will one man say it must be a previous Whig? Another that it must be a former Democrat? If so, where are we? What general criterion of integrity have we? We repudiate any such attempt at scouring up antecedents."

As the *Manchester American* made a specific denial of the *Patriot's* charge, it is evident that Rollins was at Manchester when the *Patriot* article was brought to his attention, and gave then and there an authorization for the denial. As Manchester had a candidate for this Republican Congressional nomination in David Cross, the *American's* tribute to Rollins's party fealty is all the more emphatic. The *Patriot* made no further reference to its charges, and the incident was closed for the campaign. The charge and denials both occurred several weeks before the convention was held.

The Republican newspapers of Concord advocated editorially the claims of no candidate. The *Nashua Telegraph* supported Aaron F. Stevens, of Nashua. The *Statesman,* however, gave space to a communication advocating Rollins's nomination as well as space to one the following week setting forth the claims of George W. Nesmith, of Franklin.

The convention met at Manchester, January 20, 1859. An informal ballot was first taken, which resulted as follows: Charles H. Campbell, Amherst, 1; George W. Nesmith, Franklin, 7; William H. Gove, Weare, 16; David Cross, Manchester, 29; Aaron F. Stevens, Nashua, 34; Edward H. Rollins, Concord, 39; Mason W. Tappan, Bradford, 71.

After the announcement of the result of this ballot, Rollins, Cross, and Nesmith withdrew. A formal ballot was then taken with this result: Frederick Smyth, 1; David Cross, 2; Edward H. Rollins, 10; Aaron F. Stevens, 31; William H. Gove, 54; Mason W. Tappan, 99; and Tappan was declared the nominee.

There was a spirited contest in the other two Congressional districts. In the first district, the active candidates were Gilman Marston, of Exeter, and Joel Eastman, of Conway. The former was nominated on the second ballot.

In the third district, Thomas M. Edwards, of Keene, was nominated on the first ballot, having as competitors Aaron H. Cragin, of Lebanon, Jacob Benton, of Lancaster, and Levi Barton, of Newport.

The Republican State convention met January 4, 1859, at Concord. Napoleon B. Bryant, of Concord, who was Rollins's successor as Speaker of the House, was chosen president. Bryant was one of the recent converts to the Republican party, having been a Democrat up to the Presidential election of 1856. After serving two years as Speaker, he went to Massachusetts, where he practised law until his death. He was a man of distinguished appearance and an eloquent speaker, frequently taking part in New Hampshire campaigns. His interest in New Hampshire continued through life, his summer home being in Andover.

George G. Fogg reported the resolutions, all relating to national affairs. Although it was certain that Ichabod Goodwin would be the nominee for governor, a ballot was taken. Out of 373 votes cast, Goodwin received 368. A great storm blocking roads and preventing travel occurred just before the convention, which accounted for the small attendance.

The *Patriot,* in commenting upon the Republican ticket for governor and Congressmen, said that it was made up of old enemies of the Democratic party, all Whigs, no former Democrat being among the number.

The Democratic convention met January 6, 1859. Asa P. Cate, of Northfield, was renominated for governor by acclamation. At the Democratic Congressional conventions, Daniel Marcy, of Portsmouth, was nominated in the first district, John H. George, of Concord, in the second, and William Burns, of Lancaster, in the third.

The campaign was most vigorously waged in the second district, where the Democratic candidate immediately took the stump. He issued a challenge to Tappan, his Republican opponent, to meet him in joint debate. Tappan declined on the ground that his duties as Congressman required his presence in Washington where Congress was assembled in the short session. Later George's challenge was taken up by Charles C. Woodman, of Boston, who was assisting the Republicans on the stump, and, in a letter to George, he requested the opportunity of taking Tappan's place. George declined the request on the ground that Woodman was not a voter in the district, or a resident of the State.

To no part of the State did Rollins devote more personal attention than to the second district. All through the campaign he kept in close touch with the voters of that district. Immediately after Tappan's renomination, he gave to it prompt and unequivocal endorsement. Tappan wrote him a most appreciative letter.

" House of Representatives, Washington, D. C.
" January 28, 1859.

" Friend Rollins: — I have been intending for some time to drop you a line for the purpose of thanking you for the early and cordial endorsement you gave the nomination made at Manchester on the 20th. I do so now with all my heart. I have entertained none but the kindest feelings toward you personally, and have none other now. I could hope that nothing has occurred to mar the friendly relations that have always existed between us. I endeavored to act honorably and frankly throughout the canvass. Whether I did so others must judge. I trust the nomination will prove for the best and that all will come right in the end. Let me hear from you as to the prospects and, believe me, truly your friend."

The political rallies of the campaign of 1859 were largely addressed by local speakers on both sides. To assist the Democrats, Isaac H. Wright, Sydney Webster, who had been private secretary of President Pierce, and B. F. Hallett, of Boston, appeared and spoke in the State. The Republicans were assisted in their speaking by Frank P. Blair, of Missouri, Galusha A. Grow, of Pennsylvania, Hannibal Hamlin, of Maine, John C. Underwood, of Virginia, and M. J. Parrott, a member of Congress from Kansas. The gubernatorial vote indicates the victory won by the Republicans: Goodwin, 36,326; Cate, 32,802; scattering, 27. All three Republican Congressmen were elected by good majorities, and there was the usual Republican majority in the legislature.

With a taste for public life acquired by his service in the legislature, Mr. Rollins determined to qualify himself for any future honors which might be conferred upon him. He was now considered the coming candidate of his party for Congress in the second district when Mason W. Tappan should conclude his third term, and there was a reasonable prospect that he would soon be transferred to the national field of public affairs. While Rollins had been obliged to forego a college course, he continued his education in leisure hours by extensive reading. He recognized that, if he was to take any important part in public life and participate in debates, he must acquire a facility of expression which comes only from experience. He set himself to work in the hours that were free from business cares to further equip himself.

Henry O. Kent, who had been clerk of the New Hampshire House of Representatives when Rollins was Speaker, was at this time the editor of the *Coos Republican,* a Republican newspaper published at Lancaster. Kent was a Republican leader in northern New Hampshire, and there existed between him and Rollins an intimate friendship which continued through life. Rollins asked Kent for the opportunity to write letters during the campaign of 1859 and '60 to the latter's newspaper, stating frankly his purpose in making this request, and soliciting such editorial revision of the manuscript as would be most beneficial to himself. An agreement was accordingly made, and for several months the readers of the *Coos Republican* read a chatty correspondence that dealt with politics and social affairs at the capital. The earlier letters have in them something of the crudity of expression of an inexperienced writer, but there is a noticeable improvement toward the close of the series. Throughout them all there is a directness of expression for which Rol-

lins was noted in later life. In discussing politics, he
touched upon those features of political affairs which
most readily caught the popular thought. There is
even a vein of humor running through these letters
as the correspondent appears to have given his imagination full play. No one enjoyed the quaint things of
politics more than Rollins, although he was not given
in later life to humorous speech. He thoroughly enjoyed the company of bright and witty companions,
relishing a good story, but his own sense of the ridicu-
lous he did not cultivate. These letters were written
at the time he was chairman of the Republican State
committee, and were probably composed in the back
room of his drug store, so long the headquarters of the
party. They appear over the signature of "Stark,"
and in all political references they show the intensity
of the struggle then going on. The last but one of
these letters was written after Abraham Lincoln had
made his first speech in New Hampshire, in 1860.
This was the first time Rollins had seen Lincoln, and
his impressions of the man to whom he was ever afterward ardently devoted are worth producing. He says:

"It is worth a long walk to see the man. He is
a unique specimen of the human family. Long, lank,
and awkward, he presents the picture of a real Yankee.
His voice is pitched on a high key and is anything but
musical, but these oddities and peculiarities which
would seem to detract from the efficiency of an orator
all go to gain the sympathy of his hearers and to make
his speeches what they are. For nearly two hours he

held the house in perfect silence, while by his invincible logic, interspersed with the most apt illustrations, he showed the inconsistency and suicidal position of the Democracy with reference to the slavery question. His arguments were perfectly unanswerable. His appeal to the Douglass Democrats and his charges upon Squatter Sovereignty were irresistible. I can give you no adequate description of his speech. It was, as our friends say, unquestionably the most candid, convincing, and effective speech which we have had in Concord for years. If we could have Mr. Lincoln address the people of our State for three weeks, we should triumph by ten thousand majority."

Although Rollins does not disclose his identity in this correspondence, he is continually urging upon his fellow Republicans the necessity for more perfect organization in order to secure victory.

The call for Republican State convention of 1860 was signed by Rollins as chairman of the State committee, the first call of the kind that was signed solely by the chairman. The convention met January 3, 1860. Frederick Smyth, of Manchester, was elected president. Governor Goodwin was renominated by acclamation. George G. Fogg reported the resolutions, and they all dealt with national affairs, except the one commending Goodwin's administration.

The Democratic State convention was held October 11, 1859. Walter Harriman presided over its deliberations. Asa P. Cate, of Northfield, who had twice been the candidate of the party for governor, was again a candidate. James S. Cheney, of Manchester, was also presented to the convention for the nomination. On the first ballot there was no choice, Cate receiving 102 votes, Cheney, 94, and 28 scattering. On the second ballot, Cate was renominated by 21 majority. Although educated for the bar, Cate was not an active practitioner. He was rather an office counsellor, his advice being sought by a large clientage. Few men have possessed more largely the confidence of the community.

It was in this campaign that Abraham Lincoln made his first appearance in New Hampshire. He spoke at Concord, Manchester, Dover, and Exeter. His first meeting was at Concord. At this meeting Rollins presided. All of Lincoln's speeches made a deep impression upon the Republicans of the State. It was his appearance in New Hampshire that gave him, in the National Convention, on the first ballot, seven of the ten delegates from the State.

The March election of 1860 was most important as bearing upon the Presidential election that year. A week before election Rollins published the result of the State committee's canvass. It was a novel experiment, never having been done before by the State committee of either party. Rollins's canvass gave the Republican candidate for governor 4,178 majority. His actual majority at the election was 4,471.

The effect of the New Hampshire election upon the Republicans of the country is told in a letter of con-

gratulation and exultation from Congressman Tappan
to Rollins.

"HOUSE OF REPRESENTATIVES, WASHINGTON, D. C.
"March 15, 1860.

"FRIEND ROLLINS: — All hail New Hampshire!
You have done gloriously and our friends here are in
high glee over the result. My room was crowded
Tuesday night, and when my despatch from McFarland and Jenks came you better believe we had a good
time. There never was so much interest felt here in
regard to the result in our State. You ought to have
seen Gil Marston stride across my room. He is getting
very fanatical and must be sent home, and a more conservative man sent in his place, or the country will be
ruined.

"You are getting a national reputation, and your
successful management is frequently spoken of by
members from other States in the highest terms of
praise. I have named you as just the man to come
here and take charge of the Presidential canvass. I
think Perley will suggest it in his letters to the *Boston
Journal*. Would you, or could you, come if it could
be brought about?

"I sent my ' Thank God ' to New Hampshire over
the wires Tuesday night. Did it get there? What do
the Hunkers say? The reaction has indeed commenced. I trust the ball will roll on through
Rhode Island and Connecticut. Let me hear from
you."

Immediately after the election, Rollins and George G. Fogg went to Connecticut to participate in the campaign in that State, its election occurring at that time the first Monday in April. There was frequently an exchange of talent in the campaigns of the two States. The election this year in Connecticut was a hard fought contest, and the Republican victory which followed was a fitting supplement to the Republican triumph in New Hampshire. The Republican newspapers in Connecticut were very complimentary of Rollins's efforts in that State.

Following closely the Connecticut victory was the Republican State convention of New Hampshire to choose delegates to the Republican National Convention to nominate candidates for President and Vice-President, called to meet at Chicago, May 16, 1860. Republican sentiment was divided in the State over candidates for the Presidency. Fogg was inclined to the renomination of Fremont. In answer to a correspondent, he expressed the opinion in his newspaper, *The Independent Democrat,* that, while the politicians were not for Fremont, the people were. In an editorial as late as April 19th, a week before the Republican State convention, he names as Republican candidates for the Presidency John C. Fremont, Salmon P. Chase, William H. Seward, Edward Bates, and John McLean. In his newspaper of April 26th, he gives the names of those mentioned for the Chicago nomination in this order: William H. Seward, Salmon Chase, John C. Fremont, John P. Hale, Abraham Lincoln, William P. Fessenden, Nathaniel P. Banks, Simon Cameron, Edward Bates, John McLean, Benjamin F. Wade, and Henry Wilson. This was his first mention of Lincoln as a candidate. In the same issue of his newspaper, he quotes correspondence of the *New York Tribune* in favor of Fremont.

Rollins from the time of Lincoln's first speech in New Hampshire became a champion of his nomination. In the advocacy of Lincoln, he was in accord with Chandler, Ordway, Tuck, and others. No attempt was made to commit the convention to any candidate, but the individual preference of the delegates chosen was pretty well known, and the sentiment of the convention was favorable to Lincoln by a large majority.

The Republican State convention was held April 26th. Joel Eastman, of Conway, was elected president. No platform was adopted, this work being left to the National convention. Only one ballot was taken for four delegates at large. This was as follows: Austin F. Pike, of Franklin, 1; Nathaniel Hubbard, of Tamworth, 1; Lemuel N. Pattee, of Concord, 64; David Steele, of Goffstown, 84; George M. Herring, of Farmington, 133; Amos Tuck, of Exeter, 381; William Haile, of Hinsdale, 385; Aaron H. Cragin, of Lebanon, 499; Edward H. Rollins, of Concord, 514. The last four were declared elected delegates.

The delegates from the three Congressional districts were as follows: First District: George Mathewson, of Dover, and Nathaniel Hubbard, of Tamworth. Second District: Benjamin Martin, of Manchester, and Francis H. Morgan, of Francestown. Third District: Jacob Benton, of Lancaster, and Jacob C. Bean, of Enfield. Rollins was made chairman of the delegation.

On the first ballot for President at the Chicago convention, New Hampshire cast seven votes for Lincoln, one for Chase, one for Fremont, and one for Seward. On the next ballot, ten votes of New Hampshire were given for Lincoln. The latter was especially gratified with the support he received from this State. With the exception of Tuck, who had been in Congress with him, Lincoln had no personal acquaintance with the Republican leaders of the State until the spring campaign of 1860. While he had made a deep impression by his speeches in that campaign upon the Republicans of the State, he had little reason to look for their support on the first ballot. New Hampshire was the birthplace of Chase, and it was natural to suppose that her delegates would at least compliment him with their votes. Chase himself expected their support. Then there was, as Fogg had said, " a lingering affection in the State for Fremont," the first candidate of the party, while Seward, as the most conspicuous and best known of the candidates, was likely to be preferred before Lincoln. There is no doubt that Rollins's enthusiasm for Lincoln had much to do in shaping the course of the New Hampshire delegation. Lincoln's appreciation of the help of New Hampshire in securing his nomination was shown all through his life, and his relations with the Republican leaders of the State were always cordial, and with Rollins, Ordway, and Tuck most intimate.

Fogg was continued as a member of the National Committee, and made a member of the executive committee. He was also chosen secretary. Rollins, as chairman of the delegation, was on a committee to notify the candidates, and Fogg accompanied the notification committee on their trip.

With the return of Rollins and Fogg to Concord a great ratification meeting was held at the capital, at which Rollins spoke for an hour, giving a graphic account of the proceedings of the convention. He was followed by Fogg in a similar vein of speech.

There was no doubt of the result in New Hampshire, but Rollins's conduct of the campaign was as earnest as though the result depended upon getting out every vote. Quite a number of the prominent Republicans of the country participated in the New Hampshire canvass. These were Salmon P. Chase, of Ohio, Frank P. Blair, of Missouri, Nathaniel P. Banks, Anson S. Burlingame, and Henry Wilson, of Massachusetts, Charles H. Van Wyck, of New York, and Andrew G. Curtin, of Pennsylvania. Other speakers from outside the State were Israel Washburn, C. J. Gilman, and C. W. Walton, of Maine, Charles A. Phelps, of Boston, and E. D. Culver, of New York. Rollins presided at a great meeting at Concord, October 6th, at which Curtin and Burlingame spoke. The meeting was followed by a large torchlight procession in the evening.

In a circular issued to the Republicans of New Hampshire by Rollins, October 29th, he gives a canvass of the voters. From this he figures a plurality of 6,400 for Lincoln and a majority of 5,572. In commenting upon the returns to the State committee, Rollins says: "The committee is well aware of the difficulties attending an accurate canvass of the legal voters of the State at this time, owing to the uncertain position of many Democrats, and, therefore, will not be at all surprised, nor will their confidence in the ability of the working men of the party to correctly canvass be in the least degree diminished, if the actual Republican majority far exceeds the above figures."

In this same circular, which was written after the October elections had forecast the choice of Lincoln for President, Rollins said:

"The condition of political affairs in New Hampshire is such that it should render us as energetic in this campaign as in any of our earlier conflicts. In no State has proslavery Democracy waged a more desperate warfare or struggled harder to regain lost position. Nowhere have they remained better united or more formidable as a party, and in some form the elements of opposition will be united in future State contests. Now is the time, in the flood tide of our fortune, to make our majority so strong as to render opposition powerless for years to come. Now is the time to carry for the Republican cause towns that have been heretofore with the opposition, and to acquire in

those towns a firm and enduring majority.   Let it be
the immediate duty of the Republicans of this State
to obtain such a majority for Lincoln and Hamlin
that beyond a doubt through all the coming administration New Hampshire, by the assistance of all its members of Congress and by the moral support of Republican officers in every branch of its government, will
sustain the measures of that President whom it has
labored so zealously to elect."

The actual vote of the State was as follows: Lincoln, 37,519; Douglas, 25,881; Bell, 4,441; Breckenridge, 2,112.   Lincoln's plurality over Douglas was
11,639.   His majority over all was 5,145.

CHAPTER VI.

The Democrats began the spring campaign of 1861 immediately after the Presidential election of 1860. Complete returns of that election had not been received before they were holding conventions to nominate candidates for Congress in the first and second districts. November 13, 1860, Daniel Marcy and John H. George were nominated by the Democrats for Congress, the former by acclamation in the first district, and the latter by ballot in the second district. A faction of the party which had supported Breckenridge in the Presidential election held conventions and nominated B. W. Jenness for governor, Robert Morrison and Paul R. George for Congress in the first and second districts respectively. Later in the campaign, these candidates of the Breckenridge wing withdrew, and their followers were advised to support the regular Democratic nominees. In the third Congressional district, William Burns, of Lancaster, was renominated by the Democrats.

The Democratic State convention was held January 8, 1861. Ira A. Eastman, of Concord, presided.

The contest for the gubernatorial nomination was between George Stark, of Nashua, and Edward W. Harrington, of Manchester, the former winning by a vote of 311 to 177, with seven scattering votes.

The Republican State convention met the same day, and was presided over by Samuel Upton, of Manchester. Governor Goodwin, who had been twice elected, had considerable support for a third nomination, while Nathaniel S. Berry, of Hebron, Joel Eastman, of Conway, Lemuel N. Pattee, of Antrim, and Levi Chamberlain, of Keene, were active candidates. Two ballots were taken, and on the second Mr. Berry was nominated.

The nomination of Berry, who had left the Democratic party to become a Free-soiler, and who had been the Free-soil candidate for governor from 1846 to 1850 inclusive, was particularly distasteful to the Democratic party. The *Patriot* was especially vehement in its attacks upon him.

The greatest interest, however, centred in the Republican nomination for Congress in the second district. The candidates were Edward H. Rollins, David Cross, of Manchester, and Aaron F. Stevens, of Nashua. The canvass for delegates was an earnest one. All three were leading Republicans active in the service of the party, and all had devoted supporters. Rollins undoubtedly profited by the fact that Hillsborough County was divided in its support between two candidates, while he had his own county of Merrimack practically solid in his interest. The convention was held at Manchester in January. A large number of the prominent Republicans of the district were delegates to this convention, many of them young men just coming upon the political stage.

It was a very strong convention. The reader familiar with New Hampshire politics for the generation following Lincoln's first election would recognize the names of a large number who became prominent in State and national affairs. The convention contained many of Rollins's friends, men who were attached to his ambitions and interests while he remained active in politics. Of these none was more devoted than Richard N. Batchelder, of Manchester. Starting in a business career, Batchelder early became interested in politics. He was at one time a leader among Manchester Republicans. On purely political grounds, he favored Rollins's nomination rather than that of one of his own townsmen, and to Batchelder's individual efforts and influence Rollins was indebted in a large degree for his nomination. From this time forward Batchelder became Rollins's most intimate and trusted friend. Batchelder's public career was an honor to himself and a credit to his State. On the breaking out of the Civil War, he enlisted in the First New Hampshire Regiment, rising rapidly in rank until he became Chief Quartermaster of the Army of the Potomac, a position he held during the last year of the war. With the return of peace, he was commissioned in the regular army. In 1890, he was appointed Quartermaster General by President Harrison, being promoted over the heads of six of his seniors on his military record. Batchelder was one of the great men of New Hampshire. His interest in public affairs continued unabated to his death. His counsel was sought by all the leading men of New Hampshire, and his silent influence was felt on many an occasion where the interests of his native State were at issue. In executive ability and equipment he could have conducted any department of the federal government, yet his modesty was as pronounced as his ability.

Immediately after organization with George G. Fogg as president, the convention proceeded to ballot for a candidate for Congress. Five ballots[1] were necessary to secure a choice, Rollins slowly gaining, but Cross and Stevens holding their support until the last ballot. The convention was harmonious throughout, and at the close of the balloting Rollins's nomination was made unanimous.

The day following his nomination the *Statesman* pays Rollins this tribute:

" The gentleman whose name stands at the head of this article, and whom the people of this district, in this grave juncture in public affairs, have honored with a seat in the National Councils, was born in 1824

[1] CANDIDATES	1st	2d	3d	4th	5th
Mason W. Tappan, of Bradford . .	1			5	13
Austin F. Pike, of Franklin . .	3				
William H. Gove, of Weare . .	4				2
David Cross, of Manchester . .	45	42	48	52	38
Aaron F. Stevens, of Nashua . .	62	66	59	49	37
Edward R. Rollins, of Concord . .	86	92	94	95	108

in that section of Somersworth which is now embraced
in the town of Rollinsford, and is consequently thirty-
seven years of age. . . . In the years 1850 and '51 he
was one of the leading members of the Whig State
committee, and when the American party was initiated
in this State, in 1855, he early, and with all his political forecast and ardor, enlisted in that organization.
He was the second official in rank in that association,
and, by his ceaseless and truly marvellous activity in
that position, actually saved the State from the slough
of Hunkerism in 1856. And when, in that year, as
an inevitable result of the breaking up of the Missouri
Compromise, and of the consequent opening of the
flood-gates of agitation, old party landmarks were
obliterated, Mr. Rollins was one of the most active and
efficient leaders in the organization of the Republican
party, which grew out of that commotion, and was at
once raised to the head of its State committee by the
unanimous voice of the far-sighted, energetic spirits
who headed the grand movement; a position which he
has continued, by the same unanimity of expression,
and with the most conspicuous ability, to occupy down
to the present period. At the head of this committee
he devised and put into practical operation that rigid
and accurate system of canvassing which has been a
fortress around the Republican organization; which
has, again and again, been in the most flattering terms
commended as a model scheme by the leading presses
throughout the country, and has been the wonder and

admiration of leading political managers in Washington.

" In 1855 he was elected to the popular branch of the legislature from the most populous ward in this city, and returned to that position in 1856 and 1857, by increased majorities, in both of which last mentioned years he was Speaker of that body. He discharged the duties of the presiding officer with eminent acceptance, and the journals of that assembly for those years are conclusive evidence of the expeditious manner in which business was transacted under his direction.

" In 1859, his name was one of the most prominent before the convention as a candidate for Congress; but when the harmony and efficiency of the party seemed to demand it, he promptly and cordially withdrew his name from the canvass, that Mason W. Tappan, whose Congressional career has shed lustre upon the whole State, might be returned for his third term.

" Few men in New Hampshire have done so much, and no man has done more, for the organized strength and vigor, and for the complete, unwavering triumphs of the Republican party in this State, than Edward H. Rollins, and he has never failed in the full and efficient discharge of every public duty and trust hitherto confided to his care. With the impulses of an exalted ambition, it is known that he has for years made political economy and the general philosophy of government a subject of careful study. He has a familiar knowledge of the legislative history and policy of the government, and no man better than he understands the political convictions and wants of the people whom he is called to represent."

The *New Hampshire Patriot* in commenting upon Rollins's nomination said: "Mr. Rollins was the candidate of the 'Yield not an inch' section of his party, that portion who, having forced their party into the extreme position and the adoption of the ultra doctrines which have brought the Union to the brink of ruin, and the country to the imminent danger of civil war, are now laboring to prevent a settlement of the difficulties, and declaring that they will make no concessions to avert the calamities impending over their heads. This is Mr. Rollins's position, and to support him is to endorse this ground and to aid in bringing upon the country the untold calamities which must follow its adoption."

The *Independent Democrat,* George G. Fogg's newspaper, said:

"Considering the animated contest for delegates which preceded the convention, its proceedings were remarkably free from anything like ill feeling. Several ballots were required to make the nomination, but, when made by a majority vote, the friends of the other candidates came promptly forward and moved to make it unanimous. This was done with a will, and, after short and eloquent speeches by Mr. Rollins and Judge Cross, the convention adjourned. Of the candidate selected we need say but little. He is known to nearly every prominent Republican in the district.

Having held the position of chairman of the Republican State committee ever since the organization of the party, he has had opportunity to show his devotion to Republican principles. How he has improved that opportunity the efficient and almost perfect organization of the party sufficiently attest. We have had peculiar advantages for understanding the nature and extent of his services and the thorough business manner in which he has discharged all the duties of his difficult and responsible position. Without participating actively in the canvass which has resulted in his nomination, it gives us pleasure to endorse him as eminently deserving the support of every Republican of the district. Possessed of indomitable energy, eminent practicable ability, and thorough acquaintance with the politics of the country and hearty devotion to the purposes and principles of the Republican party, we predict that the people of this Congressional district will find in him a representative thoroughly faithful to their interests and principles and at all times ready and able to defend them."

The Republican majority in New Hampshire at the Presidential election of 1860 was so large that the Democrats had little hope of redeeming the State. Yet they made great efforts to unite their party and were not without expectations of defeating Rollins for Congress. His nomination had not been secured without disappointment to other aspirants and their friends. All of Rollins's competitors for the nomination were lawyers, and the triumph of a merchant over members of the bar caused no little chagrin to these men. This feeling was fostered by the Democratic press in their efforts to compass Rollins's defeat. His preëminennce in the party had been largely acquired through his successful leadership in political campaigns, and the Democrats made it their policy to sow seeds of discontent by belittling Rollins's equipment for public life. Their efforts in this direction were not without effect in his subsequent career, when he had as competitors for the United States Senate men eminent in the legal profession who had served like himself in Congress. It is not strange, therefore, that Gilman Marston, Aaron F. Stevens, Mason W. Tappan, and other distinguished members of the bar, conscious of their own fitness and training for public life, should look askance at the promotion of a merchant to the highest honors of the State. The Democrats never allowed this feeling to slumber. In their view, to defeat Rollins's ambition was to eliminate him from the management of political campaigns. If defeated and disappointed he retired from political life, they expected to recover their control of the State.

Having centred their attack upon the second Congressional district, the Democrats sought to strengthen themselves by a change of candidates. The all-absorbing issue at this time was the preservation of the federal Union. Several Southern States had already seceded, and others were sure to follow. Lincoln would not be inaugurated President until within a few days of the State election in New Hampshire. There was every indication that he would be President of a divided country. Both political parties in New Hampshire proclaimed their love for the Union, but they differed widely in their views of how its integrity should be preserved. The Democratic candidate for Congress in the second district, John H. George, was a pronounced State rights Democrat. Some other Democrat of less pronounced views, the Democratic leaders thought, would receive more votes. In this view George coincided, and, in a open letter, withdrew as a candidate. The Democratic convention was reassembled, and without dissent Samuel D. Bell, of Manchester, chief justice of the supreme court of the State, was nominated. Bell had been a Whig until the annexation of Texas. He then identified himself with the Democratic party, but at no time had been active in politics. He was a man of large legal and literary attainments. He had been appointed to the bench by the Democrats in 1849, and was not displaced when the Republican party came into power and reorganized the courts. His appointment as chief justice was an acknowledgment of his eminent fitness for the position.

Judge Bell was nominated upon no platform, but put forward by the Democrats as an independent candidate who would subordinate party to the salvation of the Union. He did not resign from the bench, and took no active part in the campaign. Paul R. George, the candidate for Congress of the Breckenridge Democrats, immediately withdrew and advised his supporters to vote for Bell. The whole interest in the campaign now centred in this Congressional district. Few speakers from other States were brought into New Hampshire by either party, nor was there a large number of political rallies. Rollins, besides conducting the campaign as chairman of the State committee, spoke in various towns of his district. He had acquired the art of speech-making, and had become an earnest and forceful campaign speaker. The *Independent Democrat*, referring to his speech at Nashua in this campaign, said: " Mr. Rollins spoke for two hours. Yet the gratified audience hung untired upon his words, and called earnestly for more." The time occupied by speakers in those days testifies to the intensity of interest in political issues. At a rally held at Warner, addressed by Rollins, Allen Tenny, and Nehemiah G. Ordway, Rollins is credited in one newspaper as speaking for two hours, and in another as speaking for three hours. John H. George, in writing to the Democratic State committee of one of his meetings in this campaign, said that he held his audience for three hours and a half, and reports of other rallies refer frequently to speeches of from two to three hours in length.

Rollins's style of stump-speaking was always a challenge to his political opponents. He never spared the shortcomings of the Democratic party. If his speeches were not calculated to win converts, they roused the enthusiasm of Republicans to the highest pitch. A thorough master of details, Rollins was at his best when any of his statements were questioned by his audience, and interruptions at his meetings were of frequent occurrence. His preparation of speeches was by topics, with plenty of data for reference. He wrote out no speeches beforehand, and, therefore, had no set speech to deliver. An interruption or a question from the audience was likely to develop an entirely different speech from the one he intended to make. He threw down the gauntlet to the Democratic party at the opening of every meeting, and, if it was picked up by any one present, he was ready to both defend and further attack. His speeches stirred Republicans to renewed activity while they exasperated Democrats. He invariably closed with predictions of victory in the State. The verification of his canvasses gave to his predictions the stamp of prophecy, and, however angered his opponents might be at his speeches, they left the meeting with the depression which comes of the feeling that the fight is hopeless. Rollins understood this as well as any one, and his attendance at a political rally in a debatable town was a source of strength to his party.

The returns on election night showed the Republican victory to be complete. The vote for governor was as follows:

Scattering, 24; George Stark, Democrat, 31,452; Nathaniel S. Berry, Republican, 35,467. The Republicans had a majority of the legislature, and elected all three Congressmen, Rollins's majority being about nine hundred.

When the legislature organized the following June,

Edward Ashton Rollins, a cousin of Edward H. Rollins was elected Speaker of the House. These two cousins were sometimes confounded in public life, owing to the similarity of their names. Ashton Rollins, after serving two terms as Speaker, was appointed Commissioner of Internal Revenue, a position he held until he removed to Philadelphia, where he engaged in business, becoming president of the Centennial National Bank of that city. His interest in his native State continued through life. One of his public gifts to New Hampshire is the handsome chapel at Dartmouth College.

CHAPTER VII.

IN THE THIRTY - SEVENTH CONGRESS

THE thirty-seventh Congress was called by President Lincoln in extra session to meet July 4, 1861. Fort Sumter had been fired on by the Confederates, and war between the States was actually begun. Congress was called upon to provide ways and means for subduing the insurgent States, and had to face many new problems. Rollins met as associates in the House of Representatives a number of men, some of them new members like himself, who were to play a prominent part in the subsequent history of the country. Of this number were Justin S. Morrill, of Vermont, Henry L. Dawes, of Massachusetts, Roscoe Conkling, Reuben E. Fenton, William A. Wheeler, and Charles H. Van Wyck, of New York, William D. Kelley, Thaddeus Stephens, Galusha A. Grow (Speaker), and John Covode, of Pennsylvania, George H. Pendleton, Clement L. Vallandingham, Samuel S. Cox, John A. Bingham, and James M. Ashley, of Ohio, William S. Holman, George W. Julian, Daniel W. Voorhees, and Schuyler Colfax, of Indiana, Elihu B. Washburne, Owen J. Lovejoy, and John A. Logan, of Illinois, Aaron A.

121

Sargent, of California, and William Windom, of Minnesota. Rollins afterward served in the Senate with Morrill, Dawes, Conkling, Van Wyck (then of Nebraska), Pendleton, Voorhees, Logan, Sargent, and Windom, with William A. Wheeler presiding over the Senate as Vice-President, from March 4, 1877, to March 4, 1881.

Of the New Hampshire delegation, Gilman Marston and Thomas M. Edwards were serving their second term. In the committee assignments, Marston was put on the committee of military affairs, and Edwards on Indian affairs and public expenditures. Rollins's assignments were the committees on District of Columbia and accounts. Roscoe Conkling was chairman of the committee on the District of Columbia. From this association with Conkling sprang up an admiration for the Senator from New York which Rollins entertained through life.

The extra session lasted until August 6th. Rollins's activity was confined to committee work during this session. The most important measure which he introduced, and afterward championed before the committee, was one to " repeal certain laws and ordinances in the District of Columbia relative to persons of color." This measure, which had for its object the amelioration of the condition of the negroes in the District of Columbia, was referred to the district committee of the House, and subsequently was reported favorably by Rollins. He had the satisfaction of securing its immediate passage.

It was while Congress was in extra session that the first battle of Bull Run occurred. The troops called for by the President's proclamation were assembling in Washington; the North was impatiently demanding an advance on Richmond, which demand was being persistently urged by their representatives in Congress. General Scott, the commander - in - chief, protested against such a movement with undisciplined troops as hazardous. Civilian advice, however, prevailed over military protest, and an advance of the Union forces was ordered. Many Congressmen and Senators obtained passes to ride in the rear of the army and witness the conflict, which was sure to occur when the Union forces met those of the Confederates. Rollins was among the number who went to the battle-field. He barely escaped capture after the battle. Writing his wife, he thus describes his experience:

" MY DEAR ELLEN: — On my return from the battle-field this morning, I find your interesting letter. I was glad to hear from you all at home. It made me sad, however, to read it, particularly that part where you allude to the lost one and Edward's mourning so for him. It is a great loss for us all, and we must long mourn his early departure. I could not keep back the tears, but perhaps I was the more sad, for I had just witnessed the retreat of our troops.

" Senator Lane, of Indiana, George Marston, and I, with single carriage and one saddle-horse, left the city Saturday afternoon for the seat of war. I mounted the horse and we proceeded as far as Fairfax Court-house, seventeen miles, the same evening, and spent the night with a secessionist, who gave us some supper and good beds.   This is the town from which our forces drove the Confederates a few days since.   Early the next morning we went on to Centreville, nine miles beyond.   When we reached this point, we found the troops had been in motion for hours.   We took our position on the high ground, where we saw the move-ments of the troops in the valley below as they marched to make the attack upon the enemy's lines. The attack began about 10.30 A. M., after a march of about ten miles.   Our soldiers had been under arms for hours, and some of them, including our regiment, had gone without breakfast.   Where we stood, we could have a pretty good view of the scene of action, but trees prevented us from seeing the troops.   We could see the smoke and hear the sharp crack of the rifle and musket and the roar of the cannon.   It was very exciting, I can assure you, and we remained there watching the progress of the battle until about four P. M.   All the early part of the fight, and, in fact, until about four in the afternoon, our people had the best of it and were driving the Confederates back.   Our forces engaged were not really over twenty thousand, while those of the Confederates were estimated at more than double that number, with a good artillery support.   The battle seemed to be a victory in our favor, when suddenly a panic appeared to seize our army, perhaps because the enemy had received large reinforcements, and then began a very disorderly retreat.

" Our Second Regiment fought bravely and were among the last to quit the field. Colonel Marston is wounded in the arm and breast. I cannot tell how many we have lost from our regiment, but I hope not many. The loss generally in the battle is very heavy, for it was strongly contested. Many of our troops, after leaving the field, thought the enemy in immediate pursuit, and the utmost confusion prevailed.

" We remained in our position until dark watching the forces as they retreated toward camp. The officers were unable to rally the men, and the retreat was now turned into a rout. The road was full of men, horses, and wagons, and it was pretty difficult for us to move. Having no confidence in the alarm or that the enemy were pursuing, we made no haste to return to Washington. After being on our way a short distance, we retraced our steps to Centreville, put up our horses, and took tea with a friend of Senator Lane. We then stretched ourselves out upon the floor for some sleep. About eleven o'clock that night, a man on horseback rode into the yard and said the order had been given that all must retreat and that we must go. I had not slept a wink. We harnessed up and started off. Our stop was no doubt hazardous, for we were very near the enemy, who would have been glad to have taken us prisoners. There were many members of Congress and Senators upon the field, and it is reported that some of them were taken. We took up our

line of march for Washington and, in a very brief
time, overtook the retreating army, which we found in
the utmost disorder and confusion. All mixed together were officers and men, artillery, baggage, and
ambulance wagons, following no orders, but each man
for himself. Now think of our ride. I was in the
carriage and Lane on horseback for twenty-six miles
over bad and, in many places, narrow roads, in the
midst of an army retreating in disorder, with men,
horses, wagons, and artillery cumbering the highway.
We soon found ourselves in the midst of all this confusion pushing forward to get to the capital as early
as possible. Sometimes we would be between artillery-
wagons and at others between baggage-wagons which
might crush our light vehicle at any moment. Sometimes we would be pushing through a dense mass of
moving men, with wounded and tired ones asking us
for aid. We took in one wounded fellow and brought
him here. It was a night's ride I never shall forget.
We reached Washington at eight o'clock this morning,
some of our friends fearing we were captured. Just
before reaching the city, we gave our last lunch to
some of the Goodwin Rifles who were glad enough to
get it. You may think it strange that we ran the risk
we did, but I do not regret it, although I must admit
that there were many moments when I would have been
quite willing to have exchanged my place for a seat by
your side at the old mansion at Rollinsford, with a
bowl of sweet milk that I always find there, not lessened in quality by being robbed of its cream.

" The troops were fearful of an attack from cavalry at Fairfax, so the ranks were opened and a big gun placed in the advance. We were in the midst of a jam all the way, and only got relief at Long Bridge, where all the soldiers were halted and cared for. I send Edward a relic of the enemy. You better not let any one read my letters. They are nothing but scrawls. Yours affectionately."

While in Washington, Rollins was in constant correspondence with the Republican leaders of the State, keeping in close touch with the political situation. It was just after the battle of Bull Run that he received the following letter from Bainbridge Wadleigh.

" In accordance with my promise I will drop you a few lines in reference to matters in New Hampshire. You are, of course, aware that the disaster at Bull Run produced a profound impression upon the public mind here. It lifted the curtain, and showed us the magnitude of the preparations that the rebels have made for a sanguinary war. Many of our timid Republicans shrink aghast from the prospect which has been unfolded to their view. But with other of our friends their spirits rise to the magnitude of the occasion.

" As for myself, I am convinced that there is but one course left for us, and that is to keep fighting until we beat the rebels. Large as the country is, it is not large enough for two governments so adverse to each other in character as ours and that of the rebels. A division of the Union must result in long, harassing, and bloody border wars like the contests which for ages raged along the English and Scottish frontier. I am glad that the administration and Congress look at things in the same light and that the war is to be vigorously prosecuted. . . .

"One thing is pretty evident, ——— is doing all he can to shape public opinion so as to procure a result in the next election which will gladden the ears of Jeff. Davis and his co-conspirators. Many other Democrats are helping him. Many of our men will be absent at the war, and many others shaken by the wholesale charges of corruption hurled at so many of our office-holders by Democrats and Republicans alike. You should be at home here so that we may have the benefit of your skill in carrying on an election."

This letter discloses the political situation in New Hampshire. It was critical. The Bull Run defeat had dampened the courage of the Republicans. The curtain was indeed lifted and the magnitude of the conflict disclosed. Would the Republican administration at Washington be equal to the emergency? The faint-hearted were inclined to doubt. Love of the Union was paramount with many to the destruction of slavery, the cause of the war, and not a few were inclined to further compromise with the slave power if thereby the integrity of the nation could be preserved. The administration at Washington must be supported by the Republicans of New Hampshire, yet that support must not be made so partisan as to consolidate the Democratic party in opposition. Care

must be taken in preparing the call for the approaching Republican State convention, and in conducting
the canvass so as not to alienate the Democrats, who,
when Sumter was fired upon, had cast aside party
ties in their patriotic efforts to put down the rebellion.
To Rollins, therefore, as chairman of the State committee, the Republican leaders in New Hampshire
looked to outline the policy to be pursued.

Returning home after the extra session of Congress,
he gave his attention to this work. Realizing that his
duties as a member of Congress would require his presence in Washington during the winter months each
year, and that, therefore, he could give but little personal attention to the affairs of the State committee,
he determined to retire from the chairmanship when
a new committee was elected. The preliminary work
of the campaign, however, devolved upon him, and he
gave it his most zealous attention. The call for the
State convention was prepared under his direction,
and signed by the entire Republican State committee.
Its tenor will be readily seen from the opening para-
graph.

" A delegate convention representing all the people
of the State of New Hampshire in favor of sustaining
the national administration in the vigorous and effective prosecution of the war against treason and rebellion, and of maintaining at all hazards in their
original integrity the constitution and union of the
United States, will be held at Phenix Hall, in Concord,
January 1, 1862," etc.

There was considerable sentiment among Republicans in favor of the nomination of some war Democrat or some Republican of Democratic antecedents as the party candidate for governor. Responding to this sentiment, Governor Berry addressed a patriotic letter to the Republican convention offering to waive any claim to the party usage of a second nomination if it were felt that a stronger candidate than himself could be selected. This letter was read to the convention after it had organized with the choice of Aaron H. Cragin as president. The informal ballot which followed disclosed the following result: Scattering, 3; John Sullivan, of Exeter, 107; Paul J. Wheeler, of Newport, 111; Nathaniel Berry, of Hebron, 260.

A formal ballot was then taken, which gave Berry a majority, and his nomination was made unanimous. At a meeting of the Republican State committee Anthony Colby, of New London, was elected chairman, and Benjamin F. Prescott, of Concord, secretary.

The Democratic State convention met a week later. The party was divided on both the platform to be adopted and the candidate to be nominated. The ultra State rights Democrats, led by John H. George, favored the renomination of George Stark, and a declaration in the platform that slavery as an institution should not be disturbed in the prosecution of the war. The more conservative Democrats desired a new candidate, less pronounced in his views, and a platform more in keeping with the spirit of the times. Forestalling any discussion which might ensue over the plat-

form, George addressed the convention in a vigorous
speech as soon as it was organized, and, working its
members up to the highest pitch of enthusiasm, he
closed with a motion that Stark be renominated by
acclamation.   The convention was carried away by
George's vigorous eloquence, voting his motion without dissent.   The nomination of Stark settled the
platform.   It contained a declaration "that this war
should not be waged in any spirit of conquest or subjugation, or for the purpose of overthrowing the rights
or established institutions of any of the States, but to
defend and maintain the supremacy of the constitution
and the rights of all the States in the Union, and to
preserve the Union, and that, as soon as these objects
are accomplished, war should cease."

This plank marked the difference between the two
parties of New Hampshire in their attitude toward
the war, a difference which continued pronounced on
this and other questions throughout the conflict between the North and the South.

The call for a third, or "Union Convention," was
issued immediately, and the convention met February
6th.   It was presided over by Ira Perley, of Concord,
one of New Hampshire's most distinguished jurists.
He was a member of the State supreme court for
fourteen years and chief justice at the time of his
retirement.   Of positive convictions, he reached conclusions uninfluenced by popular feeling.   Although
an earnest Republican, he frequently acted inde-
pendently of his party, and in this instance he was

undoubtedly actuated by a high sense of public duty.

The leading spirits of the " Union Convention " were Edward D. Rand, of Lisbon, James W. Johnson, of Enfield, William C. Clarke and Samuel G. Clarke, of Manchester, George W. Stevens, of Laconia, and Samuel M. Wheeler, of Dover. Paul J. Wheeler, of Newport, was nominated for governor. He had been a lifelong Democrat, and, as a candidate for governor, had received considerable support in the late Republican convention. The " Union " party endorsed the policy of President Lincoln, and pledged him its support, but repeated almost word for word the plank in the Democratic platform to which reference has been made.

The campaign was earnestly conducted by both the Republicans and Democrats. For a time the nomination of Wheeler seemed a menace to Republican success, but toward the close of the canvass it was apparent that but few Republicans would be attracted to his support. The total vote fell off nearly four thousand, but the Republican party was victorious, as shown by the following returns: scattering, 45; Paul J. Wheeler, 1,709; George Stark, 28,566; Nathaniel S. Berry, 32,150.

At the regular session of the thirty-seventh Congress, which convened on the first Monday of December, 1861, the question of the abolition of slavery in the District of Columbia came to the front. Early in December, Henry Wilson, of Massachusetts, introduced a bill in the Senate providing for the immediate emancipation of the slaves in the District, and for the compensation of their owners. This bill, after debate and amendment, passed the Senate April 3, 1862, by a vote of 29 to 14, and was taken up in the House the next week. It gave rise to a brief but spirited debate, in which Rollins participated. The bill passed the House by a vote of 92 to 38, and received the approval of the President April 16, 1862.

Rollins's hostility to slavery was pronounced. He was in the vanguard of Republicans who favored its extinction. He had not been identified, however, with the early apostles of freedom, like Garrison and Parker, who believed in the destruction of slavery, regardless of the perpetuity of the Union, but he looked upon the institution as a blot upon the country, to be wiped out at the first favorable opportunity. In his campaign as the Republican nominee for Congress, he had been charged by the Democratic press of New Hampshire with being an abolitionist, a charge he never denied, and he was ready to strike a blow at slavery whenever it could be done with safety to the Union. That he foresaw the destruction of slavery in the United States, as the final result of the war, can be seen in his speech on the bill emancipating the slaves in the District of Columbia. He was prepared to use all the war powers of the government to eradicate this institution. In this, his first speech in Congress, he said:

"The abolition of slavery in the District of Co-

lumbia is to the few slaves therein a deed of justice
and mercy that this people cannot omit to perform at
this golden opportunity. Slavery has forfeited all
claims to any implied obligation for immunity at the
capital of a nation by its mad attempt to throw down
the pillars of the government under which it claims
protection. . . .

"With what ill grace does it come from the apolo-
gists of slavery to charge that the Republican party is
waging war for the emancipation of the slaves! One
would think that the free States had started a crusade
and marched their hosts into the heart of the South
while yet the whole population thereof were quietly
pursuing the accustomed tenor of their lives, loyal in
their hearts and cheerfully submitting to the proper restraints of constitutional law and performing all the
obligations of good citizens. . . . In the whole history
of this contest, in the records of the doings of the Cabinet or the proceedings of Congress, nowhere can be
found a single declaration to give color to the charge
that this is a war for the destruction of slavery. On
the contrary, we have been altogether too tender of the
institution, and our leniency has been our fault.

"It is because the South knows that, by all the laws
of war, we should be justified in seeking the heart of
the foe and annihilating forever the inspiring cause
of all our present woes, that their frighted consciences
start at the thought of what they know the whole world
would applaud.

"For more than sixty years, the free people of the

North, as they came to visit the capital of the Union, have been compelled to come in contact with this revolting and offensive system, and, for fifty years, to witness the cruel barbaritites incident to the slave trade.   The laboring men of the free States have been obliged for half a century to submit to the humiliating degradation thus heaped upon them. . . . Why should slavery be allowed longer to remain in the District? It is not surprising that now, when this same institution, in addition to all the other evils it has caused, seeks to destroy the Union and the government, the toiling millions of the North are determined at least to see it banished from the capital. Thus much they demand, and they will take nothing less. There is to be no further delay, no putting off until next year. Now is the time and the only time acceptable to the people. The abolition of slavery in this District is demanded as some slight indemnity for the past and as full security for the future. The capital should be inhabited by a loyal people, ready to defend it in rebellion, and not by a people any considerable portion of whom are ready to take arms to destroy it. Slavery makes a people disloyal, and, therefore, has no claims to consideration or favor from loyal hearts anywhere. Our own self-defence requires that it should be abolished wherever Congress has the power.

" Our honor demands the abolition of slavery in the District of Columbia. It is world-wide disgrace to the nation that its capital bears the curse of involuntary servitude. It is our reproach in every land upon

the face of the earth. It is an anomaly in the history
of the world, a fraud without parallel. It is a huge
blot upon our otherwise fair escutcheon, which should
be removed with the least possible delay. We have
borne with the innumerable evils necessarily incident
to the presence here of the peculiar institution full too
long already, and it must come to an end. Who will
mourn its departure? Who will be sad when it is
gone? No true lover of his country, no one who places
a higher estimate upon the honor and welfare of his
country than upon the perpetuity of slavery."

Five weeks later, Rollins made another speech in the
House. This speech was in support of the bill confis-
cating the property of those in arms against the government. There was no doubt in his mind that rebellion
is treason against the government, and he was for met-
ing out to the enemies of the Republic all the penalties
of treason. He scorned the argument that seeks to find
protection in the constitution for the property of those
who are attempting to destroy the Union. "It is time,"
he says, "that the Republic receive no loss, or, if too
late for that, to drain dry the sources upon which this
treason feeds. I am amazed at what I hear that seems
to hold so sacred all the rights that by every act of
rebellion have been forfeited, and should be held as lost
by every law of reason and every rule of self-defence.
No man has the hardihood to deny that we will meet
and overcome the rebels in battle. The utmost energies
of the nation should be exerted to crush out this treason, even to draining the country to the last man and

the last dollar of its treasure. But it is said our enemies' resources must remain untouched by us, to continue to nourish and keep alive the baleful body of this treason. . . . If there is anything that will tend to make the constitution a less sacred thing in the minds of the people, it is the use that is made of it to shield those who are in open rebellion against it."

Referring to the scrupulousness shown for the " constitutional rights of slave-owners," he exclaims, " Their constitutional rights! They scorned them all. They have trampled the constitution beneath the bloody hoofs of war, and we still seek to pack their breastworks with the rent parchment, so that our shot shall not reach the cause and support of this rebellion. . . . The revolted States are but the enemies of the government. The people regard them in no other light, and they look to us to crush them. They will stand by those who seek to accomplish this most effectually. If we tell them we are so hampered by the constitution that, although we may overcome their enemies in the field, we must leave their implacable foe possessed of all his resources, with the poison still treasured in his fang, we teach them to disrespect that instrument, the most sacred of all legacies. It is so sacred that whatever threatens it must be destroyed. If it be men, they must pay the forfeit with their lives. If it be institutions, they must be overthrown. . . . There is no act in the whole category of crimes that have culminated in this rebellion that slavery did not inspire. It has sought to build a government of its own. If its success were among the things possible, slavery and slavery alone would be the preamble and the close of its constitution. Its laws would be framed to extend and perpetuate slavery. Its tariffs would be imposed to protect it, and its people taxed to feed it. This is the enemy we have to meet and conquer. This country has no other that it need fear, and, while it lives, it will be a perpetual terror."

The *Independent Democrat* published both of Rollins's speeches in full, and called attention to them editorially. Of the first, it said:

"The recent speech of Hon. Edward H. Rollins in the House of Representatives upon the bill abolishing slavery in the District of Columbia will be found printed upon our first page this week. We are confident that our readers will peruse it with pleasure. It is an excellent speech, one of the very best which has been delivered in Congress in the present session. It is the first effort of Mr. Rollins in Congressional speaking, and we are happy to chronicle it a brilliant success. He could have chosen no better theme for his début. He has shown much tact in the selection of his points of view of the subject, and great skill and cogency of argument in discussing them. The speech admirably reflects the loyal sentiment of the Granite State, and is fully up in its tone and spirit with the demands of the hour for bold thought and decisive action."

Of his speech on the Confiscation Bill, the *Independent Democrat* said: "It is characterized by sound argument, clothed in appropriate and oftentimes eloquent expression. Its tone, too, is all right. It is the tone of the popular heart of New Hampshire."

The labor devolving upon Rollins during this and the subsequent Congress was prodigious. In committee and the routine work of the House, he was kept busy. Few members are capable or willing to take upon themselves the arduous details of legislation which afford little or no public credit to the individual. Rollins's aptitude for this class of work was soon recognized by his associates, and, being willing to undertake it, he had it pressed upon him in abundance. In addition, he had to attend to the calls of constituents in two Congressional districts, as his colleague, Gilman Marston, was doing service as an army officer in the field. Hundreds of inquiries came from the families and relatives of New Hampshire soldiers at the front, all of which Rollins answered. These were often supplemented by requests for passes to go within the Union lines to care for some father, son, or brother, wounded in battle or stricken with disease, and languishing in a hospital. Then there were countless applications for furloughs, sick leaves, transfers, and promotions from officers and soldiers in the service. The appeals from home were frequently most pathetic, and sometimes impossible to grant. Yet, no matter how insurmountable the obstacles seemed to be, Rollins never shrank from undertaking to aid a constituent. His success in bringing about results soon gave him a reputation that overshadowed that of any of the

Senators or Representatives from New Hampshire, and constantly added to his daily toil.

With Lincoln and Stanton, Rollins stood on intimate terms. Both appreciated him for his industry, loyalty, and executive capacity, and seldom did he ask a favor of either that was not granted. Most Senators and members of Congress stood in awe of Stanton. Rollins appears never to have feared him. Stanton appreciated a man who did things, and, if he refused less requests of Rollins than of others, it was because he looked upon Rollins as fitted for the sphere in which he was acting.

The experience of Supply W. Edwards, of Temple, New Hampshire, in the fall of 1862 was only one of many who, having relatives or friends in the army, applied to Rollins for his influence to secure for them some alleviation of their unfortunate conditions. Edwards, years afterward, in 1876, was elected to the legislature of New Hampshire. Rollins was then a candidate for the United States Senate. When Edwards reached Concord, he was importuned by a number of Representatives who endeavored to persuade him to support some other candidate for Senator. After hearing them all through, Edwards gave his reasons for supporting Rollins in these words:

" Gentlemen, listen to my story and my reasons for supporting Edward H. Rollins, and, if there is a man here who would not support him in like circumstances, the people who have sent him to the legislature have made a mistake. In the fall of 1862, I went to Wash-

ington to try and save the life of my sick boy, who had
enlisted in Company G, Thirteenth New Hampshire
Volunteers, and was reported sick in the hospital at
Falmouth, Virginia. I had some friends in Washington, and I told them what brought me there. They
informed me it would be difficult for me to get a pass
to go down the river, but said that if I would call on
Senator Daniel Clark he would probably fix it for me.
I had letters to both Senators Clark and Cragin. When
I told my story to Senator Clark, he shook his head,
and said, ' It's a hard thing to do, but I will try. Call
on me to-morrow.' The next day the Senator told me
an order had been issued not to allow any citizen to go
down the Lower Potomac, and that he could not get
me a pass. I then applied to Senator Cragin. He
also made an effort and failed. I felt almost heart-
broken, as my boy had written me that if he could only
see his father he was sure he could get well. My money
was most gone, and I was in despair. Some of my
friends suggested that I go and see Ed Rollins. Without any hope of success, I called upon him. I went to
the Capitol building and was shown to a room where
some committee was in session. A messenger notified
Mr. Rollins that a man from New Hampshire desired
to see him. Mr. Rollins, whom I had never met, came
out into the corridor in his shirt sleeves, an unlighted
cigar in his mouth. His salutation was, ' Well, my
good man from New Hampshire, what is your name
and what can I do for you ? ' I was somewhat con-
fused, and, before I could speak, tears were streaming

down my cheeks. I finally got my voice, and I told him what I was in Washington for and what fortune I had had with the two Senators from New Hampshire. Before I could say anything more, Rollins said, 'Wait a moment.' He hurried into the room, got his coat and came out, putting on the coat as he travelled along. 'Come with me,' he said. I could hardly keep up with him down the long steps of the Capitol to the avenue. He called a carriage, shouted to the driver, 'White House,' and told me to get in. When we reached the White House, he left me at the door of the President's room, and said, 'Wait here until I return.' He was gone twenty minutes to half an hour. When he returned, he caught me by the arm, rushed out to the carriage, and said to the driver, 'To the War Department.' Arriving there, we went to the door of the Secretary of War, where he bade me wait. Here he was gone another twenty minutes, but, when he came out, he handed me a pass from Abraham Lincoln, countersigned by Stanton, permitting me to go down to the army and see my sick son. Gentlemen, do you think there is anything you can say that would lead me to support any other man than Edward H. Rollins?"

The Washington correspondent of the *New Hampshire Statesman,* in a letter to that newspaper about this time, thus speaks of Rollins's service in the national House of Representatives:

"Without in any manner detracting from the faithful labors of other members, I cannot forbear mentioning the member of the House from Concord as a true

specimen of a working Congressman. Since Colonel
Marston has served in the army, the people of the first
district have put a vast deal of labor upon Mr. Rollins.
No man could have proved more ready to serve the
interests of the people of this district than has the
member from the second district, and his attention to
the wants of Colonel Marston's constituency in addition to those of his own has been most marked and
unremitting. Mr. Rollins is a good business man and,
although it may be at the risk of imposing greater
labors upon an already too hard worked member, yet
I cannot forbear saying that no man in the New
Hampshire delegation in Congress seems to have alike
the equal ability and inclination to follow up the interests of his constituents through the mazes of circum-
locution which abound in Washington."

CHAPTER VIII.

RE - ELECTION TO CONGRESS

THE adjournment of Congress brought no respite to Rollins. The calls of his constituents were constant whether he was in Washington or at home. Then he had his part in stimulating enlistments to fill the calls made by the President for additional troops. A great war meeting was held at Concord in the summer of 1862, which he addressed with Governor Berry and others. The approaching campaign of 1863 also loomed large upon the political horizon. A new candidate for governor was to be selected by the Republicans, and certain indications pointed to a nomination not likely to add strength to the ticket. It was the Congressional year, and Rollins himself must go before the people to secure approval of his stewardship.

The war as yet had brought no decisive success to the Union arms, while the Emancipation Proclamation of the President was to issue in the new year. It was by no means certain that the voters of New Hampshire would approve of this forward movement of the Republican party. There were a number of Republicans who doubted its wisdom, while there were others who thought the step had been too long delayed. As in other States, the Republican party of New Hampshire was weakened by the army enlistments, for, besides Republicans who were absent at the front, there were many Democrats from the State in the army who had no sympathy with slavery. These voters could not be brought home, and there was as yet no provision for counting the votes of soldiers in the field.

The Democratic press of New Hampshire, thoroughly hostile to emancipation, charged that the Republican administration was violating its pledges made early in the war. " It was to be a war," they said, " for the preservation of the Union and not for the destruction of State institutions like slavery." This attitude of the Democracy, which later was so disastrous to that party, did not at first impair its solidarity. When the loyalty of that party was questioned, its leaders resented it. While antagonizing the administration of Lincoln, they still asserted their opposition to secession and their attachment to the Union. They insisted upon a distinction being drawn between opposition to the war and opposition to the civil and political measures of the administration. This distinction for a time held loyal Democrats to the support of the party ticket. It was only when in platform and in speech the Democratic leaders declared the war a failure, and demanded peace at any price, that disintegration of their ranks began. At the opening of the New Hampshire campaign of 1863, it was not apparent that a single Democratic voter could be won to the support of the Republican ticket by the Republican party's declaration in favor of the emancipation of the slaves. The prospect of Republican success in the State was, therefore, far from propitious, and, as events proved, the election was to be won only by the hardest kind of work. The situation in the fall of 1862 was one of grave concern to Rollins and other Republican leaders of the State.

The Democrats were first in the field in New Hampshire with a State convention. It was held November 20, 1862. Ira A. Eastman, of Concord, was nominated for governor. He had served ten years on the bench of the supreme court of the State, and was highly esteemed by the people of New Hampshire. Previous to his appointment to the bench he had been Speaker of the House and a member of Congress. His nomination was the strongest the Democratic party could have made at this time.

Among the resolutions adopted was the following:

"*Resolved,* That we unqualifiedly condemn the late proclamation of the President relative to emancipation as unwarranted by the constitution, in violation of the solemnly plighted faith of the administration at the commencement of the war and, if persisted in, fatal to all hopes of a restored Union."

Daniel Marcy was renominated for Congress in the first district, and William Burns, of Lancaster, in the third district. In the second district, John H. George, of Concord, who had withdrawn after nomination in the previous campaign, was again nominated as a candidate to meet Rollins. The platform adopted in this convention was in consonance with that of the State convention, only more pronounced. It declared that the Democratic party had no sympathy with radical abolition at the North, and denounced the recent Emancipation Proclamation of the President to be " not only unconstitutional, but fraught with more evil than good, not only to the government, but also to the class of individuals upon whom it was designed to operate."

The platform adopted at the convention which nominated Daniel Marcy declared it to be its " solemn conviction that this bloody and fratricidal strife ought, as soon as practicable and prudent, to be arrested by an armistice and steps taken by means of a commission or a convention of the States to restore and save our glorious Union in the spirit of justice, compromise, and concession, in which it was framed and transmitted to us by our patriotic fathers."

George, in his letter of response, said: " I can only regard the Emancipation Proclamation as disgraceful in its futility, disastrous in its policy, palpable in its violation of the constitution, and atrocious in its purpose."

The Republican State convention met January 1, 1863. Ichabod Goodwin, of Portsmouth, presided. The prominent candidates were Onslow Stearns, of Concord; Frederick Smyth, of Manchester; Walter Harriman, of Warner; and Joseph A. Gilmore, of

Concord, the latter being the leading candidate. Gilmore was the superintendent of the Concord Railroad. He was a man of forceful character, actively interested in politics, and ambitious of political preferment. His connection with the railroad aroused hostility to his candidacy for governor, first at the convention and later at the polls. The support of Harriman came from Republicans who thought it would be both politic and wise to nominate a war Democrat and a soldier, and who were also apprehensive of Gilmore's strength as a candidate. Rollins appears to have been one of those who doubted the advisability of Gilmore's nomination at this time. An informal ballot being taken, it was found that Gilmore lacked only eight votes of a majority of the convention. After this vote was declared, a letter from Harriman was read, in which he said that he must not be considered as a candidate. In spite of this letter, he received a large vote on the formal ballot which followed, and which resulted in the nomination of Gilmore by thirty-eight majority.

The platform was reported by Amos Tuck, of Exeter. This platform congratulated the President that his patriotism, honesty, and singleness of purpose had never been questioned and that his " proclamation (emancipation) this day to be issued enrolls his name with imperishable renown upon the records of time."

In the Republican conventions of the first and third Congressional districts, there were spirited contests. In both conventions there were three candidates. In the first district, John D. Lyman, of Farmington, Gilman Marston, of Exeter, and Joel Eastman, of Conway, were the candidates. On the fourth ballot, Eastman was nominated.

The nomination of the latter was a great disappointment to Marston and his friends, who confidently expected his second renomination. Eastman was of Whig antecedents, prominent in that party's councils as early as 1838, when he was its candidate for Congress. He was United States district attorney for New Hampshire under the elder Harrison, and he had considerable support as a candidate for United States Senator in the legislature of 1854. Uniting with the Republican party at the time of its formation, he became one of its influential leaders in his section of the State.

In the third district, the candidates were Thomas M. Edwards, of Keene, James W. Patterson, of Hanover, and Jacob Benton, of Lancaster. Patterson and Benton tied on the fourth ballot, and, on the fifth, Patterson was nominated.

In the second district, Rollins was nominated by acclamation. He was endorsed by the convention as follows:

"*Resolved,* That Edward H. Rollins has by his industry, activity, and faithful discharge of his public duties proved himself a talented and useful legislator and an eminently practical and worthy representative, and we commend him for reëlection to the voters of the district as a public servant true in every respect to the vital interests of his district, his State, and the country."

As Rollins was not present at the convention, he was notified of his nomination by letter. In this letter, the committee say:

"The cordial manner with which your name was presented by the convention to the electors of the district we regard as a just and fitting tribute to a faithful public servant. During the short time you have been in Congress, you have been called upon to act upon some of the most solemn and momentous questions that were ever submitted to a legislator, and the skill and fidelity that you have manifested in guarding the numerous interests that have been committed to your keeping cannot fail to meet the entire approval of a large majority of your constituents. We have been gratified to notice the faithful and steady support you have given to the President while he has been laboring to put down treason and rebellion in the country, preserve the constitution, and restore the union of the United States. We confidently believe that, should you again be returned to the national legislature, you will continue constantly to oppose any surrender of those great and immutable principles of liberty and equality that constitute the foundations of a Republican government."

To this Rollins replied, thanking the delegates for their expressions of confidence, and outlining the issue of the campaign. He said: "The continuance of this great struggle for the maintenance of a free government and for the preservation of the constitution and the Union renders it necessary that all questions of minor consideration should be held in abeyance and that the patriotic people of the loyal States should stand by and support the constituted authorities in all their earnest efforts to put down the rebellion, on the battle-field, before the people, at the ballot-box, or wherever they may be called upon to act or speak. . . . Propositions for an armistice or a temporary peace that would allow the rebels to recuperate their wasted energies for a more desperate struggle, and declarations that ' the conflict has raged more than a year and a half with no other result than a frightful sacrifice of blood and treasure,' whether made in Congress or political conventions in New Hampshire, all point unmistakably to a disgraceful surrender of our rights and liberties, a final dissolution of the Union, and an ignominious peace dictated to us by Jefferson Davis and his coworkers in treason. Most earnestly do I desire to behold again permanent peace restored to our bleeding country, and to welcome back thousands of noble men and war-worn veterans, who have gone forth to do battle for the right, to the ordinary pursuits of life, to a generous people, and to happy homes, but I want a peace which shall be honorable and consistent with past history, a peace which shall be an earnest of our future triumphs, and upon such terms as shall cause the stars and stripes to be respected throughout the Union."

The *Statesman* spoke of Rollins's renomination as

follows: "The first term of Mr. Rollins is now near its close, and it may without qualification be said that New Hampshire never had a representative in Congress more attentive to his legislative duties, or more unweary in his efforts to promote her welfare in the calamitous period upon which we have fallen."

The *Independent Democrat* said: "In the second district, Edward H. Rollins is a candidate for reëlection. He was nominated by acclamation. This token of confidence and respect he has fully and nobly earned by his career in Congress. A more active and efficient representative, one more untiringly devoted to the interest of his constituents than Mr. Rollins, New Hampshire has never sent to the capital of the nation. Both a worker and a speaker, he has already achieved a national fame. His earnest support of the government in its present deadly encounter with rebellion is the outgrowth of true patriotism, a patriotism that embraces our whole country as the God-given heritage of freedom. He will be, as he ought to be, triumphantly elected."

It was apparent from the beginning that the contest in New Hampshire would be close, and that, whichever party won, it would win by a narrow margin. The campaign was one of the hardest fought in the history of the State. The previous fall elections had resulted in great gains of Democratic Congressmen. Upon the outcome of the spring elections in New Hampshire and Connecticut might depend the organization of the next national House of Representatives. Gilmore, the

Republican nominee for governor, did not command the united support of the party and the failure of the convention to nominate a soldier disappointed many Republicans. At one time in the campaign there was every indication of the election by the people of Eastman, the Democratic candidate. The defeat of all the Republican candidates in Congress also seemed probable.

Nehemiah G. Ordway, of Warner, was elected chairman of the Republican State committee. Associated with him in the conduct of the campaign was William E. Chandler. It was a trying campaign from start to finish, taxing all the energies and resources of both the chairman and his assistants. Charles H. Roberts, for many years a member and officer of the Republican State committee, says of this campaign:

" It was the most strenuous in my experience. The committee had the greatest difficulty in procuring speakers, and was equally embarrassed by lack of funds to conduct the canvass. Everything seemed to combine for our defeat. Our candidate for governor was unpopular, while the Democratic candidate stood high in the estimation of the people. The Republican party was not united on the slavery question, and it suffered by reason of the absence of voters who had enlisted in the army, a majority of whom would have voted the Republican ticket if they had had the opportunity, whatever their prevous political predilections. At no time in the campaign could the committee figure out success. Ordway, as chairman, did excellent service, while Rollins earnestly coöperated from Washington, but a large share of credit for our victory was due to Chandler."

When it became apparent that Gilmore was likely to be defeated at the polls, a third party organization was inspired by the Republican leaders. A union convention, so-called, was held in Manchester, February 17, 1863. William C. Clarke, of Manchester, presided. Walter Harriman, then a colonel of one of the New Hampshire regiments, was nominated for governor. Harriman at the time was what was known as a "War Democrat." The resolutions adopted were vigorous and patriotic, but indicated no party spirit. The Democratic press denounced the convention as a Republican subterfuge, and were especially bitter in their reflections upon Harriman for permitting the use of his name as a candidate.

The *Patriot* of January 28, 1863, said: "The Democratic position is fully and clearly defined in few words. The party is for the maintenance of the constitution as it is and the restoration of the Union as it was."

The Democrats were very confident of success, being inspired by the victories of their party in the previous fall elections. Assisting them as speakers in the campaign were William A. Richardson, United States Senator from Illinois, Charles Levi Woodbury, A. O. Brewster, E. D. Kelley, T. H. Sweetser, Richard S. Spofford, and W. D. Northend, of Massachusetts.

Aiding the Republicans were William D. Kelley, of

Pennsylvania, Lot M. Morrill, Israel Washburn, and Charles J. Gilman, of Maine, William A. Howard, of Michigan, John A. Bingham, of Ohio, A. J. Hamilton, of Texas, Governor John A. Andrew, E. W. Hincks, and Charles W. Slack, of Massachusetts, and B. F. Flanders, of Louisiana.

The last act of the thirty-seventh Congress, which expired March 3, 1863, a few days before the New Hampshire election, was the Conscription Act authorizing the draft to supply troops for the Union armies. This act the Democrats had opposed in Congress, and their New Hampshire brethren now took up the refrain of their Congressional leaders, denouncing the draft as unconstitutional. They argued that a war which could not be sustained by the patriotism of the people ought to cease. The Emancipation Proclamation had made the draft necessary. If the administration at Washington had held to its original declaration to wage war for the preservation of the Union, there would be no trouble about volunteers. Men, however, would not enlist to fight for the emancipation of the negro. The Republican party had repeatedly ignored the constitution in the conduct of the war. Now all its sacred guarantees were violated. The war had become one of conquest and subjugation.

No Union victory in the field occurred to inspire the Republicans of New Hampshire. The draft was recognized by them as a necessity, but it was not popular with the people. Between the ages of eighteen and forty-five no able-bodied man was exempt from its provisions. The bread-winners might now be drawn from any home for service in the army. It was the most gloomy period of the war. None could foresee the end. There had been almost two years of strife, and yet the Southern confederacy seemed invincible. Coming at a time when the Republican State committee of New Hampshire almost despaired of success, the Conscription Act seemed to ensure defeat. Yet somehow the rank and file of the party were inspired to greater determination the more the issue seemed doubtful. The State committee redoubled its efforts, and the closing week of the campaign saw the Republicans wrought to the highest tension. Republican appeals were to the patriotism of the people, and the people did not fail them, although the election was close, and, for some time after the returns began to come in, the result was in doubt. Democratic bulletins the night of election announced the defeat of Gilmore and the election to Congress of Marcy and George over Eastman and Rollins.

The total vote was increased more than four thousand over the vote of the previous year, and Eastman, the Democratic candidate for governor, came within less than five hundred votes of an election by the people. The choice for governor was thrown into the legislature, which the Republicans carried by a greatly reduced majority. In the Congressional districts, the Democrats carried the first, electing Daniel Marcy by 76 plurality. Rollins was elected in the second dis-

trict by 351 plurality, and Patterson in the third
district by 376 plurality.

The margin of Republican victory in the State was,
therefore, very slight. There was no election of governor by the people. The Republican majority in the
legislature was reduced one-half, and the Republicans
had lost one member of Congress and elected the other
two by very small pluralities. The tide of Democratic
victory in the October and November elections of 1862,
however, was checked by the New Hampshire election,
and the result in that State was hailed by Republicans
throughout the country as encouraging. Rollins's part
in the campaign was considerable, although his duties
in Washington, the thirty-seventh Congress being upon
its last session, prevented him from personally participating therein. The chairman of the State committee visited him in Washington for conference, while,
by correspondence, Rollins stimulated the activities of
leading Republicans in various parts of the State. This
New Hampshire election had an important influence
in national affairs. The Emancipation Proclamation
and the draft had been vital issues in the campaign,
and Republican victory in the State showed that the
people would sustain the administration at Washington. To the national Republican leaders this victory
was as welcome as a triumph in the field.

CHAPTER IX.

IN THE THIRTY-EIGHTH CONGRESS

CONGRESS met in regular session in December, 1863, making choice of Schuyler Colfax as Speaker of the House. Nehemiah G. Ordway was elected sergeant-at-arms. The New Hampshire members were assigned to committees as follows: Rollins was made chairman of the committee on accounts and a member of the committee on public expenditures; Patterson had Rollins's place on the committee of the District of Columbia, and was made a member of the committee on expenditures of the Treasury Department; and Marcy was given a position on the committee on Revolutionary pensions and the committee on expenditures of the Navy Department. The committee on public expenditures appears to have been busy making investigations, the New York custom-house being one of the subjects of their inquiry.

It was during the first session of this Congress that Rollins was brought into prominence by an attempt made by the Republicans of the House to expel Representative Alexander Long, of the second Ohio district, for alleged treasonable utterances in debate. It

158

was at a time of intense feeling over the war. General
Grant had been recently appointed to the command
of the Union armies, and was beginning his advance
on Richmond. News of a battle was momentarily expected. The North was making strenuous efforts to
fill its quota of troops. Grant's successes in the West
had created a confidence that, under his leadership, the
war would be speedily brought to an end. It was felt
that the tide had turned in favor of the Union forces,
and that, with a united front, the rebellion would be
crushed. Therefore, Long's speech made a deeper impression than would have been the case if it had been
delivered at an earlier period of the war. Long dis-
tinctly avowed that his Democratic associates were in
no way responsible for what he said, and nearly all of
them repudiated in the discussion which followed the
particular sentiments for which it was sought to expel
him, though opposing his expulsion as a blow at freedom in debate.

On Friday, April 8, 1864, Long obtained the floor,
the House having resolved itself into a committee of
the whole on the state of the Union upon the President's message, with George S. Boutwell, of Massachusetts, in the chair. Long's speech was a carefully
prepared and written address, and, in the main, it was
an argument against the constitutional right of the
government to coerce a sovereign State in rebellion.
This feature attracted no attention, as it had been frequently advanced from the Democratic side, but he
followed it with the assertion that, in the conduct of

the war by the administration, not a single vestige of the constitution remained and that " every clause and every letter of it had been violated." Despairing of a restoration of the Union as it once existed, he said: " I now believe there are but two alternatives; and they are either an acknowledgment of the independence of the South as an independent nation or their complete subjugation and extermination as a people; and, of these alternatives, I prefer the former."

Garfield, of Ohio, immediately replied in an impassioned speech which electrified the House. He characterized Long as a Benedict Arnold, and a running debate between him and Long followed, which lasted until the committee rose and the House adjourned. Long's speech greatly incensed the Republicans, and there was a general feeling that action should be taken to condemn such sentiments.

When the House assembled the next morning (Saturday) a motion was made to dispense with the reading of the Journal, which was carried. Then the Speaker, calling Rollins to the chair, took the floor and offered a resolution for the expulsion of Long on the ground that he had violated his oath of office by " giving aid, countenance, and encouragement to persons engaged in armed hostility to the United States." He followed the resolution with a speech sustaining it. The debate then became general and continued until the following Thursday, to the exclusion of all other business. The Republicans lined up in favor of the resolution and the Democrats against it. The debate was participated in by the leaders of both sides and became both personal and acrimonious. The proceedings were further complicated by the inflammatory utterances of Benjamin G. Harris, a Democratic member from Maryland. Obtaining the floor, he proclaimed that he endorsed every word uttered by Long. Growing more vehement as he proceeded, he exclaimed: " The South asks you to let them live in peace. But, no, you said you would bring them into subjugation. This is not done yet. God Almighty grant it may never be. I hope you will never subjugate the South."

Harris was immediately called to order by Washburne, of Illinois, who demanded that his words be taken done and read to the House. This was done, and the Speaker *pro tem,* upon the point being made, ruled that Harris was out of order and could not proceed. Soon after, the pending question of the proposed expulsion of Long was postponed until Monday, and a resolution was also offered expelling Harris. No defence of Harris was undertaken by his Democratic associates, but they made points of order against the resolution for his expulsion. After these were overruled by the chair, the resolution came to a vote. It failed of the constitutional two-thirds, the Democrats voting against it. Immediately a resolution censuring Harris was introduced and carried, only eighteen Democrats voting against it. Then the House adjourned for the day. On Monday, the debate was renewed and continued day and evening without interruption except for adjournment until the final vote of

Thursday. The alignment on the Harris resolution showed that no Democratic votes could be secured to expel Long. So a substitute resolution was offered as follows:

" *Resolved,* That Alexander Long, a Representative from the second district of Ohio, be and he is hereby declared to be an unworthy member of the House of Representatives."

A point of order was made against the substitute, which was overruled by the chair and his decision sustained by the House on appeal. This resolution was finally adopted by a strict party vote.

During the debate, Rollins, as Speaker *pro tem,* was frequently called to rule on points of order made by the minority, which he did with prompt decision. Only once was an appeal taken from his decision and that in the case referred to. The galleries were crowded during these days, and the House was often in a turmoil. It was a trying ordeal for the presiding officer, and, as the records show, Rollins acquitted himself with credit and justified his selection by the Speaker. He had previously presided in committee of the whole, and Speaker Colfax had opportunities of judging of his qualifications for the chair. Ready knowledge of the rules and quick decisions were required in this partisan debate, and Rollins showed that he was not only well acquainted with parliamentary practice but was ready in his application of it.

The *New Hampshire Statesman* of April 29, 1864, made this comment: "New Hampshire Congressmen seem to be in great favor as presiding officers. Mr. Rollins presided in the House to universal acceptance during the stormy debate in the matter of the expulsion of Mr. Long, of Ohio, and, about the same time, Mr. Clark was temporary presiding officer in the Senate. Since then, Vice-President Hamlin gave notice of intended absence the remainder of the session, and Mr. Clark was chosen President *pro tem* of the Senate."

Just prior to this occurrence, another political campaign was fought in New Hampshire. Large national interest centred in the State election of March, 1864, although no Congressmen were to be chosen. It was the first election in the Presidential year. Candidates for President were being discussed, especially by the Republican party. Would New Hampshire Republicans endorse the candidacy of Abraham Lincoln for reëlection? And, if so, would the New Hampshire election about to follow presage a national Republican triumph? There were Republican leaders in the country who doubted the policy of renominating Lincoln. The opposition to his selection as a standard-bearer was already expressing itself in the press and in the utterances of influential Republicans. Both the action of the Republican convention of New Hampshire and the forthcoming election were of especial interest to Lincoln himself. If the convention favored his candidacy, and the Republicans carried the State by a good majority, the attitude of New England in the Presidential contest would be settled. These results would have an important bearing upon the action of Republican conventions in other doubtful States.

That Lincoln awaited the result in New Hampshire with solicitous interest is well known. No outsider knew better than he the strenuous contest waged by the Republicans of the Granite State. Nor was he lacking in appreciation of the loyalty to his administration of the Republicans of New Hampshire. To their requests made to him through Rollins and other representatives of the State at the capital, he was ever a patient and responsive listener. With Rollins, who was the creator and representative of the effective Republican organization of the State, and who in Congress bent all his energy to the support of the administration, he was on terms of intimacy.

New Hampshire never had greater importance in national politics than during Lincoln's administration. The Republicans of the State had at no time failed the hope of the administration. The last election had been won by a narrow margin, but, with the exception of the loss of one Congressman, all the fruits of the victory were with the Republicans. Seven of the ten delegates from New Hampshire to the Chicago convention had voted for Lincoln's first nomination. In the main, the Republican leaders in the State approved of the acts of his administration, but, as in other States, there were some who doubted the policy of his renomination, or of his endorsement at a State convention preceding the one to choose delegates to the national convention. Rollins, Chandler, and Ordway, now rec-

ognized as "the triumvirate," potential in shaping
Republican policies in the State, were outspoken for
the endorsement of Lincoln and in favor of New
Hampshire leading the way. Both Rollins and Ordway were detained in Washington by their duties
there, and the leadership of the administration forces
devolved upon Chandler.

William E. Chandler was then twenty-eight years
of age, having served one term as Speaker of the New
Hampshire House of Representatives, the youngest
occupant of that position in the history of the State.
Before he was of age, he was active in politics, doing
much of the literary work of the State committee prior
to his appointment as its secretary. From the time of
his entrance into politics, for a period of forty-five
years, his influence was felt in all the shifting scenes
of New Hampshire politics, and, for a greater part of
this time, he was the most striking personality in the
State. No man in New Hampshire more thoroughly
enjoyed the turmoil of political strife. None possessed
greater courage, and none made more bitter enemies
or more earnest friends. He was always in the thick
of the fray, attacking or defending, giving or parrying
blows. He spared not the feelings of friends in his
encounters if these friends stood across his path. Yet
his success was due to his faculty of reconciling to his
personal interests those whom he had angered by his
caustic criticism. No politician of the State ever had
so many ups and downs, and none had so many obitu-
aries written on the passing of his political career. He

won the highest honors of the State, compelling support from many through admiration for his ability.

The Republican State convention to nominate a candidate for governor met January 6, 1864, and was presided over by Mason W. Tappan. Governor Gilmore was renominated by acclamation. His administration had been successful and opposition to his nomination, so pronounced the year before, had entirely disappeared. The platform was reported by Aaron H. Cragin. It contained no endorsement of Lincoln for renomination. The committee, desiring to be conservative, had listened to the advice of those who, while admitting the probability of Lincoln's becoming the Presidential nominee, did not wish to take premature action. Another convention to choose delegates to the national convention would be held in a few months, and to that convention more properly belonged the expression of views as to a Presidential candidate. The events of the next few months growing out of the progress of the war might present a clearer view of the best course to pursue.

Although the failure of the committee to report a plank in the platform endorsing Lincoln's candidacy came as a surprise to the convention, the platform was adopted without dissent. Immediately after its adoption, Chandler, against the advice of older men, presented a resolution declaring Abraham Lincoln to be the people's choice for President in 1864. Without debate, it passed unanimously amid great enthusiasm, showing, that while some of the leaders hesitated, the rank and file of the Republican party in New Hampshire were ready and anxious to express their choice.

The Republican platform endorsed the administration of Lincoln, opposed any proposition of peace so long as there was found a rebel in arms against the government, and expressed confidence in the financial ability of Secretary Salmon P. Chase.

The Democratic State convention followed two days after the Republican convention. It was presided over by William H. Duncan, of Hanover. Ira A. Eastman having signified to the party that he did not desire a second nomination, a ballot was taken for a candidate for governor. Edward W. Harrington, of Manchester, received 518 votes of the 535 cast, and his nomination was made unanimous. The platform denounced the financial policy of the Republican administration, declared its plan of emancipation of the negro to be " unwise, impolitic, cruel, and unworthy the support of a civilized and Christian people," and maintained that the war should be conducted solely for the restoration of the Union.

The campaign lacked none of the intensity of previous campaigns. It was fought wholly on the war issues. Both parties called to their aid speakers from other States. For the Democrats, there came William W. Eaton, afterward United States Senator, and James Gallagher, of Connecticut, A. Oakey Hall and John M. Harrington, of New York, and William D. Northend, of Massachusetts.

Assisting the Republicans were Gen. E. W. Gantt,

of Arkansas, who had served in the Confederate army and recently renounced his allegiance to that cause, Frederick Montgomery, of Virginia, Paul Dillingham, of Vermont, Richard Busteed, A. H. Chase, Rufus F. Andrews, of New York, Mark H. Dunnell and Lewis Barker, of Maine, E. W. Hincks, of Massachusetts, and William C. Doane, of Washington, D. C.

How the Republicans regarded the campaign may be judged by the following extract from an address to the voters of New Hampshire issued by the chairman of the Republican State committee:

"Union Citizens of New Hampshire: — The election of this year possesses more national importance than that of any previous year. A triumph of the so-called Democracy would be hailed with rejoicing by Jefferson Davis and every other rebel leader; it would afford aid and comfort to traitors in arms; and by its effect upon the Presidential campaign would do more to prolong the war than a rebel victory in the field.

"A victory of the Unionists of the State would rejoice the hearts of the friends of the government — of union and liberty everywhere, and would discourage and dishearten the leaders of the rebellion, because it would be a certain indication of the choice of a Union Republican President at the ensuing election.

"The chief hope of the rebels is now, as heretofore, in a division of sentiment in the North. Proclaim to them that they cannot by prolonging the war gain the privilege of negotiating with men in power at the North who have been during the whole struggle sym-

pathizers with the rebellion, and every reason for prolonging a hopeless struggle is at an end; the advance
of our armies will result in the submission of the
people of the seceded States to the power of the national government, and substantial peace may be obtained within the present year."

The vote was larger by nearly two thousand than the
previous year and the result a great Republican victory. The Republican majority for governor approxi-
mated six thousand. Such a majority had not been
equalled in New Hampshire since the Presidential
election of 1860. It was a surprise to both Republicans and Democrats. The *Patriot* attributed it to
Republican soldiers from New Hampshire home on
furlough. The official vote was: Scattering, 79; Edward W. Harrington, 31,340; Joseph A. Gilmore,
37,006.

Following closely after the March election came the
Republican convention to elect delegates to the Republican national convention, to be held at Baltimore.
There was no question now as to the candidate for
President whom the New Hampshire delegates would
support. The interest in the convention was in the
personnel of the delegates, and there was a large number of candidates. William E. Chandler, as chairman
of the State committee, called the convention to order,
and William Haile, of Hinsdale, presided. A ballot
was taken for four delegates at large, with the result
that Onslow Stearns, of Concord, John B. Clarke, of
Manchester, William Haile, of Hinsdale, and Thomas

E. Sawyer, of Dover, were elected. As district delegates Benjamin J. Cole, of Gilford, and Joseph B. Adams, of Portsmouth, were chosen from the first district; Edward Spalding, of Nashua, and David Cross, of Manchester, from the second; and Shepard L. Bowers, of Newport, and Enoch L. Colby, of Lancaster, from the third.

John B. Clarke, who was one of the delegates at large, was the proprietor of the *Manchester Mirror*, a newspaper with both a daily and a weekly edition, the latter of large circulation. Of genial temperament and original ideas, he had already made his impress upon the people of the State. Through his newspaper he continued until his death to exert a large influence in New Hampshire politics.

Of the other delegates Haile had been governor of the State, Stearns was president of the State Senate, Cross was the most prominent candidate for Congress to succeed Rollins, Cole was then and for years after the leading Republican in his section of the State, and Sawyer was an influential citizen of Strafford County. At the next election Sawyer became the candidate for Congress in the first district of the Republicans who bolted the renomination of Gilman Marston.

Upon the legislature which convened in June, 1864, devolved the duty of electing a successor to Senator John P. Hale, whose term would expire with the thirty-eighth Congress. The reputation that Rollins had made as a Congressman led a large number of his friends to suggest him as a candidate for the Senate.

Other avowed candidates were John P. Hale, Aaron H. Cragin, Gilman Marston, Amos Tuck, and Thomas M. Edwards. It was apparent, with so many strong candidates, that no one could have anywhere near a majority on the first ballot. The outcome of the caucus, therefore, was doubtful, and the interest was intense until the ballot was taken. So far as Rollins's candidacy was concerned, it was embarrassed by the State-house contest, which had become acute through the offer of Manchester citizens to give a large sum of money sufficient to build a new State-house, provided the capital of the State was transferred from Concord to Manchester. The question came up at this time because of the necessity of enlarging and repairing the State-house. It was recognized as a life and death struggle of the citizens of Concord to maintain their city as the capital of the State, and civic pride called for the sacrifice of all personal ambition to the attainment of this end. If Concord secured the United States Senator as the result of what was a strenuous contest, there would follow in the wake personal disappointment that might count against the capital city. Rollins's love of Concord was second to that of no other citizen. The city had been his home for nearly twenty years. Here he had begun business for himself, and here was the scene of all his early triumphs in politics. As the time approached for the meeting of the legislature, it became apparent both to him and to Chandler, who was interested in his Senatorial canvass, that his candidacy would militate against Concord's interests. They both concluded that it would not be wise to present Rollins's name to the Senatorial caucus. But, that his withdrawal might count as much as possible for Concord's benefit, he continued a candidate until the night of the caucus. Just before the ballot was taken, Chandler withdrew Rollins's name. Five ballots were necessary to secure a choice.[1]

Tuck's name was withdrawn after the third ballot, and his support went to Cragin in preference to Marston. John H. George was the Democratic candidate for Senator.

The Presidential campaign was not a long one. Not much doubt was entertained by Republicans of the result in New Hampshire. Their majority in the spring election seemed too large for the Democrats to overcome, yet the Democratic party made a determined effort to carry the State. Rollins entered this campaign with enthusiasm, it being the first in which he had personally participated since he took his seat in Congress. He made many speeches throughout the canvass, besides assisting in the work of the State committee. George Thompson, the English abolitionist,

	First	Second	Third	Fourth	Fifth
[1] Anthony Colby, of New London	1	1			
Ira Perley, of Concord	4	4	3	2	
Thomas M. Edwards, of Keene	24	19	9	1	
Amos Tuck, of Exeter	32	37	27		
John P. Hale, of Dover	35	27	20	12	
Aaron H. Cragin, of Lebanon	49	58	72	97	126
Gilman Marston, of Exeter	57	59	73	89	75

Vice-President Hamlin, and Edwin C. Bailey, editor of the *Boston Herald,* took part in the campaign for the Republicans.

The Democrats were assisted in their stump-speaking by C. T. Russell, William D. Northend, Josiah G. Abbot, George S. Hilliard, and G. H. Devereau, of Massachusetts, C. C. Burr, of Connecticut, and A. M. Dickey, of Vermont. The Republicans were successful, but their majority was much smaller than in the spring election.[1]

After election, Rollins returned to Washington to the closing session of the thirty-eighth Congress. Early in the session, he introduced a resolution of inquiry regarding the treatment of Union prisoners of war in the Confederate prisons, with instructions to the committee on military affairs to report upon the expediency of providing by law for retaliation if such treatment of Union prisoners was continued, to the end that the Confederate authorities may be compelled to treat their prisoners according to the rules and usages of civilized warfare. The resolution was immediately adopted, but the next day, it occasioned a stirring debate, the Democrats claiming that they did not understand the purport of the resolution at

---

[1] The official vote as given in the *Statesman* of December 2, 1864, is as follows :

		LINCOLN	MCCLELLAN
Home vote	. . . . .	34,382	32,200
Soldier vote	. . . . .	2,018	671
Total,		36,400	32,871

the time of its passage. Other resolutions were introduced during the debate, and the whole subject was finally referred to the committee on military affairs.

It was during this session that an assault was made upon Congressman William D. Kelley, of Pennsylvania, by A. P. Field, of Louisiana, who claimed a seat in the House, and labored under the impression that Kelley's influence prevented him from obtaining it. The assault was brought to the attention of the House, and a select committee, of which Rollins was one, was appointed by the Speaker to investigate and report. After inquiry, they reported the facts to the House, and Field was brought to the bar of the House, and reprimanded by the Speaker.

The calls upon Rollins on the part of soldiers and their families were not confined to members of his party, nor did he show party preference in responding to them. All the people of New Hampshire were his constituents, and he gave to each his best effort. In the midst of the political campaign of 1863, when the Democrats of the State were making strenuous efforts to defeat his reëlection, he received a letter from Ira A. Eastman, the Democratic candidate for governor that year, in behalf of a New Hampshire soldier convicted of desertion and sentenced to be hanged. Eastman's letter is a type of many he received and is expressive of the faith that both Democrats and Republicans entertained of his potential influence. Eastman writes:

"I learn that you have interested yourself to pro-

cure commutation of the sentence of Private ———,
Tenth New Hampshire Volunteers, and that the President has or will reprieve him preliminary to commut-
ing his sentence. I believe the governor sent the application for his commutation and you presented it to
the President. If so, you saw the facts of the case.
It should be especially borne in mind that he was a
volunteer who enlisted in 1862 without any of the
large bounties. It should also be borne in mind that
at the time of his desertion the offence was a very common one, and not severely punished. Had he deserted
within the last few months, it would be a very different matter. His wife is a very reputable, well-appear-
ing woman, and has one or two children. Of course,
she is deeply interested in his welfare, as well as his
other friends. I hope you will see to it that there is
no mistake about the matter. The life of a man is of
some consequence to his friends at least, and, if he is
released, he will, no doubt, make a good soldier. He
must have suffered much with this sentence hanging
over him. I have told his friends that I have no doubt
that you will look close to it so as to save him."

The endorsement on the letter in Rollins's hand-
writing is " A general order issued when first application made to suspend sentence in Butler's district.
Have now had a special order sent by telegraph in
this case and there is no doubt."

CHAPTER X.

THE Democratic party had been so thoroughly beaten in the Presidential campaign that it was impossible for its leaders in New Hampshire to evoke much enthusiasm among the rank and file in the spring campaign of 1865. Both leaders and followers were too dispirited to take advantage of Republican dissensions, of which there was soon to be abundant evidence. Then again, it was difficult for the party to abandon wholly the theories and principles for which it had fought for so long a time. The Democratic party did not, and could not, arise to its opportunity in this campaign.

The Republican Congressional conventions in the first and second districts were held December 21, 1864. In the first district Marston was again a candidate for renomination. There was strong opposition, especially among the supporters of Eastman, the candidate of two years before, who had charged his defeat at the polls to the indifference of Marston. Eastman was not again a candidate, but the opponents of Marston concentrated largely on Samuel M. Wheeler, of

176

Dover.   Only one ballot was necessary for a choice. The votes of the delegates were distributed as follows: Benjamin J. Cole, of Gilford, 7; Jacob H. Ela, of Rochester, 10; John D. Lyman, of Farmington, 19; Samuel M. Wheeler, of Dover, 72; Gilman Marston, of Exeter, 135.

Dissatisfaction with the nomination at once made itself manifest, and charges were openly made that it had been brought about by unfair means and by the pernicious activity of federal office-holders.   Immediate steps were taken to call another convention.   An address was issued to the Republicans of the district charging that the will of the party had been defeated by methods deserving rebuke.   There were also arrangements made for holding a bolting convention at Dover.   The *Monitor* and its weekly, the *Independent Democrat,* gave encouragement to the bolt by not only publishing the address but also by favorable comment thereon.   The convention at Dover nominated Thomas E. Sawyer of that city, who accepted the nomination.   Among the reasons advanced for the defeat of Marston was the fact that he had had two terms in Congress, which at that time and for years after was looked upon by many people of the State as the full complement to be given a Congressional candidate.

Rollins, in seeking a third nomination, had this rotation theory to overcome.   He himself had been a candidate against Mason W. Tappan, in 1859, when the latter was seeking a third nomination, and had withdrawn only after an informal ballot showed Tappan largely in the lead. He had been an advocate of rotation, and continued so when later he aspired to the Senate. A formidable candidate had arisen in the rival city of Manchester. David Cross, who was voted for in the convention of 1859, and strongly supported in the convention of 1861, was seeking the nomination in this district. Rotation would send the nomination to Manchester. Nor was this the only contest between these two cities, whose rivalry for so many years interfered with political ambitions. There were two active candidates for gubernatorial honors, Frederick Smyth, of Manchester, and Onslow Stearns, of Concord. The holding of the Congressional convention ahead of the State convention is quite likely to have been part of Rollins's plan to secure for himself in the division of prizes the one going to Concord. The Democratic *Patriot* later charged that he was responsible for the gubernatorial nomination going to Manchester.

The election of delegates to the second Congressional convention showed that the contest between Rollins and Cross would be close. The personal popularity of Cross and the rotation principle seemed likely to outweigh the advantages to the State of keeping an experienced legislator in Congress. Just before the convention, however, an adjustment of the contest was arranged by the mutual friends of Rollins and Cross. The pension agency for New Hampshire was then a lucrative office. Its emoluments were greater than the salary of a Congressman. A lawyer holding this place could at that time still keep in touch with his clients, and not entirely neglect his practice, which was not possible if he were serving in Congress. This phase of the case appealed to Cross, and he virtually withdrew from the Congressional race to become a successful candidate for the pension agency, a change of ambition he has repeatedly said he never regretted.

David Cross's political activities pertain to almost three generations of contemporaries. So well preserved is he to-day (1906) that he seems to have all the elasticity of a man in middle life. Yet, he was first a candidate for Congress forty-seven years ago, and was influential in Whig politics at an earlier date. Giving up political ambition after he accepted the pension agency, his life-work has been in his profession, where he has ranked among the leaders both as a counsellor and as an advocate. Now the Nestor of the bar of the State, he is regarded with filial affection by all his juniors in the profession. This attachment is but a just return, for his whole life has been one of helpfulness to young and struggling attorneys. Although not aspiring to office, he has most cheerfully responded at all times to calls for party work. His active campaigning covers quite half a century. His last public service was as a member of the constitutional convention of 1902.

The Congressional convention for the second district was held at Manchester and was largely attended. An informal ballot showed fifty-five votes for Cross and one hundred and thirty-four for Rollins. The name of Cross was then withdrawn, and the nomination of Rollins made by acclamation. The convention then adopted the following resolution:

"*Resolved,* That Edward H. Rollins has by his eminently patriotic and laborious endeavors, and by his faithful service for the country in most trying and difficult circumstances during his four years of public record, proved himself a most talented and useful legislator and a representative whose influence, labors, and experience can be regarded as indispensable in the present juncture of our affairs, and we heartily commend him to the voters of the district."

The Democratic newspapers of the State assailed the nomination with vehemence. The *Union,* of Manchester, attributed it to the power of the " apothecary shop " to manipulate things. The *Patriot* said:

" The renomination of Rollins was expected, for it had been fixed beforehand. The administration acts generally upon Mr. Lincoln's theory that it is bad policy to swap horses while crossing a stream. Having proved Rollins and found him to be reliable, always ready to do its work without question as to its character or tendency, it deemed it best to retain him two years longer, and, therefore, gave him the power to secure his own nomination. . . . The nomination was virtually made at Washington. Every intelligent man knows that the unbiassed action of the Republican party of the district would have resulted in a very different manner, but Rollins had the patronage of the administration at his bestowal, and that was used to effect the desired result."

The *Statesman* said:

"Edward H. Rollins was placed in nomination for a third term of service as a member of Congress by the cordial and unanimous vote of a convention of nearly two hundred members. This is a procedure in the highest degree creditable to the convention, and took place under circumstances which cannot but be very gratifying to the intelligent, efficient, and laborious member from the second district of our State. A complimentary vote was given to David Cross, of Manchester, a gentleman for whom men of all parties entertain deep respect for his high personal character, and who has secured the universal regard of the Republican party for effective service rendered the cause at home and abroad."

Patterson was renominated in the third district by acclamation.

The Republican State convention was held January 5, 1865. It was called to order by Nehemiah G. Ordway in the absence of William E. Chandler, chairman of the Republican State committee. Nathaniel G. Upham, of Concord, presided. The platform, reported by Austin F. Pike, pledged the party anew to a vigorous prosecution of the war, and declared for the complete extermination of slavery from the soil of the republic. The nomination of Rollins for Congress precluded the possibility of the gubernatorial nomination going to Concord, but the friends of Stearns clung tenaciously to him as a candidate. The ballot showed 445 votes for Frederick Smyth, 221 for Onslow Stearns, 8 for Walter Harriman, and 6 for Milan W. Harris, of Dublin. Smyth was declared the nominee.

Frederick Smyth, whose occupation was that of a banker, was an eminently successful business man. He had been mayor of Manchester, and had served in the legislature. A product of the school of stern necessity, he made his way in life by his self-reliance, foreseeing opportunities, and taking advantage of them. A close student of human nature, he had a pleasing address, and possessed those attributes which contribute to personal popularity. Energetic and resourceful, acting where others hesitated, he made a successful chief magistrate at a time when large executive ability was required.

A change was made this year in the method of electing a State committee. The Republicans of the several counties were authorized to choose committees to work within the counties. The chairmen and secretaries of the county organizations constituted *ex officio* the State central committee. "This plan," remarked the *Statesman,* "will, it is hoped, remove all complaint of 'central cliques,' 'Concord dictation,' etc." The new plan survived just one campaign.

The Democratic State convention was held January 12, 1865. Dr. A. P. Stackpole, of Dover, presided. Edward W. Harrington, of Manchester, was renominated by acclamation. The platform was very brief. After reciting the preamble of the United

States constitution, the convention resolved " That the delegated Democracy of New Hampshire in convention assembled accept as a platform of principles the constitution and the Union."

After the convention had voted to accept this as a declaration of principles, a commotion was created by an amendment offered endorsing the Kentucky and Virginia resolutions of 1798 and 1799, calling for a convention of States for the adjustment of present troubles, and protesting against the Republican party's purpose of abolishing slavery. After a spirited debate, the amendment was rejected by a vote of 73 yeas to 14 nays. This contest over the platform destroyed whatever chance the Democratic party had of profiting by Republican dissensions.

At the Democratic Congressional conventions, Daniel Marcy was renominated in the first district, while new candidates were presented in both the second and third districts. Lewis W. Clark, of Manchester, was selected in the second district, and Harry Bingham, of Littleton, in the third.

Rollins's opponent, Lewis W. Clark, was a brilliant man of fine legal attainments. He stood well at the bar, was a pleasing speaker and personally popular. He afterward became attorney-general of the State and subsequently was appointed to its supreme bench, where he remained until retired by age limitations. Although a Democrat to the close of his life, both political parties had confidence in him, and he was made chief justice by a Republican governor and council with the entire approval of the people of the State.

The bolt in the first Congressional district encouraged the opposition to Rollins to attempt like action in the second district. Stearns regarded his defeat for the gubernatorial nomination as due to Rollins's third nomination for Congress, and was lukewarm even if not opposed to the latter's election. Governor Gilmore, who was at odds with the Republican party over the soldiers' voting bill, which was passed by the previous legislature, and which he attempted to veto, was especially hostile to Rollins and Ordway. At his instigation, a meeting of Republicans was called at Concord to determine whether action should be taken to bolt the nomination. Many of those opposed to Rollins were invited to the meeting by Gilmore. Chandler invited others friendly to Rollins. Gilmore informally presided at the meeting and called for opinions. These were given, and, while some were in favor of taking formal action, no one was ready to take the responsibility of contributing to the election of Clark. The project failed largely through the efforts of Chandler, assisted by Austin F. Pike, who was then chairman of the State committee.

The campaign was not enlivened by much speaking on either side. Few local speakers took part. A few meetings were arranged by the Republicans, which were addressed by Dr. George B. Loring, of Massachusetts, William C. Doane, of Washington, D. C., and Edward McPherson, of Pennsylvania. The *Statesman* commented upon the quietness of the canvass and occasionally warned the Republicans not to be caught napping. The *Monitor* and *Independent Democrat* voiced a dissatisfaction which was felt by disappointed candidates, their friends and others who thought that Rollins, Chandler, and Ordway had too much to do with shaping the affairs of the party. So independent were these two newspapers that talk was made of starting at the capital an administration daily. Referring to a report of this, the *Monitor* satirically welcomed the proposed paper and boldly disclaimed being an administration organ. It said: "If, in the first Congressional district, Gilman Marston, in the second district, Edward H. Rollins, and in the State at large, Nehemiah G. Ordway are the administration, we are not an administration daily."

The Democratic *Patriot,* commenting upon the situation, said: "It is apparent to every one that there is much dissatisfaction among Republicans of this [the second] district and that many of those who finally vote for Rollins will do so with great reluctance and, as the *Monitor* says, under protest. Indeed that paper declares that even greater dissatisfaction exists here than in the first district, where there is much reason to believe the abolition candidate will be defeated. The *Monitor* says this dissatisfaction is not with the principles of the party, but with the men who claim to be the exponents of those principles — with Rollins, Chandler, and Ordway, in fact."

There were frequent and anxious conferences of

the Republican leaders, and Rollins was in constant correspondence with his friends in the district. No canvass gave any indication of the extent of the dissatisfaction. The canvass put out by the Republican State committee showed less than three thousand majority. The committee itself was far from sanguine of attaining even this majority. Therefore, the returns came in as a happy surprise. The Republican victory was overwhelming. The vote for governor was as follows: Scattering, 57; Edward W. Harrington, 28,017; Frederick Smyth, 34,145.

The majority exceeded that of the preceding year on a much lighter vote. The Republican majority in the legislature was very large. All three of the Republican candidates for Congress were elected. Marston had fifteen hundred majority in the first district, Rollins seventeen hundred in the second, and Patterson eighteen hundred in the third. The vote for Sawyer, the bolting Republican candidate in the first district, was but about five hundred.

CHAPTER XI.

IN THE THIRTY - NINTH CONGRESS

THE national events immediately following the March election of 1865 in New Hampshire obscured for the time being all thoughts of politics. In quick succession came the surrender of Lee, the assassination of Lincoln, and the final collapse of the confederacy. Rollins was in Washington at the time, although Congress had adjourned. He was one of the few who were at the bedside of Lincoln when he died, and he was one of the committee accompanying the remains of the President to Illinois. From Lincoln's home, he returned to Concord, to remain until the thirty-ninth Congress should assemble in the following December.

It is interesting to note that the last official signature of Abraham Lincoln is in the possession of the Rollins family. About five o'clock on the afternoon of April 14, 1865, Rollins called upon the President to secure his endorsement on a petition from New Hampshire addressed to the Secretary of War. Lincoln had finished his day's business and left his office in the White House, going up-stairs. On receiving Rollins's card, he returned to meet him. Lincoln took

187

the petition on his knee and wrote his endorsement, dated it, and signed his name. As Rollins took his departure, Lincoln gave orders to the doorkeeper to admit no one to the White House. As Lincoln's assassination followed that evening, Rollins did not present the petition, but kept it as a memento of the martyred President, forwarding the request of his New Hampshire constituents in another way. A few years later this petition was shown to Schuyler Colfax by Senator Rollins's son, Edward W. Rollins, and the time and circumstances connected with the President's signature related. Colfax said that it was undoubtedly Lincoln's last signature, as he dined with the President that night and after dinner escorted him to the carriage which was to take him to the theatre. Colfax said that while he was at the White House in the evening Lincoln performed no official act.

Hon. Secretary of War, please see and hear Hon. Mr Rollins, & oblige him if you consistently can,

A Lincoln

April 14 1865.

The time intervening between the assassination of Lincoln and the meeting of Congress in December was a period of mourning for the martyred President, and of speculation as to the policy of his successor. The question of the reconstruction of the South was overshadowing all else, and the whole country watched every move and utterance of Andrew Johnson with eager interest. He was a Southern man and, before the war, a Democrat. His attitude toward the South, now that peace had come, was unknown, but the Republican leaders were hopeful that he would continue in accord with the party that elected him, and this hope was not fully dispelled until after Congress had assembled.

Rollins was sworn in for the third time as a member of the House. He was made chairman of the committee on accounts, and a member of the committee on public expenditures. Marston was put upon the committees on military affairs and mileage, while Patterson was advanced to the committee on foreign affairs. The committee on accounts had oversight of the expenditures of the House for supplies and for salaries of employees. To keep the expenditures within reasonable limits and to respond to the constant request of members for increase of compensation of their friends upon the pay-rolls of the House was no easy task. At times the House in an economical mood would sit down hard upon the report of the committee for a necessary expenditure, while at others Rollins had to fight with all the persistency of his nature some generous impulse of members to increase salaries all along the line. To the committee on public expenditures was assigned various investigations of the larger custom-houses and alleged frauds in the internal revenue, and the committee was kept busy a good share of its time.

Rollins's third term in Congress was marked by the same patient industry, close attention to the business of the House, and constant activity in behalf of his constituents that characterized his previous terms of service. Being better known, the demand upon his time was greater. He had been a member of the committee on the District of Columbia but one term, giving place in the thirty-eighth Congress to Patterson, his colleague from New Hampshire, but he continued to take an interest in the affairs of the District, which the people of Washington appreciated. The welfare of the recently emancipated slaves of the District engaged his attention, and he had the satisfaction of contributing by his efforts to the improvement of their condition. With the experience that comes of service in the House, he participated more frequently in debates, but he made no set speech. In the stormy times which followed the break of President Johnson with the Republican party, Rollins stood firm with the Republican leaders in opposing the policy of Johnson, all the time watchful of opinion in New Hampshire and earnestly at work to keep the State in line with Republican principles.

At the very beginning of Johnson's administration,

the question of appointments to office became acute.
Not many appointments had been made by Lincoln
in his second term prior to his death. New Hampshire men in federal position were desirous of remaining. Some of them, like Amos Tuck and George G.
Fogg, were holding important offices. The advent of
Johnson upset all plans made with his predecessor,
and it early developed that Johnson had preferences
of his own to gratify. So long as the latter appeared
to act with the Republicans, Rollins undertook to
assist in retaining the New Hampshire federal officials in office. As more was expected of him than of
other members of the delegation, so he had to share
a larger part of the responsibility for failure. No
small part of the enmity of influential Republicans
in New Hampshire which he incurred dates from this
period. As the management of the party in New
Hampshire was attributed to Rollins, Chandler, and
Ordway, so to them was laid the blame for individual
disappointments of office-holders and office-seekers.
From this time on, the attacks upon them from within
the party became more pronounced. While President
Johnson was slowly drifting into alliance with the
Democratic party, another campaign occurred in New
Hampshire.

The Republican State convention was held January
5, 1866. It was called to order by Benjamin F. Prescott, the secretary of the State committee. George G.
Fogg presided. Governor Smyth was renominated by
acclamation. The platform adopted was a somewhat

guarded document in its reference to the administration at Washington. It commended Andrew Johnson as a just citizen, sincere patriot, and distinguished statesman, approved the tone and temper of his late annual message, and pledged him hearty support in all his efforts to restore harmony and mutual trust between different sections of the Union upon the basis of universal liberty and justice to all.

The Democratic State convention did not meet until February 7, 1866. The attitude of the President was now clear, and the Democrats were able to take a decided position on his policy. Their convention was called to order by Lewis W. Clark, chairman of the State committee, and Charles R. Morrison, of Manchester, was elected president. On the ballot for a candidate for governor, John G. Sinclair, of Bethlehem, was nominated, receiving 305 votes to 38 for Hiram R. Roberts, of Rollinsford, 28 for John W. Sanborn, of Wakefield, and 5 scattering.

The platform, quoting from President Johnson that " propositions to amend the constitution are becoming as numerous as resolutions at town meetings called to consider the most ordinary questions of local affairs," resolved that " we disapprove of all amendments to the constitution at the present time and under the present circumstances."

It further pledged to Andrew Johnson the support of the Democratic party " in the efforts he is making to secure to all the States immediate representation in Congress and their full rights under the constitution as States of the Union." It promised to stand by him so long as he stands by the constitution. It invited all patriotic citizens to unite with the Democratic party in this purpose. The Democrats were further encouraged by the report that the President would appoint no men to office who did not support his policy.

The campaign was a quiet one. With a new candidate for governor, the Democrats expected to make an improved showing on the popular vote, and were not without hope that the defection of Andrew Johnson would contribute to their success in the State by unsettling the convictions of New Hampshire Republicans. They were, however, disappointed. The returns showed the reëlection of Governor Smyth by nearly five thousand majority. The vote was as follows: Scattering, 18; John G. Sinclair, 30,484; Frederick Smyth, 35,136.

It devolved upon the incoming legislature to choose a successor to Senator Daniel Clark. Including himself, there were four candidates who aspired to his seat in the Senate. The others were Rollins, Patterson, and Marston, all of whom were then members of Congress whose terms expired at the same time with Clark's. Patterson had come rapidly to the front during his service in the national House, attracting the attention of the country by his forceful and eloquent speeches. He was strongly supported for the position. Rollins had withdrawn two years before as a candidate on account of Concord's interest in remaining the capital of the State. Marston had come very near to the goal at that time, having been defeated by the transfer of Amos Tuck's support to Aaron H. Cragin. The cry of rotation in office was taken up by Rollins, Patterson, and Marston, and it became a contest with Clark against the field. Clark, though lacking elements of personal popularity, was strong as a candidate because of the prominence he had attained in the Senate. It was evident that those favorable to rotation in office could more easily unite on Patterson than on either Rollins and Marston, both of whom bore scars from their recent Congressional contests. One had been openly bolted and the other seriously threatened with a bolt. Although both had been reëlected by large majorities, the feeling engendered by their contests for renomination still remained. Four ballots were necessary for a choice and Patterson was nominated.[1]

Rollins expressed no disappointment at his defeat. He returned to the short session of the thirty-ninth Congress with the hope that he might be again returned to the House. In this hope he was somewhat encouraged by his friends. A large majority of the working Republicans of the State looked upon him as the most effective member of the delegation in that his work, though not so conspicuous as that of some

	First	Second	Third	Fourth
[1] Clark	72	76	79	77
Patterson	62	69	82	124
Marston	36	35	27	2
Rollins	36	25	15	2

of his colleagues, usually brought about results. His most formidable opponent was Aaron F. Stevens, of Nashua, an able lawyer of political prominence. A vacancy on the supreme bench of the State was soon to occur, to which it was thought Stevens might be appointed. If so, the field would be reasonably clear for Rollins's fourth nomination. Stevens was postmaster of Nashua at this time. Rollins, therefore, wrote to his friends in the district asking their advice as to his candidacy. In the meantime, delegates were elected to the convention which was to assemble at Manchester, December 27, 1866. Rollins himself was chosen a delegate from Ward 4, Concord. A number of Rollins's staunch friends, like Ordway, Austin F. Pike, John Kimball, of Concord, Edward Osgood and David Foster, of Canterbury, were also chosen as delegates.

Referring to the approaching Congressional convention in the second district, the *Statesman* said: " In our own district Mr. Rollins, the present efficient Representative, has been so uniformly right upon all questions presented to Congress and his name is so interwoven with the true men who have been returned from nearly all the loyal States to the fortieth Congress that we confess it would give us pleasure to see him returned again. The great issue now presented to the people is whether Congress shall be sustained or the President. The question is presented as one of policy solely, whether Mr. Rollins shall be reëlected or a new Representative chosen. It is not whether we shall adopt a fourth term rule, but whether, under existing circumstances, Mr. Rollins be returned as a direct rebuke to Andrew Johnson. At the same time, we are not unmindful of the claims of distinguished and worthy gentlemen of the district. The popular choice seems to point strongly toward Gen. Aaron F. Stevens, of Nashua, as the successor of Mr. Rollins whenever a new man is chosen. His election would be a fitting recognition of his eminent service in the State and in the field. Messrs. Pike, of Franklin, and Briggs, of Hillsborough, are both mentioned in the same connection, and the responsibilities of the office might be safely left in their hands."

The convention being in the recess of Congress, Rollins attended. After the convention was called to order, he addressed it, and the conclusion he had reached is set forth in his speech. He said:

" I propose to submit a few remarks to this convention which in my judgment will have a tendency to promote that harmony and unity of action which are so essential to the welfare and prosperity of the Republicans of the district. I am well aware that there are gentlemen present, and many in the district, warm friends, who would be pleased to see me renominated and reëlected to Congress. I confess with entire frankness that there was a time when, considering the question whether Congress or the President would be sustained by the people, observing that generally the members of the thirty-ninth Congress had been returned, and listening to the kind and flattering words of ardent and devoted supporters, I thought it possible, aye probable, that this constituency would depart in this instance from the time-honored doctrine of rotation in office. That time has passed. Distrusting my own judgment and desiring full information to enable me to arrive at an intelligent conclusion, and to act agreeably to the wishes of the Republican party, I wrote letters to influential gentlemen in various parts of the district, seeking counsel as to the sentiments of the people in their immediate localities. To some of these letters I received prompt reply, but many replies were so long delayed that they have but recently come into my hands. While the tone of the responses was with scarcely an exception of most kind and cordial character, assuring me of full and unqualified endorsement of my official record, it was apparent that there was a strong inclination to adhere to the doctrine of rotation. To the doctrine I have been committed in the past, and I submit to it cheerfully in the present.

" I wish now to express my hearty thanks to my friends, here and elsewhere, and to the Republican party of the district for their many expressions of confidence, and the unfaltering support which has been given to me during the nearly six years I have held a seat in Congress. At the expiration of my present term, I shall again return to the ranks, where, I flatter myself, I have heretofore done some service for the cause, and where I hope to do still more in the future."

Mr. Rollins then moved the nomination of Stevens by acclamation. The name of James F. Briggs, of

Hillsborough, was withdrawn, and Stevens was nominated. The convention then adopted the following resolution:

"*Resolved,* That we are proud of the official career of our present able and efficient Representative in Congress, Edward H. Rollins, and that we fully and heartily endorse the same and pledge ourselves to push forward to consummation the work in which he in Congress is engaged."

In the Republican convention of the first Congressional district, Jacob H. Ela, of Rochester, was nominated after several ballots, the other candidates being Gilman Marston, Samuel M. Wheeler, and Edward Ashton Rollins, the latter being a cousin of Edward H. Rollins.

Ela was a hard-working Republican, and a very earnest man. As a public speaker he made a favorable impression upon an audience. After serving two terms in Congress, he was appointed an auditor of the Treasury Department at Washington, a position he held for many years. Throughout life he was a familiar figure in New Hampshire campaigns.

In the third district, Jacob Benton, of Lancaster, was nominated by acclamation, the other candidates withdrawing before a ballot. Benton had a rugged and strong character, and a well-balanced mind. A man of positive convictions, he would have been a leader in any walk in life. Educated for the bar, he held a prominent place in the profession. After his Congressional career he drifted into business pursuits, making and losing a fortune. Settling in full with his creditors, he took up the burden late in life and again acquired a competence.

The Republican State convention, which met January 8, 1867, excited wide-spread interest because of the intense contest made for the gubernatorial nomination. Onslow Stearns, who had been a candidate two years before, was again in the field. In the natural sequence of politics, the nomination would have been accorded to him without opposition. But this was the first State convention in New Hampshire since the close of the war, and there was a demand for a soldier candidate on the part of many Republicans of the State. Walter Harriman, then Secretary of State, who had stepped into the breach four years before as an independent candidate to save Gilmore from defeat, had enthusiastic support. Rollins, Chandler, and Ordway, who were dissatisfied with Stearns's course after his defeat in the previous convention, favored Harriman. The *Manchester Mirror* opposed Stearns because he was a railroad president, and supported Harriman. The *Statesman* early in the canvass came out strongly for Stearns, but later urged the third nomination of Governor Smyth in the interest of party harmony. The last nomination was also favored for the same reason by the *Portsmouth Journal,* the *Dover Enquirer,* and the *Claremont Eagle.* The canvass became very earnest, with much display of personal feeling. Other candidates were mentioned during the canvass, but the strife between the friends of Harriman and Stearns forced all dark horses from the field. Governor Smyth, before the convention assembled, declined to be a candidate for a third time. Simon G. Griffin, of Keene, presided over the convention. Harriman was nominated on the first ballot, the vote standing, Harriman 349, Stearns 318, and scattering 8. The *Patriot* attributed the defeat of Stearns to the efforts of "the ring," meaning Rollins, Chandler, and Ordway.

The Democratic convention met January 16, 1867, with a confidence its members had not shared for several years. The administration at Washington was no longer in sympathy with the Republican party. The Republican office-holders had either been supplanted by Johnson men or coerced into inactivity. The threatened breach in the Republican ranks gave great encouragement to the Democracy. The convention was presided over by Edmund Burke, of Newport. John G. Sinclair was renominated by acclamation. The latter on motion of John H. George was instructed to challenge Harriman to meet him upon the stump and discuss before the people the issues of the day. The challenge was accepted, and meetings were arranged.

Harriman at the time of this debate was fifty years of age. He had been educated for the ministry, and had preached for several years. Retiring from the ministry, he engaged in trade at Warner. Being an effective and eloquent speaker, his drift into politics was easy and natural. From about 1850 to 1862, he

was one of the most popular campaign speakers of the
Democratic party of New Hampshire.   As a war Democrat he had enlisted and gone to the front at the head
of a New Hampshire regiment, and had been breveted
brigadier-general.   His affiliation with the Republican party dated from about 1863.   The New Hampshire Democrats bitterly resented his change of politics, and he was the target in subsequent campaigns
for virulent denunciation.   As recalled at a little later
period, Harriman was a man of imposing presence,
long, flowing, white hair, a resonant voice, captivating
audiences by his well-rounded periods and apt Scrip-
tural quotations.   He was always in demand during
the campaign both at home and abroad, and ranked
among the best stump-speakers of the country.   He
was afterward appointed naval officer of customs at the
port of Boston, a position which he held for two
terms.

John G. Sinclair was one of the giants of the Democratic party of New Hampshire.   A self-made man,
endowed by nature with shrewdness, sagacity, and a
ready wit, he early in life came to the front in the
politics of the State.   There was a vein of irony in
his speech nettling to an opponent, but evoking the
delight of his partisans.   He served many terms in the
House of Representatives of New Hampshire, and was
the most brilliant debater of that body during his term
of service.   He would delight the House with a fund
of anecdotal and humorous illustrations with which
he punctured the argument of an opponent, and, while

the merits of the question most frequently left him in the minority when the vote was taken, he almost invariably carried off the honors of the discussion. Any unfortunate lapse of speech of an opponent was his opportunity, for he was quick at repartee, and his greatest forensic triumphs seemed to be won when, without warning, a debate was precipitated upon the House. He was afflicted with deafness, but this infirmity appeared in no way to impair his effectiveness. It used to be said that he always heard all that it was necessary to hear for the purposes of reply, and certainly no vulnerable point in an opponent's argument escaped him. Such was the antagonist whom Harriman had to meet in the joint discussion which was to be held in different parts of the State.

There had been no joint discussion in the State of any note since the meeting of Franklin Pierce and John P. Hale in the Old North Meeting-house at Concord twenty years before, and the Harriman-Sinclair debate attracted the attention of the entire State. The issues discussed by Harriman and Sinclair were national, and the meetings drew throngs of people. So intense was the partisan feeling at the time that no contemporary opinion of the merits of the speakers was unbiassed. At the close of each meeting, the Republicans were positive that Harriman had the best of the discussion, while the Democrats were equally certain that Sinclair had worsted his opponent. Harriman had the better cause and he won, but it is no discredit to him to say that Sinclair at that time was probably without his equal in the State as a debater in the political forum.

For Congress the Democrats renominated Daniel Marcy in the first district, and Harry Bingham in the third, while Edward W. Harrington, of Manchester, was put forward as the candidate in the second district.

The friends of Stearns were very bitter over his defeat, and for a time a bolt of the convention seemed possible, with Stearns running as an independent candidate. A meeting of the prominent Republicans of the State was called in Concord, and about one hundred and fifty were present, having in view the nomination of Stearns as an independent Republican, with the expectation that the Democrats would endorse him. Sinclair favored this course, and stood ready to withdraw. Fear of the disruption of the Republican party alone prevented action, and Stearns himself, in a letter to the chairman of the meeting, declined to have his name used, saying among other things: "Whatever my opinions may be relative to the manner in which the canvass was conducted and the false representations made in regard to one of the most important interests of the State with which I am and have been for a long time identified, I cherish too strong an attachment to old associations to allow my personal feelings to control my political action, and, whatever measures you may see fit to adopt to express your disapprobation of the course pursued, I must respectfully decline to allow my name to be used as a candidate for governor at the ensuing election."

Stearns was assured by the Republican leaders that he would be nominated as Harriman's successor, and united action was secured in behalf of the Republican ticket. It was largely through the instrumentality of Austin F. Pike, chairman of the State committee, that a bolt was prevented. There still remained enough of personal dissatisfaction to give the Democrats encouragement in the campaign, but the returns showed a Republican victory by a somewhat reduced majority. The vote was as follows: Scattering, 136; John G. Sinclair, 32,663; Walter Harriman, 35,809.

CHAPTER XII.

ROLLINS RESUMES THE CHAIRMANSHIP

ROLLINS's third term in Congress expired March 4, 1867. He returned home to give some attention to his private affairs. As he had said in his speech to the convention which nominated his successor, he still hoped, while returning to the ranks, to be of service to the cause. He held himself subject to call by his party, and he had not long to wait before being drawn into service. The fall elections of 1867 were far from gratifying to the Republicans, while they encouraged Democratic activities all over the country. In the October State elections of that autumn, the Democrats carried Pennsylvania by a small majority on the popular vote and secured the legislature of Ohio, defeating Benjamin F. Wade for reëlection to the Senate, while Rutherford B. Hayes, Republican candidate for governor, received only three thousand majority. In the November elections following, the Democrats carried New York by fifty thousand majority and New Jersey by twelve thousand. Preceding as these elections did the Presidential year, the Democrats were buoyant with courage, while the Republicans were correspondingly depressed. The March election of 1868 in New Hampshire would be the next State election, and the eyes of the whole country were focussed upon this State, always debatable, for a further indication of the probabilities of the impending national contest.

Elated by the success of their brethren in other States, the Democrats of New Hampshire assumed the offensive and called their convention early. It was held November 14, 1867, Lewis W. Clark presiding. There was a lively contest for the nomination for governor. Sinclair, who had been defeated twice, was again a candidate, but a very large number of the party favored a new candidate. These people rallied about Ellery A. Hibbard, of Laconia, a lawyer of good standing at the bar, and a Democrat not so scarred in political warfare as Sinclair. Hibbard was a practitioner in his profession whose counsel led to the settlement of controversies, a man of quiet tastes, one respected by all who knew him, and against whom nothing could be urged in public or private life. No stronger candidate could have been selected at that time by the Democratic party. A local support of Hiram R. Roberts, of Rollinsford, deflected just enough votes in the convention to defeat Hibbard. Two ballots were necessary for a choice. On the first ballot the vote stood: Sinclair, 312; Hibbard, 302; Roberts, 31; and scattering, 17. On the second ballot Sinclair was nominated by a vote of 331 to 269. The contest in this convention was the beginning of a struggle for leadership which was soon to divide the Democratic party into factions. However, the renomination of Sinclair was acquiesced in, and the Democratic party, united for the time being, entered the campaign for one of its most desperate struggles to regain control of the State.

Joshua L. Foster, of Portsmouth, afterward of Dover, reported the resolutions. These denounced the Congressional plan of reconstruction as a revolutionary usurpation and characterized the attempt of Congress to establish supremacy of the negro race (in the South) as " a most atrocious crime against the principles of Republican government and the civilization of the age." Anson S. Marshall, of Concord, was chosen chairman of the Democratic State committee. He was a man of brilliant attainments, a leader at the bar, self-reliant, and with capacity for organization. Under his leadership the party was brought into its best fighting trim, and labored incessantly for victory.

The Republican State convention met December 18, 1867. Onslow Stearns was elected president. Walter Harriman was renominated by acclamation. William E. Chandler reported the resolutions, which in vigorous terms endorsed the policy of Congress, accepting the gage of battle thrown down by the Democratic party, and declaring for General Grant as the next Republican candidate for President. This declaration for Grant precipitated the Presidential canvass into the State campaign, and the issues at once became wholly national. Rollins was again elected chairman of the State committee after an absence of six years from this position.

The Democratic campaign was opened at Concord soon after the conventions by a meeting which was addressed by John Quincy Adams, of Massachusetts, grandson of President John Quincy Adams. He was followed in the campaign by an array of speaking talent seldom seen in the State. The Democratic National committee saw the advantage to accrue if New Hampshire could be detached from Republican control, and responded to all calls of the party in the State. Some of the ablest Democratic speakers in the country participated in this campaign. The list included Daniel W. Voorhees, of Indiana, Montgomery Blair and Charles E. Phelps, of Maryland, Richard O'Gorman, C. C. Burr, John A. Thompson, E. O. Perrin, and James S. Thayer, of New York, James R. Doolittle, of Wisconsin, Thomas Ewing, Jr., of Ohio. Richard Vaux, of Pennsylvania, Henry Clay Dean, of Iowa, Lewis W. Ross, of Illinois, Eben F. Pillsbury, of Maine, E. S. Cleveland and James F. Babcock, of Connecticut, Charles Levi Woodbury, Augustus O. Brewster, Patrick A. Collins, James K. Tarbox, and John E. Fitzgerald, of Massachusetts. Assisting these were all the local Democratic speakers who could be mustered into service. Democratic meetings were largely attended and Democratic enthusiasm reached the highest pitch. There was hardly a hamlet in the State that did not have its political rally, some of the smaller localities being visited by speakers of national reputation, and meetings were held out-doors when halls were not large enough to hold the people assembled.

Rollins always regarded this as his hardest campaign, and he frequently referred to it as his most successful one. The Republicans of the State were alarmed at the activity of the Democrats and continued apprehensive of the result until the votes were counted. None saw more clearly than Rollins the magnitude of the contest and its bearing upon the subsequent Presidential campaign. The Republicans of New Hampshire had been so universally successful that it was somewhat difficult to impress the Republican National committee with the danger of their defeat. There was none too good feeling among the Republican leaders of the State. Rollins, Chandler, and Ordway led and controlled the Republican organization. Opposition to their control was growing. If suppressed in the midst of this campaign, it was nevertheless smoldering to break out in force later. Chandler and Ordway were relied upon by Rollins to present the importance and magnitude of the contest to the national leaders, and the work these two performed contributed greatly to Republican success.

In the midst of the canvass, the impeachment of Andrew Johnson by the Republican majority in Congress occurred. What its effect would be upon the New Hampshire election no one could foretell. Of its embarrassments Chandler writes Rollins under February 23, 1868, as follows:

" Of course this impeachment business has discour-

aged everything. The Republicans of the House are
unanimous for it and will so vote to-morrow. I suppose I have not changed my mind as to its expediency.
We exchange, by embarking on an unknown sea, a certainty for an uncertainty. I hope for the best and, if
it can be done at once, it may not destroy us. If the
work lingers, we are gone, provided the enemy is wise
enough to take advantage of our indiscretion. It will
break up the arrangement of speakers from Congress,
and our members will not start home so soon as otherwise. You must do the best you can. . . . I don't
suppose the impeachment project will effect you one
way or another in New Hampshire, certainly not to
hurt, I should think."

Henry O. Kent, writing Rollins from Lancaster
about this time, said: "The impeachment matter
roused our people like the uprising of 1861. They
are all sound here for Congress." The impeachment
trial probably did not effect one vote in New Hampshire, the Republicans being enthusiastic in its support, and the Democrats earnest in defence of Andrew
Johnson, who was now recognized as in thorough accord with their party. It was, however, the source
of the greatest embarrassment to Rollins in conducting the campaign. The Democrats were making an
aggressive canvass, holding meetings everywhere in the
State and putting forward their ablest stump-speakers.
Republican demands for meetings poured in upon the
State committee, and Rollins in turn invited and implored, personally, and through Chandler and Ordway,

leading Republicans of the country to come to his assistance. The difficulty in obtaining speakers is explained by a letter of Ordway to Rollins. He says: "I have labored, coaxed, and prayed to induce the members to keep their appointments and leave to-night, not wholly without effect. The articles of impeachment are being discussed and each man wants to make a speech. The managers on the part of the House are to be elected to-morrow or Monday, and all want to be here to vote for their friends. I cannot do more than I have done, yet all seem to fail. I don't dare leave the Speaker. Don't think it safe for me to do so until after the articles of impeachment are disposed of, as the discussion is very exciting at times. The Capitol has been double-guarded at night, and double-locked from bottom to top. I know what a bad fix it places you in to have these members disappoint you, but I have done all in my power to have it otherwise."

In spite of these disappointments, Rollins was able to put into the field a corps of speakers equal in national fame to those sent out by the Democrats. These were Hannibal Hamlin, of Maine, William B. Allison, of Iowa, Horace Maynard, James Mullins, and William B. Stokes, of Tennessee, Daniel E. Sickles and John Cochrane, of New York, James W. Nye, of Nevada, John A. J. Cresswell and John L. Thompson, of Maryland, Joseph R. Hawley, of Connecticut, Henry Wilson, of Massachusetts, Governor Austin Blair, of Michigan, Governor George S. Woods, of Oregon, T. M. Hite and George W. Anderson, of Missouri, Ignatius Donnelly, of Minnesota, William Williams and Henry D. Washburn, of Indiana, John C. Caldwell, of Maine, John Covode, of Pennsylvania, and George G. Gorham, of California.

Both sides put forth their greatest efforts to bring home absent voters and to get all voters to the polls. Senator Cragin wrote Rollins from Washington: " I am digging up all the votes from here and many will go. I start two from Virginia. I am now going through the Interior Department and I shall get some there." Ordway wrote: " I have helped on the expenses of some clerks who are willing to go home to vote and I am willing to aid others who cannot go without aid."

There were no laggards on either side in this campaign. Whatever position a man occupied, he stood ready to do his part. A letter to Rollins from Judge Charles Doe, who, in later life, affected an indifference to all political matters, shows the intense individual interest. He says: " I send by express a quantity of Walter Harriman's speeches on the negro question and a slip on impeachment. We are using these with capital effect in this part of the State, sending them around to every store and house. Please send them to different towns for distribution and charge the expense to me. This is a part of my contribution to the cause."

February 25, 1868, Ordway wrote to Rollins: " I went to see Edwin M. Stanton last night, found him in possession of the War Department and in good spirits. He said to me, 'Tell Rollins we rely on him to carry the State.'" As the campaign progressed, the Democrats became very sanguine of victory. Rollins published his canvass of the State a short time before election, showing a comfortable majority for the Republicans. To this challenge Marshall, chairman of the Democratic committee, replied by publishing his canvass. Rollins gave 2,891 doubtful votes and Marshall 2,506. Each divided the doubtful equally between the parties. Including the doubtful thus divided, the two canvasses are shown below.[1]

The *Manchester Mirror* says of the Republican canvass: "The canvass was returned March 1st, and the excess of Democratic votes over the canvass is owing to the naturalization of six hundred foreigners between that time and election."

The feelings of Republicans throughout the country when the news of the New Hampshire election was received is expressed by the *Boston Transcript* editorially in referring to the result. That newspaper said: "The Republicans of the Granite State achieved the most

	ROLLINS'S	MARSHALL'S
[1] Harriman	39,883	34,462
Sinclair	36,648	37,336
Total Vote	76,531	71,798

ACTUAL VOTE

Harriman	39,771
Sinclair	37,241
Total vote	77,012

remarkable victory it was ever their good fortune to win. By common consent, as it were, throughout the country New Hampshire has been selected as a battle-ground by the two parties for the purpose of testing the popularity of General Grant and ascertaining whether his strength with the people has been materially affected by the present aspect of national affairs. For the past three or four years the New Hampshire Democrats have been beaten by their opponents only through the exercise of the most unremitting vigilance and by systematic efforts that have made the Republican canvasses of the State historical. This year the Republicans labored under disadvantages and were met by obstacles absolutely sufficient to discourage any set of men but those who have continued for many years to uphold the banner of Republicanism against odds such as are not encountered by Republicans elsewhere."

After complimenting the speakers, the *Transcript* says: "But it was not the public speaking that did the most of the work. Every Republican in New Hampshire talked and exerted himself as though the destinies of the State rested upon his shoulders. Their efforts were rendered effective to the utmost degree by an organization so complete as to comprise almost every voter in the State. The thoroughness of their organization enabled the Republican State committee at Concord to know all the weak points along the line and strengthen them, and a large measure of its success is due to the committee, at the head of which stands that celebrated organizer of political campaigns, Edward H. Rollins."

After election, the Democratic *Patriot* said: "The Democrats confidently expected to reduce the Republican majority to a small figure and hoped to win. The Republicans feared defeat and hoped only to escape by 'the skin of their teeth.' To say that we are disappointed, that our friends are disappointed, does not begin to express their feelings. They feel the result to be a just cause for sadness and grave apprehension on the part of all true friends of constitutional government."

The Democrats polled in this election the largest vote they had ever polled by nearly five thousand. The Republican victory was rendered more significant by the fact that in the Connecticut election, April following, the Democrats triumphed by an increased majority over the previous year.

The election of delegates to the national convention was the next consideration of the Republican party of New Hampshire. The State convention met May 5, 1868, for this purpose. Rollins called the convention to order and Mason W. Tappan presided. The previous State convention having declared for General Grant as the Republican candidate for President, the action of this convention was merely a formal ratification of the well-known views of the Republicans of the State. The delegates at large who were selected were William E. Chandler, of Concord, Elijah M. Topliff, of Manchester, Charles S. Faulkner, of Keene, and

John H. Bailey, of Portsmouth. Those chosen from the districts were John E. Bickford, of Dover, and Ezra Gould, of Sandwich, from the first district, James F. Briggs, of Hillsborough, and Francis B. Ayer, of Nashua, from the second, and Edward A. Vaughan, of Claremont, and Thomas P. Cheney, of Ashland.

After the nomination of Grant and Colfax, a ratification meeting occurred in Concord which was addressed by Rollins, Harriman, Tappan, Fogg, and others.

The Maine election in September was an indication of the drift of the political tide, which was confirmed by the October elections following. There was, therefore, no incentive for the New Hampshire Democrats to make a contest for the choice of electors. Their campaign was not aggressive, and the Republicans were not called upon to repeat their exertions of the spring before. Little speaking occurred on either side. Rollins, as chairman of the State committee, was desirous of rolling up a good majority, and his labors were bent upon getting out the Republican vote. In this he was successful, for the Republican majority exceeded seven thousand.[1]

As soon as the national election was over, preparations were made for the spring campaign of 1869. It was settled that Onslow Stearns would be nominated as Governor Harriman's successor. To assure the pub-

[1] Grant 37,726
Seymour 30,573
——————
7,153

lic that the breach made in the party at the convention
of 1867 was healed, Governor Harriman was invited
to preside at the convention, and accepted. The convention met January 7, 1869. The nomination of
Onslow Stearns was made by acclamation. The State
committee met immediately after the convention adjourned, and organized by the choice of Rollins as
chairman, and Wyman Pattee, of Enfield, as secretary.
The reëlection of Rollins as chairman was greeted by
the *Nashua Telegraph,* of which Orrin C. Moore had
recently become the editor, as an assurance of victory,
and Rollins was complimented for his work as chairman of the State committee.

In the spring of 1869, Rollins was elected assistant
treasurer of the Union Pacific Railroad, and secretary
of the board of directors. This position he owed to his
acquaintance with Oakes Ames, with whom he had
served in Congress. After his retirement from Congress, he had become identified with the interests of
the Union Pacific Railroad, and had been an agent of
the road in looking after its affairs in Washington.
The Union Pacific, being a land grant railroad, had
large dealings with the departments at Washington,
and was the subject of more or less inquiry by Congress. Its interests had constantly to be watched and
its side of controversies to be presented to committees
of Congress and to departments, a work for which Rollins was especially fitted. His knowledge of the routine of the departments and of parliamentary proceedings, his large acquaintance with public men and

the persistence with which he followed matters placed in his charge, made him a valuable representative of the road and led to his election, first, as assistant treasurer, and later, as treasurer of this corporation. The Union Pacific Road was under suspicion and fire at this time, and scandals later developed in connection with its management. With these scandals Rollins had no connection, but his employment by the road, first as its agent and later as one of its officers, made him vulnerable to attack, and his enemies and rivals in New Hampshire were not slow in improving the opportunity thus afforded.

To the complimentary notice given Rollins by Orrin C. Moore in the *Nashua Telegraph,* George G. Fogg referred sneeringly in the *Monitor* and *Independent Democrat,* making light of Rollins's ability as a political organizer, and saying that Rollins's connection with the Union Pacific Railroad unfitted him for chairman of the State committee. Fogg followed up this attack upon Rollins by further attacks upon him and upon Chandler and Ordway, denouncing them with all the bitterness of which he was capable. Moreover, these attacks continued throughout the campaign. About this time, Rollins, Chandler, and Ordway secured an interest in the *New Hampshire Statesman,* and this newspaper became their weapon of defence. The warfare thus begun by Fogg continued, becoming more and more vehement until the merging of the *Statesman* and the *Independent Democrat* into one paper in 1871.

Jacob H. Ela, Aaron F. Stevens, and Jacob Benton

were all renominated for Congress by acclamation, having served but one term.

The Democratic State convention was held January 20, 1869. Ira A. Eastman presided. Democratic sentiment in the State was divided between John Bedel, of Bath, and Albert R. Hatch, of Portsmouth, for a candidate for governor. Before the ballot was taken in the convention, Hatch's name was withdrawn, and Bedel received 392 votes out of 433 cast.

Ellery A. Hibbard, of Laconia, was nominated for Congress in the first district, Hosea W. Parker, of Claremont, in the third district, and Edward W. Harrington, of Manchester, was renominated in the second district. Samuel B. Page, of Warren, was elected chairman of the State committee, and Henry H. Metcalf, of Concord, secretary.

Page has had an interesting legislative career, representing at different times the towns of Warren, Haverhill, and Concord in the legislature. A fluent speaker, a skilled parliamentarian, well versed in the history of the State, he is without doubt the readiest debater the State has ever produced. His forte is in directing a parliamentary contest. For a number of sessions of the legislature he was an active leader of the Democratic minority.

Metcalf's name has been associated with New Hampshire politics for more than a generation. After reading law he embarked in newspaper work, and for nearly forty years he has been an aggressive editorial writer. Honest but intense in his convictions, he has

impartially distributed praise or criticism upon both
friend and foe. His Democracy has known no shadow
of turning, for at all times and in all circumstances he
has stood forth preëminently as the exponent and de-
fender of the principles of the Democratic party. Of
late years through his membership in the Grange he has
done much to promote the interests of New Hampshire.

The campaign of 1869 was more marked by signs of
impending trouble in the Republican party through
the quarrel of Fogg with Rollins, Chandler, and Ordway than by strenuous activities on the part of either
State committee to carry the election. Whatever hopes
the Democrats had of making gains in this election
were based upon Republican dissensions. The Republican victory in the Presidential campaign of 1868 had
been so pronounced that a Democratic triumph in the
State was not probable. Besides this, a Republican
national administration would be inaugurated just
before the New Hampshire election in March, and
this, with the assurance it gave of superseding Johnson men in federal positions by Republicans, kept the
latter in line for the election, however much they might
afterward give countenance to Fogg's warfare upon
the Republican leaders. The election resulted in the
choice of Stearns as governor by more than thirty-five
hundred majority, and the election of all the Republican candidates for Congress. The legislature was
also Republican by a good majority. The vote for
governor was as follows: Scattering, 42; John Bedel,
32,057; Onslow Stearns, 35,772.

CHAPTER XIII.

HOSTILITY TO THE ORGANIZATION

THERE were early signs that the campaign of 1870 would be troublesome to the Republicans. The causes of apprehension were numerous. There was pronounced dissatisfaction with the administration at Washington. The attacks upon President Grant from within the party, which culminated in the liberal Republican bolt of 1872, had begun. There were indications in New Hampshire of Republican disloyalty to the national administration. There were also dissensions in the Republican party of the State. There were Republicans who felt that they had not been sufficiently recognized, and attributed their failure of recognition to the "machine," as those who guided the Republican organization were called. Rollins, Chandler, and Ordway, who for a decade had been acting together in party management and in the distribution of patronage, were, in the minds of the dissatisfied, the "machine."] Neither Rollins nor Chandler then held office, but Ordway was still sergeant-at-arms of the national House of Representatives, a position which gave him a large acquaintance with public men and no inconsiderable political influence. Rollins, however, was chairman of the Republican State committee, and Chandler was secretary of the national committee. These party recognitions gave them prestige both in the State and in the country at large, while in the popular mind they were thought to exert a greater influence upon nominations and appointments in the State than they really did. Republicans whose ambitions met with disappointment attributed their failure to the machinations of these three men.

George G. Fogg, editor of the *Daily Monitor* and *Weekly Independent Democrat,* was openly attacking the Republican "machine," giving expression in his newspapers to his personal enmity to Rollins, Chandler, and Ordway, while he encouraged the grievances of discontented Republicans. Fogg had been a free-soil Democrat. He had been elected Secretary of the State at the time John P. Hale was first sent to the United States Senate. He was a vigorous and aggressive writer, and as a newspaper editor did valiant service in the cause of freedom. His trenchant pen contributed to the overthrow of the Democratic party of the State, and in the contest for the abolition of slavery he was a power. With the success of the American party in 1855 he had been made law reporter of the State, a position he held until 1859, when he was succeeded by William E. Chandler. The State printing, which even in those days was a tidy bit of patronage, went to his printing-office at various times after the Republican party came into power. In the campaign of 1860 he was secretary of the Republican national committee. When Lincoln was inaugurated President, further recognition was given to Fogg by his appointment as minister to Switzerland, a position both honorable and lucrative. With the accession of Andrew Johnson to the Presidency, Fogg was removed. He felt that his removal was due to the influence of Chandler and the indifference of Rollins. Such, however, was not the case. The correspondence of Rollins and Chandler of that period shows that an earnest effort was made by Chandler, then Assistant Secretary of the Treasury, supported by Rollins, to secure the appointment of Fogg as minister to Denmark, after it was ascertained that he could not remain in Switzerland. Fogg was later appointed United States Senator to fill a vacancy occasioned by the resignation of Daniel Clark. He served in this position from August 31, 1866, to March 4, 1867. This appointment was made within a year after his return from Switzerland. With Fogg's retirement from the Senate began his opposition to the management of the Republican party of New Hampshire by Rollins, Chandler, and Ordway, an opposition which in 1870 had ripened into open hostility.

Another troublesome feature of this campaign was the attitude of the extreme Prohibitionists of the State. They were dissatisfied with the enforcement of the prohibitory law and they charged the party in power with lack of sympathy with the law. At the previous session of the legislature they had demanded the passage of a State constabulary law, to provide a State police to enforce the prohibitory statute. This demand was granted on condition that it be approved by popular vote in November following. At a special election called for this purpose the law was beaten by a large majority. The disappointed Prohibitionists now demanded the formation of a third party. At the head of this movement was the Rev. Dr. Lorenzo D. Barrows, a Methodist minister, who at that time was president of the Methodist school at Tilton. Doctor Barrows occupied a similar position in New Hampshire in regard to prohibition to that held by the Rev. Dr. Alonzo A. Miner in Massachusetts. In many ways there was a strong resemblance between these two men. Both were self-educated, and both were at the head of educational institutions. Both were men of uncompromising natures, and ready at all times to lead a forlorn hope in defence of the principles they espoused. Both had been earnest advocates of the abolition of slavery.

A call for a convention to meet at Concord, January 11, 1870, to consider the question of the formation of a Prohibitory party was issued. At the election in March, 1869, Governor Stearns had been chosen by a majority of about 3,700, with only 42 independent and scattering votes, out of a total vote of 67,829. Yet, a third party movement at this time menaced Republican success, especially as another call for an independent political convention had been issued in behalf of the labor reformers to meet the last of the month. The energies of the Republican leaders were, therefore, directed to heading off any third party organization. In this work they were aided by many friends of the prohibitory law, who believed that a third party would contribute to the success of the Democrats, who were known to favor the repeal of the law. The convention from start to finish showed two determined factions — one to force a separate nomination for governor, and the other, to question the wisdom of such a course. Nearly all the delegates were Republicans. The third party Prohibitionists won by a large majority with Doctor Barrows as their standard-bearer. About a third of the delegates· withdrew from the convention and, holding a conference in another place, declared their opposition to a third ticket at this time.

The labor reformers' convention met at Concord, January 28, 1870. This movement had gained some headway in Massachusetts the fall before, the party there polling several thousand votes. Several of the Massachusetts reformers had been doing missionary work in New Hampshire since the Massachusetts election. The narrow margin of Republican ascendency in New Hampshire gave promise that a new party might hold the balance of power and perhaps produce a political upheaval in the State. The jealousies of the Republican leaders were known, and the State seemed a good field for the formation of an independent political party. Engaged in the enterprise were some disaffected Republicans, but the larger number of the promoters were Democrats. Both of the old party leaders were apprehensive of the movement and the party newspapers referred to it gingerly. The Republicans made some effort to control the convention, but in this they were unsuccessful.

The leading delegates of Republican antecedents were John H. Goodale, of Northfield, Andrew J. Fogg, of Concord, and Samuel Flint, of Lyme. Goodale was a writer and lecturer of some repute, a man of pleasant address, with much capacity as an organizer. He was undoubtedly the directing force of the movement, although not prominent in its preliminary work. Fogg was a newspaper writer with a penchant for statistics, and later compiling a gazetteer of New Hampshire. Flint was a farmer, with a leaning to soft money principles, who had come before the public as a declaimer against bondholders.

After organization an informal ballot was taken for a candidate for governor, which showed an almost equal vote for Samuel Flint, of Lyme, and James A. Weston, of Manchester. The latter had been reëlected a second time mayor of Manchester by the Democrats. Before the formal ballot was taken, Goodale warned the convention not to take their candidate from a minority party if they hoped for success. Heeding this warning, the convention nominated Flint, and adopted a platform of principles.

The Republican and Democratic conventions had already met and nominated their candidates. At the Republican convention, Governor Stearns, who had made a very acceptable chief magistrate, was renominated by acclamation. The Democratic convention renominated John Bedel, of Bath. The Democratic party at this time was divided into two factions struggling for control of the organization. John H. Pearson, a wealthy merchant of Concord, who was a man of indomitable will, had broken with the leaders of the party after his defeat for State Senator in 1868, and had established a newspaper at the capital called *The People.* His slogan was anti-monopoly, and he soon acquired an extensive following in the State. Affiliated with Pearson were Edmund Burke, of Newport, Harry Bingham, of Littleton, and other leading Democrats who were hostile to the leadership of John H. George, Josiah Minot, John M. Hill, and William Butterfield; the latter disciples of Franklin Pierce and his successors in the control and leadership of the party. A climax in this struggle for control was reached later in the campaign and contributed materially to the reëlection of Governor Stearns by the people.

At an early meeting of the Republican State committee for organization, Rollins declined to be a candidate for reëlection as chairman. The hostility of George G. Fogg to the triumvirate of Rollins, Chandler, and Ordway led him to take this step, in which he was supported by both Chandler and Ordway, who felt as he did, that Fogg and his followers should be given no excuse for not heartily supporting the ticket. The committee refused to consider his declination, and on the motion of one who had previously opposed his continuing at the head of the organization he was unanimously reëlected. The present peril of the party was dwelt upon by members of the committee and Rollins was urged to sink all personal considerations and stand by the ship. Reluctantly he took the matter under consideration pending a later meeting of the committee. He then wrote Chandler as follows:

" I am forced to believe that we have leading men who would welcome defeat rather than success under present circumstances. For the cause I am willing to make any sacrifice necessary. I have no aspirations in the way of duty. I can easily clear the track and let other ambitious men have the field if that will help the cause and assure our success. At any rate I desire and intend to be relieved of the chairmanship so that the great leaders may feel at liberty to do something to help the cause."

At the second meeting of the committee early in February, he again tendered his resignation, and was met with the same objections that the peril of the party did not permit it. He was, therefore, persuaded to accept. Writing immediately to Chandler, he said:

" We have had our State committee meeting and I am still chairman. I read your telegram and also Ordway's, and wanted very much to resign, but could not find a single member, friend or foe, who would consent. I may have made a mistake in remaining, but have listened to the advice of friends who are very anxious about the result in the State. I did not want to do anything that would look like deserting them or the ship, and you and Ordway must make the best of my blunder, if I have made one, and do all in your power to help us through. . . . We had a full meeting and many of our folks are somewhat alarmed about the Labor Reform movement. I hope we can head it off. The Labor League is at work. It organized in this city to-night."

To this letter Chandler replied three days later, as follows:

" Yours of the 5th inst. is at hand. On the whole, you probably did right in remaining chairman. If you had resigned immediately after you were unanimously elected it would have been better. You could have done just as much work in the campaign for yourself and the cause, without increasing those confounded jealousies and continuing an impression that it is necessary to your influence in the politics of New Hampshire that you should remain chairman of the committee. As it stands now, it is useless to expect certain men to give you any credit if the State is carried, while any mishap that takes place will be charged to your account, but you are in it and must go through."

At a later date, when Rollins did retire from the chairmanship of the State committee, and assisted others to guide the party to victory, he increased his prestige and following in the State. As Chandler predicted, he gained no credit from his enemies for his work in this campaign after the victory was won. Whether in this particular campaign his work would have been as effective, had he been at headquarters without official recognition, it is difficult at this time to say. There existed a confidence among the rank and file of the party in Rollins's management, which no other chairman could have inspired, and, with the exception of Fogg, even his enemies and rivals were free to admit this.

The problem which confronted Rollins at that time is always a difficult one for any individual to solve. It comes home occasionally to every political leader, even though his leadership comprises only a small community. Rollins could hardly be unconscious of his superior equipment for the post of chairman, for his friends and admirers were constantly asserting it and his enemies conceding it. Whatever a regard for his own future might dictate, his love of the party and the appeals of party men to him to stand by the organization for just one more campaign overcame his scruples. He knew the jealousies his acceptance would provoke, but he doubtless thought that his successful leadership would neutralize these with the people of the State. It was understood that he would be a candidate for the United States Senate before the legislature to be chosen, but there is nothing in his correspondence to show that he broached his ambition to any one until after the election. That Rollins used his position as chairman of the State committee to advance his Senatorial ambitions is refuted by all those who were ever intimately associated with him at party headquarters, but his rivals honestly thought that he did, and they knew that there is a distinct advantage to any Senatorial aspirant in being brought into immediate association with candidates for the legislature during the campaign, as must necessarily be the case with the chairman of the committee. Charles H. Roberts, who was for several years associated with Rollins as secretary or treasurer of the committee, says: "Rollins was one of the most unselfish political leaders I ever knew. He fought campaigns for the whole party until the battle was won."

John Kimball, of Concord, who was treasurer of the State committee for many years, and Daniel Hall, who was chairman at a later period, speak in the same vein of Rollins's fairness in conducting political campaigns.

James A. Wood, for thirty years an active member of the State committee, and for several campaigns a member of the executive committee, says that Rollins disregarded all personal considerations while leading the Republican forces.

In the same tenor both Senator Jacob H. Gallinger and Congressman Frank D. Currier, who were associated with Rollins in the campaign of 1882, bear witness to his sinking all personal ambitions when a campaign was in progress.

In this very campaign of 1870 Rollins wrote William E. Waterhouse, of Barrington, as follows: "Don't trouble yourself about the election of a United States Senator. That will settle itself after the election, but do make sure to send us two good, true-blue Republican Representatives, as that is the important matter in the present crisis of our political affairs."

Senator Cragin, who was a candidate for reëlection as United States Senator, writing Rollins, February 10, 1870, about the election and the importance of securing Republican representatives in the close towns, said: " I know you will do your whole duty and I wish I could say as much of all our friends." Later he wrote Rollins: " I am glad you did not resign as chairman. It would have been bad policy at this time. I am sure I appreciate your efficient and untiring labors."

That all of Rollins's rivals could not take this generous view of the situation is but natural. They acquiesced in his reëlection as chairman because the party demanded it, but they probably gained as much by his acceptance in using it later against his candidacy for the Senate, as he himself gained in the estimation of the people when the victory was won and they realized that he was instrumental in winning it.

Fogg made a direct and bitter attack in his newspapers upon Rollins after his election as chairman, asserting that it was the outcome of sharp practice and that Rollins's connection with the Union Pacific Railroad unfitted him for leadership of the party. He also belittled Rollins's qualifications for the position. Strange to say, neither Democratic newspaper at the capital quotes or refers to this attack of Fogg, although it would have furnished campaign material for the Democratic party.

The Republicans of New Hampshire were further embarrassed in the beginning of the campaign by a speech in Congress made by Henry L. Dawes, of Massachusetts, then chairman of the appropriations committee of the House, severely criticizing as extravagant the estimates of the departments for the coming fiscal year, and demanding rigid economy in the appropriations to be made. The Democrats hailed this speech as convincing evidence of shortcomings on the part of the national administration. It was published broadcast over the State. It caused consternation among the Republicans and raised the hopes of the Democrats.

The outlook for the Republicans was anything but propitious. If Rollins had sought personal vindication he had but to retire from the chairmanship of the State committee to see the party go to probable defeat. The rank and file, however, demanded his continuance at the head of the committee, and hostile or jealous leaders preferred to throw upon him the responsibility of the campaign to assuming it themselves.

an The work before the State committee was to prevent
sl   \c Republican accession to the Prohibition and
to   ol'eform parties, to ascertain what disaffection
ex.   harmonize differences, to secure active work
fro   fu'blican leaders all over the State, and to
cha   \ campaign from one of defence to one of
aggr: .n. To this work Rollins gave attention with his accustomed foresight and energy.

He wrote Congressman Dawes about the use the Democrats were making of his speech, and pointed out to him the necessity of his appearing in the State to answer the Democratic charges. Dawes responded that he would speak the last week of the campaign, and this fact was announced to offset the political capital the Democrats were accumulating.

Well-known temperance Republicans were set to work to neutralize the efforts of the Prohibitionists. To counteract the Labor Reform movement Republican labor leagues were organized in manufacturing districts. Ostensibly, the work of organizing these leagues was in the hands of labor men, but the expense was borne by the Republican State committee. Lysander H. Carroll, a friend of Rollins, was elected treasurer of the State League, and through him were made the disbursements by the Republican State committee in its behalf. Thus the work was brought in touch with the direction of the chairman. All through the campaign Fogg condemned the league as out of harmony with the principles of the Republican party, because of its secret work. He insinuated that it was organized the interest of some candidate for the United Sta, Senate, implying that it was a device to promote Rol, of lins's aspirations. In spite of this back fire, the league in served its purpose, and neutralized much of the work of the Labor Reform party leaders.

The Labor Reform party started a campaign newspaper which was published at the printing-office of the Democratic *People*. Rollins emphasized this fact as proving the alliance of the Labor Reform and Democratic parties. The Prohibitionists had a newspaper published at Tilton, the home of Doctor Barrows, and edited by him, but the canvass of this party awakened little public interest. It was conceded that the ticket would poll a thousand votes, which of itself would not be dangerous. If the Labor Reform party should secure any considerable number of Republican recruits the result would be extremely doubtful.

Toward the close of the campaign the internal dissensions of the Democratic leaders cropped out in the attempt of the Pearson wing to transfer the Democratic vote from Bedel, the Democratic nominee for governor, to Flint, the Labor Reform candidate. There was no secret ballot at this time, and political parties printed their own ballots. The Democrats were confident that, with four gubernatorial candidates in the field, there would be no election of governor by the people, and they were equally confident that the Democrats and Labor Reformers together would control the legislature. The Democratic State committee was called together about two weeks before the election, and, in anticipation of victory, the question of the division of spoils was considered. While no public action appears to have been taken, certain Democratic leaders assumed that, if a Labor Reformer were elected governor, the Democrats would have the right to name the United States Senator to be chosen by the legislature. To make Flint a constitutional candidate before the legislature, he would have to be one of the two candidates having the highest popular vote. Thereupon, a large number of Democratic ballots were prepared with Flint's name at the head of the ticket. These were sent out to some of the towns. The facts were soon known at Republican headquarters and exploited in the newspapers. The campaign up to that time on the part of the Republicans had been a labored one, but Rollins immediately took the offensive and charged home to the Democrats that the Labor Reform movement was nothing but a Democratic conspiracy to attain power by false pretences. The *Patriot* and other old-line Democratic papers denounced the scheme and repudiated it. The chairman of the Democratic State committee made a *quasi* denial in behalf of the committee, but the facts could not be disputed. The Democrats of the State were astounded at the exposure, but as usual were rallied to the polls.

Congressman Dawes appeared the last week of the campaign and explained his position to the satisfaction of New Hampshire Republicans. The latter were now filled with confidence and Rollins gave out to the public, as usual, his canvass of the state in advance of election, to have it verified at the polls. Governor Stearns's majority was reduced from 3,700 the year before to 1,200 in a total vote only 600 larger. The Prohibition vote accounted for 1,135 of this reduction, and it therefore appeared that about 1,400 Republicans remained in the Labor Reform party to vote that ticket. The popular vote was: Scattering, 33; Lorenzo D. Barrows, 1,135; Samuel Flint, 7,369; John Bedel, 25,058; Onslow Stearns, 34,847.

The *Monitor,* reviewing the result, said: " The result of our late election has carried joy into Republican hearts all over the land and the more so that there was an almost universal apprehension of a different result."

The *Statesman* said: "In considering the instrumentalities that worked together to accomplish the glorious Republican triumph just achieved in this State, the active and well-directed efforts of Edward H. Rollins, the able chairman of the State committee, should be gratefully remembered."

The Republican speakers in this campaign from other States were United States Senators James W. Nye, of Nevada, and Frederick A. Sawyer, of South Carolina, Congressman Henry L. Dawes, of Massachusetts, Thomas Fitch, of Nevada, Charles H. Van Wyck, of New York, and James B. Belford, of Colorado, afterward a Representative in Congress from that State.

The contest for the Senatorship opened soon after the election. The active candidates were Aaron H. Cragin, Edward H. Rollins, Aaron F. Stevens, and Mason W. Tappan. There was newspaper mention of Gilman Marston, Frederick Smyth, Walter Harriman, and some others. Cragin had served two terms in Congress and was closing his first term in the Senate. His career in the national legislature, although not brilliant, had been creditable. He had been an industrious and hard-working Senator, attentive to the wants of his constituents, and he had escaped enmity in the State. Accepting the contest for his position in good part he succeeded in keeping his rivals more friendly to him than they were to one another. Cragin

was a practical politician, and it was not denied that he
had done his share of work to keep the State Republican. The shibboleth raised against him was the cry
of "rotation in office." This was the argument of Rollins and of the other candidates. The question was
discussed with earnestness in the party press, the *Exeter News Letter,* the *Manchester Mirror,* and the
Nashua Telegraph advocating rotation. The political
history of the State was ransacked to prove that giving
Cragin another continuous term in the Senate in addition to his two terms in the House, was without precedent, and it seemed at one time as if this argument
would defeat him. But Cragin had given his personal
attention to the election of members of the legislature
and had a strong and resourceful following.

Rollins was handicapped by his connection with the
Union Pacific Railroad. This road was not at that
time popular with the people. There was wide-spread
suspicion that its directory was not dealing justly with
the government. It was being assailed in Congress
and in the press. Fogg, in his newspapers, while
favoring no candidate, neglected no opportunity to
keep alive the prejudice against this road. Rollins,
therefore, suffered in his candidacy from this general
feeling; he undoubtedly failed to get support which
would otherwise have been cheerfully given to him.
His canvass appears to have been made wholly through
appeals to his friends in the State, and to the members-elect of the legislature. That he was to be a candidate for the Senate he was by no means early in

announcing, for Daniel Hall, in a letter dated May 2d, writes him as follows: " You will admit that up to within a few weeks you have never announced yourself a candidate for the Senate."

Toward the close of the canvass, Tappan developed a considerable following. Since his retirement from Congress, in 1861, he had been often mentioned for the Senatorship, but his easy-going disposition had led him to inactivity in politics. He was an able lawyer, and had a good practice. Large-hearted and generous, his emotions rather than his judgment controlled his political course. Even at this time he was suspected of discontent with the party by the radical Republican leaders of the State. Two years later this discontent led Tappan to support Horace Greeley for President. His ability none questioned, for he was welcomed back to the Republican party after the collapse of liberal Republicanism and made attorney-general of the State. He had, however, no turn for practical politics, and could neither organize nor direct his following. His unexpected strength as the legislature assembled alarmed the leaders and weakened Rollins's support, while it contributed to that of Cragin, whose Republicanism was unquestioned.

That Rollins was stronger than the votes in the caucus showed is evident. Henry McFarland, of Concord, writing to him from Washington, May 20th, says: " I am glad you are setting úp your pins so well. Cheney (Thomas P.) is here. He admits that you are making a good battle and that, if Cragin is not chosen, you will be." McFarland was a neighbor and intimate friend of Rollins through life. For several years he was associated with Rollins in the Union Pacific Railroad as his assistant and succeeded him as treasurer of that corporation.

The *Manchester Mirror's* editorial notes from the capital after the legislature met give currency to McFarland's opinion as follows: " The Senatorship is still in abeyance. The partisans of Cragin, Rollins, and Stevens are most active, and present appearances indicate that the selection will be made from this trio. Rollins seems to be the first choice of many active, earnest men of the party, and is evidently the second choice of a large number of members, who will at first give their influence to Cragin and Stevens, or perhaps to Marston and Tappan. We can see no chance as yet for Marston, and, notwithstanding the conceded superiority of Tappan, intellectually, there are not many aspirants for official position on his recommendation."

Chandler, who was in sympathy with Rollins's aspirations, was not able to be present to assist him, and, while having the benefit of Chandler's counsel in correspondence, Rollins felt the lack of his personal participation. Ordway also hoped for Rollins's success, but was detained in Washington until after the legislature met. Nor did any newspaper directly advocate Rollins's election. What benefit he got from the press was indirect, through their championship of rotation.

It was admitted that Cragin would lead on the first ballot, but how near he would come to a majority none could tell. Many of his supporters were partial to Rollins. The combined strength of Cragin and Rollins represented the sterling Republicans of the State. Beyond any personal preference, these Republicans were determined to elect as Senator what Rollins had earlier called a "true-blue Republican." Apprehension in the closing hours that the defeat of Cragin might be followed in the break-up of his strength by the election of Tappan settled the fate of Rollins and made Cragin's calling and election sure. Only two ballots were necessary.[1]

Rollins was disappointed not so much at defeat as at the showing he made in the caucus. His predictions in political campaigns had been prophetic, and he had encouraged his friends to believe that his chances of election as Senator were good. He himself thought so. Writing after election of his defeat, he said: "I stood a good chance until about twenty-four hours before the caucus, and had about sixty votes, which would have given me the nomination after a few ballots, when all the influences combined to get up a panic which produced a result surprising to everybody."

	First Ballot	Second Ballot
[1] Daniel Clark	1	
Frederick Smyth	3	
Nathaniel Gordon	8	5
Mason W. Tappan	21	23
Edward H. Rollins	32	21
Aaron F. Stevens	43	46
Aaron H. Craigin	95	109

CHAPTER XIV.

THE REPUBLICAN PARTY'S DEFEAT

GOVERNOR STEARNS's second administration gave general satisfaction. No State issue, unless it were temperance, appeared to trouble the Republican party, but the lack of cordiality among Republican leaders still continued. There were, however, local railroad troubles arising out of the contest for the control of the Concord Railroad, which did not strengthen the party in power. This contest went to the courts and their action occasioned criticism. As all but one of the supreme court judges were Republicans, the majority party suffered from any dissatisfaction with the court's decision. This contest, however, did not play any prominent part in the subsequent election. In national politics, the opposition of leading Republicans of the country to President Grant's administration became more pronounced. In the fall of 1870 the liberal Republican movement had its birth in Missouri in a bolt of Republicans led by United States Senator Carl Schurz and B. Gratz Brown, which triumphed in that State by a coalition with the Democrats. The other State elections that fall gave encouragement to the

242

Democratic party. The *Monitor,* Fogg's daily paper, December 29, 1870, said of the approaching Republican State convention:

"Never since the organization of the Republican party did more importance attach to the selection of the very best and strongest candidate. Party obligations have not hung so loosely upon the people for many years as at the present time. With not a few who have always hitherto voted the Republican ticket various moral questions have come to be regarded as of pressing if not paramount consequence. And it is demanded that these moral questions shall receive recognition at the hands of the Republican party, not merely in the platform of resolutions but in the selection of candidates."

One of the moral questions to which Fogg referred was that pertaining to temperance. Over eleven hundred voters, nearly all of them Republicans, had flocked to the standard of the Prohibitory party in the preceding election. If this party increased its vote, Republican ascendency in New Hampshire for a time at least was at an end. If these could be won back, there was less danger of Democratic success. The view of Fogg that not only the platform should be made to meet the wishes of these men, but that the candidate for governor should invite their support, had earnest champions. In casting about for such a candidate, the Rev. James Pike, of South Newmarket, was the choice of many. He was then fifty-three years of age, a presiding elder in the New Hampshire Methodist Conference, and one of the leading Methodist clergymen of the State. He had been in Congress two terms with Mason W. Tappan and Aaron H. Cragin as colleagues, having been first elected by the American party in 1855. On his return from Washington, he had resumed his pastoral duties. During the Civil War he was appointed colonel of the Sixteenth New Hampshire Volunteers, and served with that regiment creditably during its enlistment of nine months.

Interest in the Republican State convention held January 4, 1871, centred in the nomination for governor. There were many active candidates for this nomination. Pike was the leading candidate, while those who doubted the wisdom of his nomination divided their support principally among five prominent men of the State, with a few votes given to nine others. The first ballot was as follows: James Pike, of South Newmarket, 292; Horton D. Walker, of Portsmouth, 99; Benjamin J. Cole, of Gilford, 74; Ezekiel A. Straw, of Manchester, 65; John M. Brackett, of Wolfboro, 59; George W. Nesmith, of Franklin, 25; scattering, 32.

This vote showed a majority of sixty-two against Mr. Pike's nomination. It was confidently believed by the party leaders that subsequent ballotings would result in the nomination of one of the other candidates. Before a second ballot could be taken, however, a motion was made to nominate Pike by acclamation. It was carried in one of those critical moments of a convention when the leaders are off their guard and taken by surprise.

The Prohibitory party met in convention and voted to make no nomination. The nomination of Pike by the Republicans satisfied the majority of the Prohibition leaders of the sincerity of the Republican party in supporting prohibition. A minority of the convention, however, bolted its action and nominated a candidate for governor. For a time, the action of the Republican convention in nominating Mr. Pike seemed to be a politic move and one likely to restore the allegiance of Prohibitionists to the Republican party.

The Democrats nominated James A. Weston, whom they had three times elected mayor of Manchester. He was a civil engineer by profession, a man of business ability, respected by the community in which he resided, and enjoying its confidence. After his retirement from politics he engaged in banking.

The Labor Reformers met in convention and formally put in nomination Lemuel E. Cooper, of Croydon. Less interest was shown in this convention than the year before, as it was pretty generally understood that the party was simply an adjunct to the Democratic party.

The Republican Congressional nominations were disappointing and did not promote harmony. The *Statesman* before the conventions expressed the opinion that " Republican success would be more fully assured by an entirely new Congressional ticket than by continuing any present member upon it." This was addressed largely to the voters of the second district where Aaron F. Stevens was a candidate for a third term. He was renominated after a hard contest. He had made enemies by his appointments. The cry of " rotation " was revived and threats of a bolt followed the convention that nominated him.

In the first district William B. Small, of Newmarket, was selected after protracted balloting, defeating Samuel M. Wheeler, of Dover, whom Republicans generally expected to be nominated. In the third district the choice fell upon Simon G. Griffin, of Keene. Griffin had been a gallant soldier in the Civil War, but the very qualities which made him an excellent officer in the field were not popular in civil life. Then there were local jealousies in the district which detracted from his support as a candidate. The candidates of the Democratic party were Ellery A. Hibbard, of Laconia, Samuel N. Bell, of Manchester, and Hosea W. Parker, of Claremont, the first and last being renominated.

The Republican State committee met immediately after the State convention for the purpose of organization. The story of this organization is best told in the correspondence of Rollins and Chandler. Writing Chandler January 5th, Rollins said:

"We had a splendid convention. All were feeling pretty well, but very anxious. You will see that I was reëlected chairman by a unanimous vote. I tried to have the matter postponed, but they insisted upon organization. When elected, I positively declined and gave my reasons at length and without excitement. I defined my position fully. We must have peace or I will have nothing to do with the matter. They would not accept my resignation, but I did not agree to serve. We are to have a meeting in about two weeks, and in the meantime Durkee & Company will see what they can do for peace. I told them frankly that I would no longer act as chairman without the cordial support of all Republicans and the press."

To this letter Chandler replied January 7th, as follows: "Yours of the 5th inst. is at hand. General Stevens returned last night and I had a full talk with him. He pretends to feel good-natured but is really very bitter toward you and our crowd, says that he declined to express any opinion in reference to the chairmanship of the committee, that the Republican party of the State evidently had more confidence in your ability than they would have in that of any one else, and that he believed you would intend to act in good faith and not promote any bolting in his district, although he could not be certain what you might not be drawn into if you got angry.

"He evidently wants you to remain chairman of the committee and help elect him, but he has not frankness enough to say so. He barely admits that you would probably not be a scoundrel in the place. He will hold you responsible for all the evil that results and give you no credit for success.

"Of course I have my opinion as to what you should do under such circumstances. If I were in your place and had no well-founded political aspirations for the future in connection with New Hampshire, I would on no account be chairman of the committee for the precise reason suggested; you will be held responsible and condemned for every failure. You can get by no possibility any additional credit for any success. On any other ground than that you have future political expectations, it will be utter folly for you to take charge of and be responsible for the campaign.

"But, if you have such expectations and think there is a reasonable chance for success in them, of course you may be willing to go forward, notwithstanding the objections to it which are so apparent. On this point I do not advise you. Stevens will, of course, hold you responsible for any bolting in Concord.

"Of course the attempt of Durkee and others to make things better in Concord will amount to nothing. Fogg will simply refrain from attacking you during the campaign, which he probably would do anyhow. More than this he will not agree to."

In addition to the jealousies occasioned by Rollins's remaining chairman, he knew that he could not give the time to the campaign its exigencies required. The Union Pacific Railroad was seeking legislation of Congress to relieve it of financial difficulties, and, as an officer of that corporation, his presence would be required in Washington. It was the short session of Congress, and whatever was done must be done before the 4th of March. The second meeting of the State committee, however, secured his acceptance of the chairmanship.

It proved to be a quiet campaign. Fogg made no attack upon Rollins or any member of the "clique," and heartily supported the ticket, especially praising the nomination of Mr. Pike, saying: "The candidate agreed upon is the very best selection that could have been made." The Democrats attacked both the Republican candidate for governor and the Republican platform, the former because of his early affiliation with the American or Know Nothing party, and the latter as a surrender to the Prohibitionists. There was general apathy among Republicans. Rollins was not at headquarters to watch the campaign and to checkmate the work of the bolting Republicans. There was little public speaking, and no effort made to arouse the party. The Republican party press predicted victory. It took no note of the indifference of the rank and file. The Democrats conducted a still hunt for votes with success, although trading openly with the Labor Reformers whenever this was advantageous. Toward the close of the campaign they became bolder and openly urged their voters to come to the polls in anticipation of victory.

Affairs at Washington contributed to Democratic confidence. Mr. Motley, our minister to England, was removed by President Grant as a result of the President's differences with Charles Sumner, and, just before election day, Sumner himself was removed from the chairmanship of the committee on foreign relations by his Republican colleagues of the Senate for the same reason. This last act came as a shock to the party in New England.

The election returns were a surprise to the people of the State. The morning after election it was apparent that there was no choice of governor by the people, Weston leading Pike by nearly a thousand votes. All three Democratic candidates for Congress were elected, and the legislature was in doubt. Both sides claimed a majority of the House, on which depended the organization of the Senate, the control of the Council and the election of governor. The vote for governor was as follows: Scattering, 41; Albert G. Comings, 314; Lemuel P. Cooper, 782; James Pike, 33,892; James A. Weston, 34,700.

The *Manchester Mirror* ascribed Republican defeat to various causes, dragging temperance into the campaign, forcing the nomination of Pike against the judgment of a majority of the convention, ignoring the demand for rotation in office, the land-grabbing jobs of Congress, the San Domingo scheme, and the removal of Charles Sumner from the chairmanship of the Senate committee on foreign relations.

The *Statesman* gave these same causes of defeat, and said: " Had all these causes of embarrassment been withheld, we might have carried the State by nearly the usual majority in spite of demoralization produced in the party by forcing upon it unpopular nominations made in packed caucuses."

This was the only campaign that the Republicans

lost with which Rollins had direct connection. The explanation is given in his letter to Benjamin Gerrish, Jr., written when he was reorganizing the party for the campaign of 1872. This letter is as follows:

" In regard to the campaign of last spring, I must confess that I had but little to do with it, for I was in New Hampshire but three days before the election took place after the campaign commenced. The Pacific Railroad was having a terrific fight, a sort of life and death struggle in regard to the payment of interest on the bonds issued by the government to this company, and it was a matter of absolute necessity for me to be at Washington, and I remained until the 4th of March. We secured the legislation we needed in the very last day of the session of Congress, without which this concern would have been pretty much used up. You see, I was away from necessity and not from inclination. Had I been at home, I should have pitched into the fight as usual. Since I returned from Washington, I have devoted a very large amount of time to politics of our State, and feel confident we are getting into a satisfactory position and can carry the State at the next election. I am getting ready for just such a fight as we had in 1868, when you and I ran the machine."

Upon the organization of the House of Representatives depended the outcome of the election. Both Republicans and Democrats claimed a majority in this branch of the Legislature, and both Republican and Democratic newspapers published lists giving the political status of members elect. Several Labor Reformers had been elected to the legislature, and some of these being of Republican antecedents were claimed by both parties. There were two or more instances where there was dispute as to the right of members elect to the certificate of election held by them, notably in Ward 6, Concord, where Samuel B. Page had been declared elected. There were, therefore, complications to keep the question in doubt until the members voted.

Differences in the Republican ranks for the time being were laid aside; the leaders generally coöperating in an attempt to save the legislature. The burden fell upon Rollins as chairman of the committee to marshal the Republican legislative forces. He threw himself into this work, but he found the party leaders demoralized by the prospect of probable defeat. He at once entered into correspondence with the Republican members of the legislature and appealed to prominent Republicans in all parts of the State to assist in the work. The following is a letter addressed by him to Republican members of the legislature.

"I presume you agree with me that it is of vital importance to secure, first, the organization of the House of Representatives in June next, second, the election of Republican State officers, and third, the complete triumph of the Republican party at the next annual election. The accomplishment of the first two will render the latter more certain.

"To this end are you willing to make extra effort during the current year to bring about these desirable results? If so, please make complete reply to the circular of the State committee at Concord, and report to me in detail all the facts in your possession having a bearing upon the organization of the House of Representatives.

"We must take immediate steps to heal all local dissensions, thoroughly organize, firmly unite the party, and thus make preparation to sustain our members of the legislature and win the battle in March next."

This was supplemented by other letters to members of the legislature and to prominent Republicans of the State urging activity and vigilance. Until the night preceding the meeting of the legislature, there was reasonable assurance that the Republicans would organize the House. Then weakness on the part of some Republican leaders, together with the illness of two Republican Representatives, gave the Democrats the victory. William H. Gove, of Weare, the candidate for Speaker of both the Labor Reform and the Democratic parties, was elected by two majority over James O. Adams, the Republican candidate.

It was a memorable contest, the Democrats taking no chances of defeat. They numbered their ballots for Speaker, and on the back of each was the name of the Representative to vote it. In this way each member's vote could be accounted for. They had reliable party workers in charge of all doubtful men, who were responsible for their appearance and votes. All through the session they held their following intact against Republican assault, though in the early days of the session, before they increased their majority in the House by unseating Republicans whose seats were contested, their Speaker had several times to vote on questions to give them a majority.

The death of one of the Democratic Senators-elect before the meeting of the legislature deprived them of the fruits of their triumph. In filling the vacancy they were compelled to choose between his Republican competitor at the polls and a temperance Republican who received a few votes. They elected Alvah Smith, the temperance Republican, to this vacancy. With his vote they had a majority in a Senate of twelve members. He voted with the Democrats in the election of State officers, but, when it came to carrying out the Democratic programme for redistricting the State and removing Republican office-holders, he refused to act with them, nor could any persuasion or threat secure his support of this programme. The indignation of the Democrats knew no bounds. They accused Senator Smith of violating his pledges to them and threatened to oust him from his seat in the Senate. Nothing, however, came of these threats. The session continued exciting throughout, and gave the Republicans material for campaign purposes which they used to advantage. At the final adjournment the two parties stood in battle-array for the next campaign, which was opened immediately.

CHAPTER XV.

ALTHOUGH the Democrats had secured but little
material benefit from their control of the executive
office and one branch of the legislature, the prestige
of victory was theirs, and they were buoyed up with
confidence of success in the campaign of 1872. On
the other hand, the Republicans were more or less
demoralized by their defeat. They had gained some
courage out of the discomfiture of their opponents in
failing to control the legislature, but their dissensions
and jealousies remained. There were plenty of leaders
who could give explanations of the party's defeat, but
few who had heart to suggest how this defeat might
be retrieved. Rollins was one of the few who had confidence that the State could be redeemed, and he
began the campaign of 1872 while the legislature of
1871 was in session. He was now situated so that
he could give time to political affairs, and he immediately opened correspondence with Republicans in all
parts of the State urging activity and organization of
the party for the coming battle. While others were
suggesting candidates for governor, he gave his atten-

tion to the close towns, requesting immediate canvasses with lists of wavering and doubtful Republicans. The treasury of the State committee was empty, and a committee of ten prominent Republicans was organized to raise funds to carry on this preliminary canvass.

Any one who has had to do with political campaigns knows how difficult it is to secure contributions of money in advance of the formal opening of the campaign. When the excitement of the struggle is on, appeals for financial aid meet with response, but, with the contest months ahead, contributions are grudgingly given even by those most interested. Rollins's plan of campaign embraced the placing in the hands of every young or wavering voter of the State a Republican newspaper, whose constant repetitions of the shortcomings of the Democracy would shape this voter's thought in the right direction. He realized, as have all his successors in the chairmanship, that documents, speeches, and newspapers flooded upon a voter a few weeks or days before election are a waste of time and money, as most of them are thrown aside and never read. He knew that, if converts are to be made or backsliders regained, it must be by constant evidence of the unfitness of the opposition to hold power. Yet plain as this proposition is now and was then, it required repeated appeals to obtain even small sums for this purpose.

From his railroad office in Boston, Rollins carried on his political correspondence, and, as he himself frequently complained, he devoted more time to this work than to his railroad business. Nor was he always encouraged by the interest of Republicans in the cause. Not a few were indifferent. Some were disheartened, and here and there cropped out jealousy of his management of the party. With justifiable impatience he frequently offered to take his place in the ranks to allow the malcontents to pick out his successor as chairman of the State committee. Writing Bainbridge Wadleigh, of Milford, afterward United States. Senator, about this time, he said:

"I regret that you were not present at our meeting last evening. I did not receive any report from you in regard to the articles of association. You were chairman of the committee to prepare them. Meeting adjourned until next Tuesday at 8 P. M., at Phenix Hotel. Hope you will make it a point to be present.

"I find it necessary in order to keep things moving to devote about half my time to the politics of New Hampshire. It is considerable of a bore. Have you found somebody to take my place yet? Do you think you had better take it? You will find it a very pleasant position and your services will always be appreciated, particularly by the leading Republicans, more especially those who do not wish to do any work themselves and only growl at those who do labor."

To this letter Wadleigh replied: "Dear Rollins: Yours of the 24th inst. came to hand last evening. I received no notice of the meeting on the 23d, and was aware of none until I learned of it from your letter. I shall try to be present next Tuesday, though I have an engagement on that day which may possibly prevent me from going up. Now, my dear Ned, I cannot allow you to mistake my position in reference to yourself. You seem to credit me with some hostility to you which does not exist. I am well aware of the debt of gratitude which we all owe you, and no man ever heard me say one word to depreciate it. But very evidently your services have produced jealousy, and I think that with your coöperation we can get a little more harmony with a new figure-head, and I think — I know — that you would be the stronger for it. As for my taking it, it is out of the question, even if I were wanted, which does not appear. It is not with any view to my own interests that I think as I do, because I feel that I have no better friend than yourself. I am well aware that in the next contest we shall need all the strength we can muster, and, as for myself, though I have had nothing and expect nothing from the party, I am willing to do all in my power to give it victory."

Answering this letter, Rollins said: "Yours of the 26th inst. is received and I note your remarks with reference to the last meeting. A notice was sent you by mail and I regret that you did not receive it. You mistake me in supposing that I regard you as anything but a sincere friend. I have always believed you to be such and have no reason to change my views. Whatever you have said or now think about the 'figure-head,' I am sure you were and are prompted by the best of motives and look only to the welfare of the party. Still I think those gentlemen who agree with you in regard to the matter should present their man at once. Let us see that he is the proper man for the place. It is no use to talk about the change and still take no steps to secure the services of some proper man to take my place. I shall be delighted to be relieved from the burden and care of the campaign and should like to have the change made at once, for a great share of the hard labor will have to be performed before the meeting of the State convention, unless that is held very soon. Hoping to see you this evening, and hear from you as often as convenient, I remain," etc.

No one appeared voluntarily to take up the burden of the chairmanship of the State committee, and no one was suggested by those who criticized Rollins's control of the organization. With the exception of these outbursts of impatience at the indifference of the leaders and the personal criticism of himself, Rollins's correspondence indicates an optimism which finally stimulated the Republicans of the State to make a winning fight. With his usual grasp of details, he had the campaign fully mapped out and the local leaders at work before the State convention was held. After the nomination of governor, it was only necessary to push the campaign to a successful issue.

Another difficulty besetting the Republicans was the lack of a party newspaper at the capital which should represent the whole party and not a faction. George G. Fogg still controlled the columns of the *Independent Democrat* and the *Daily Monitor*. In these journals he continued to criticize the management of the party. The sparring between him and the editors of the *New Hampshire Statesman* delighted the enemy and discouraged Republicans. It was necessary to success that harmony should prevail, and Rollins set on foot a movement to purchase both newspaper plants and consolidate them. Frequent meetings were held for this purpose, first to secure the consent of the proprietors to sell, and, second, to secure subscribers for the capital stock of the consolidated plant. The former was no easy task. The latter proved to be an undertaking which called for the utmost patience and persistency. The stock was to be distributed in small blocks in different parts of the State, so that no individual or section would control the management. The purchase and consolidation took place in October, 1871, but the stock was not fully subscribed until some weeks later. Probably no one rendered more efficient service in this work than Person C. Chency, of Manchester.

Nothing better illustrates Rollins's subordination of personal feelings to the good of the cause than his kindly reception of a suggestion that Fogg be made editor of the consolidated newspapers. On this point he wrote Daniel Hall: "If Fogg would put on the party harness and work with the spirit he manifested in olden times, he would undoubtedly be the best man we could have, and I should be in favor of securing his services. He has ability and perhaps could aid in bringing back into the fold some of the sheep who have strayed away under his leadership."

Rollins also wrote to other leaders suggesting that the proposition was worthy of consideration, with the result that Fogg became the political editor of the consolidated newspapers, a position he held until the next summer.

The Republican State committee met November 22, 1871, to fix the time for holding the State and other conventions. This meeting was largely attended by its members and by prominent men of the party. Rollins was now able to lay before them the result of his labors during the summer and fall and to show them that with united effort the party could regain control of the State. In December, the Rev. James Pike, in an open letter, declined to be again a candidate for governor, thus relieving the party of any embarrassment which might arise from passing him over. The party was encouraged by several municipal elections which occurred this month. Dover and Portsmouth were carried by the Republicans with their usual majorities, while Manchester, which had for three years elected James A. Weston mayor, now chose Person C. Cheney his successor by several hundred majority.

The Republican State convention met at Concord, January 3, 1872. Rollins, as chairman of the State committee, opened the convention with a speech full of vigor and confidence. He said:

" You have assembled as representatives of the Republican party under very extraordinary circumstances. We have a Democratic governor. Our action to-day will, I am confident, be so satisfactory to our party and to the people that Governor Weston will be the last of his tribe. We have beaten the enemy in twenty successive well-contested campaigns, but, at the last election, he achieved a partial success, this not on account of any regard the people have for modern Democracy, or its conduct during the war, or love for copperhead principles, but rather by reason of local troubles, disaffections, and unusual apathy in our own ranks. We were in fact beaten by ourselves. One experiment of this kind is sufficient. . . . The experience of the past year has taught us a lesson which we shall not speedily forget. We know now that there must be harmony in our ranks, life and activity in our organizaton, vigor and discretion in our action, and wisdom in our counsels to render success certain. I have given much attention to political affairs since the last election, and I know that I utter but the truth when I say that the Republicans have determined in compact irresistible columns to move upon the works of the enemy and redeem the State. We have not forgotten the more than thirty-nine thousand legal votes which we gave for the Republican candidate in 1868. We can, if we so resolve, repeat that memorable campaign."

Only one ballot for governor was necessary. It resulted in the nomination of Ezekiel A. Straw, of Manchester, his principal opponent being Horton D. Walker, of Portsmouth. Straw was the agent of the

Amoskeag Corporation, of Manchester, and a man of large executive ability. His selection was the best that could have been made at that time, both on account of locality and his standing in the State.

The State committee met immediately after the convention for the purpose of organization. In spite of all his labors and what he had accomplished in re-uniting the party, there was decided opposition on the part of some of the leaders to Rollins's continuing at the head of the committee. A United States Senator would be chosen by the legislature to be elected in March. This prospective prize was sufficient to arouse all the old jealousies of Rollins's leadership. At the committee meeting, he was accused by Mason W. Tappan of neglecting the party in the previous campaign. To this accusation he replied that, as the committee had refused to accept his resignation and forced the position upon him, he considered it unjust. This seemed to be the view of most of the committee, but without action an adjournment was taken for a week.

This attack came as a surprise to most members of the State committee. It seemed for the time as if all of Rollins's work of reorganizing the party would go for naught. If the party was to be torn by dissensions at the very outset of the campaign, there was little prospect of success. If the Senatorial contest was to be precipitated in advance of the election, it was not impossible that the Democratic party would carry off this prize. Rollins's feelings are shown in letters to friends written between the time of the first and second meeting of the State committee. A sample of these letters is the following to William B. Small, of Newmarket, the defeated candidate for Congress in the first district at the previous election: "My dear Small: — Your two letters of the 9th instant received. Many thanks for your kind and encouraging words. Be assured that at the first opportunity all your efforts will be appreciated by me in a manner that will be quite satisfactory to you. I confess that I was much mortified at the attack made upon me in view of my earnest efforts since the last election to place the Republican party in a position to win the victory in March. It was wicked to have such a scene in the State committee after the magnificent convention of the day. I think our enemies have made a mistake, for I am satisfied from information received that the feeling of the Republicans is strongly in the right direction, and will manifest itself on Friday next.

"Patterson and his friends have been busy for a month trying to work up this case, but I was surprised to see Tappan, Stevens, and O. C. Moore in it. They have made a great mistake and it will react upon them. I understand that Patterson's friends are beginning to hedge by declaring that he was never in favor of the change. The result will be entirely satisfactory to me, although the ordeal is not a pleasant one. We can hardly afford such scrimmages in the party at present. I shall do my best for the cause under any circumstances. . . . I trust there will be a full meeting, not only of the committee but of leading Republicans. I hope not only to see my friends but also my enemies, if there are any, for I am sure they will be satisfied when they know all, unless their minds are poisoned by ambitious schemers."

The second meeting of the committee was very largely attended. Rollins opened it by a calm statement of his position. He reviewed his connection with the previous campaign, explained his enforced absence, repeated the assurance he had received from Prescott and Fogg, who were in charge of the State committee, that Republican success was assured, and outlined his work of reorganizing the party. He concluded by stating that he was not a candidate for reëlection, but, if selected, he should not feel at liberty to decline. His speech made a strong impression. It was supplemented by a brief statement from Mr. Straw, the candidate for governor, expressing his wishes and his desire for harmonious action. There was no discussion and, a ballot being taken, Rollins received all but a few scattering votes. His election as chairman was then made unanimous.

Writing Ordway immediately after the second meeting of the committee, Rollins said:

"I must run the machine once more, and then I hope to be quit of it. I could not retire without seeming disgrace. This I cannot afford. I think the hostility exhibited by Patterson, Tappan and Co. has done me much good and ensured me many friends whom I otherwise would not have had. The fact is the rank and file of the party are for me, and they found it out before the committee met, and accepted the situation."

The *Manchester Mirror* in its account of the State committee meeting said: "The meeting was such as will give the key-note to the present campaign. It means that the contest on the part of the Republicans is to be one of untiring and indefatigable labor. The selection of Mr. Rollins means old-fashioned warfare and an immediate movement on the enemy's works."

The *Statesman* said: "The abilities and success of E. H. Rollins in his position of chairman have become historic in New Hampshire and need not be descanted upon."

The skill with which Rollins managed campaigns in New Hampshire was known and recognized by Republican leaders all over the country. It was about this time that Rollins received the following message from Elihu B. Washburne, our minister to France, in a letter written to him by Benjamin Gerrish, Jr., of Concord, then consul at Nantes, France.

"When you write Rollins, give him my kindest regards and tell him that I am glad he is to run the next campaign in New Hampshire, for that looks like business. I know what the result will be if he takes hold in earnest. He is the best party organizer that New Hampshire ever produced."

Washburne was an intimate friend of Grant and interested in his reëlection to the Presidency. He recognized the importance of a Republican victory in New

Hampshire in March as bearing not only upon the renomination but the reëlection of President Grant.

The campaign was an active and vigilant one. The Democrats renominated Governor Weston, and a small gathering of Labor Reformers nominated Lemuel P. Cooper, of Croydon. The Prohibitionists held a convention and selected John Blackmer as their standard-bearer. The contest, however, was between the two old parties, the Labor Reformers and Prohibitionists cutting no figure in the canvass. Among the outside speakers for the Republicans were Senator Henry Wilson, of Massachusetts, Gen. Daniel E. Sickles, of New York, Mary A. Livermore, of Massachusetts, and James F. Wilson, of Iowa, afterward United States Senator from that State. Daniel Voorhees, of Indiana, then Congressman, and afterward Senator, appeared on the stump for the Democrats.

General Sickles not only spoke in the campaign, but sent his check for five hundred dollars to aid in the expenses. Acknowledging Sickles's letter, Rollins said: " My dear General: — Yours of the 4th inst. enclosing check of five hundred dollars to aid the good cause in the State is received. A thousand thanks for your generous contribution. It is the first that we have received from our friends outside of the State, and I assure you that it will not only do us much good toward getting home our absent voters, but will encourage us to make more determined efforts to redeem the State. The fight is to be a desperate one, and we need all the assistance we can have. We remember well how you turned the 'tide of battle' in our campaign of 1868, and may find ourselves again in a position where your services will be indispensable. If such should be the case, Chandler intimates that you will make two or three speeches for us. We are well aware of the changes that have taken place and the consequent different relations which you hold to the government and the people, and consequently shall not call upon you unless the necessity seems obvious. Please let me hear from you when convenient, and believe me as ever, your sincere friend."

Three weeks before the election, Rollins had prepared his canvass of the State. A copy of this canvass was given at that time to Governor Jewell, of Connecticut, and to Mr. Straw, the Republican candidate for governor.[1]

Commenting upon this canvass after election, the *Boston Advertiser's* Concord corespondent said: " It seems almost incredible that so correct a canvass could have been made, and yet the result is not any more

[1] CANVASS

Straw	38,141
Weston	36,137
Blackmer	301
Cooper	527

VOTE CAST

Straw	38,752
Weston	36,584
Blackmer	436
Cooper and scattering	460

accurate than has occurred several times before under the excellent management of E. H. Rollins, chairman of the State committee."

The election resulted in the choice of Straw as governor by the people. The Republicans carried the legislature by about sixty majority. Speaking of this campaign, the *Statesman* said:

"The chairman of the committee, E. H. Rollins, was almost literally sleepless in his vigilance, and never acquitted himself more creditably in any of his previous campaigns. It is safe to say that under any other chairman than Mr. Rollins our success would have been at best doubtful. In view of his faithful and efficient service, the Republicans of New Hampshire and of the whole country owe Mr. Rollins the heartiest thanks."

This campaign in New Hampshire enlisted more than ever the attention of the country. It was to have an important bearing upon the Republican national convention which would assemble a few weeks after the result was known. The Liberal Republican movement was on foot to defeat the renomination of President Grant by the menace of a threatened bolt. The Republicans of New Hampshire had endorsed President Grant's administration in their convention. Rollins, representing the Grant sentiment, which was strong in the State, was especially anxious to make the victory so emphatic that there would be no question of his renomination. Tappan, Fogg, and even Senator Patterson were suspected of hostility to Grant. If only a partial triumph were secured at the New Hampshire election, the opponents of Grant all over the country would hail it as an indication that he could not be elected if nominated, and that his selection would result in national defeat for the party. The anti-Grant sentiment in New Hampshire was not outspoken, but anything short of a complete victory in the March election would bring it into the open. How much of this sentiment lurked in the Republican ranks of the State became apparent after the national conventions were held. It is not too much to say that the result in New Hampshire settled the renomination of President Grant. The *Washington Star* commenting upon the New Hampshire election, expressed the feeling of Grant's supporters everywhere when it said:

" The first gun of the campaign is very emphatically for Grant, and the Republicans gained all they lost last year. As we said yesterday, the issue in this State was purely a national one between the friends of the administration and its enemies, and, this being the case, the result must be accepted as an indication that the so-called Liberal Republican movement has not seriously weakened the Republican party of New England."

The Senatorial canvass, which began immediately after election, became intense and even bitter toward its close. Rollins was the most prominent contestant for Patterson's seat, and around these two the battle raged with no small amount of personal feling. Governor Onslow Stearns, Mason W. Tappan, and Gilman

Marston were later brought into the contest, and it early became the field against Patterson. Rollins was not adverse to the candidacies of these three, believing that they would draw from Patterson where he could not, and that with Patterson's defeat their friends would come to him.

Stearns's two terms as governor had been creditable to himself and the party. He was recognized as a successful business man. Of forceful character, he showed himself popular with the people of the State. He was president of one of the New Hampshire railroads. His recognized executive ability gave him a considerable following.

The familiar cry of "rotation" was taken up, and the feeling of many Republicans of the State was expressed by Marston in a letter to Rollins dated May 24, 1872, in which he said:

"The reëlection of Cragin was a mistake which all men now see and acknowledge. It did not strengthen the party or add a ray of glory to our State. It helped nobody but himself and Ruel (Durkee). The mistake cannot now be rectified and it will not be repeated. . . . I am of the opinion that, if I could have seen you frequently and you would have taken kindly some suggestions — and I am sure you would — rotation could have been made certain. From my point of view Mr. Patterson seems strong, not so strong as he was, but still formidable. He has not a majority, but you know how difficult it is to unite the friends of several candidates upon any one."

This last suggestion of Marston was true. Rollins, Stearns, Tappan, and Marston were agreed that Patterson ought not to be reëlected, but none of them reached the point where he was ready to throw his support to any of the others. As the contest grew in intensity, it appeared to the unprejudiced that, while Rollins's candidacy might defeat Patterson, it would not elect himself. As the session of the legislature approached, a deadlock of the leaders in the caucus seemed probable. Other candidates now awakened to the possibilities of the canvass.

In addition to the argument of rotation, Patterson had to meet the suspicion that he was not in full accord with Grant's administration, as well as open attacks that he was connected with the Washington city ring then in power with "Boss" Alexander R. Shepard at its head. He was attacked in the Democratic newspapers, and, in the closing days of the canvass, two negroes from Washington appeared at Concord, where in public speeches they accused him of disloyalty to their race. The Credit Mobilier scandal had not then come to the front, and was only hinted at during the canvass. Rollins was accused of inspiring the attacks upon Patterson, a charge he denied. As many of the statements which were made about Patterson's public career were supposed to be within the knowledge of Rollins, it was easy to accuse him of giving them currency, and difficult for him to persuade the public that he had not done so. Then Rollins's association with Ordway, who openly attacked Patterson while championing Rollins's election, seemed to confirm that belief.

Chandler, who was kept busy by his duties as secretary of the national convention which met in June, was not on the ground, but he kept in touch with what was going on. Three weeks before the legislature met, he wrote Rollins a letter:

"I am satisfied that if any set of members in the caucus a resolution proposing an understanding in favor of rotation on the Senatorial question in favor of new candidate ... time and carrying it through there will be one chance of a result getting in. Others will have some difference of opinion when it comes ... Patterson will be elected."

What Chandler stated came near happening ... Patterson ... to give him a majority of ... The second ballot in the caucus gave ... he ... he had on the ... Then it was ... Rollins was arguing ... of the case, apparently the greatest ... ... he ... at that gathering. The Manchester Mirror report of the caucus ... ... of Rollins ... rough after a night ... close in the afternoon ... the caucus appearances indicated that Patterson and Rollins are pretty evenly balanced," the reporter on the ... Later in the day the current set against Rollins and in favor of Patterson in consequence of new energy on the part of Patterson's friends and the charge that Rollins had brought Ordway to his aid and imported colored men from Washington to declaim against Patterson. There is no reason to believe that Rollins was guilty of the charge, but Ordway and the colored men were present and opposed Patterson, and this gave color to the accusation."

The caucus met amid intense excitement, but proceeded immediately to ballot. Patterson lacked eight of a majority on the first vote. Rollins polled nearly a third of the caucus. Stearns's vote added to Rollins's would have placed the latter within ten votes of Patterson. On the first ballot Bainbridge Wadleigh had three votes. Patterson held his forces well in hand for three ballots. Then a break came and Wadleigh was nominated on the fifth ballot.[1]

The election of Wadleigh came as a complete surprise to the State. He had not expected the nomination, although he knew he would be voted for in the

[1] THE BALLOTS

	First	Second	Third	Fourth	Fifth
James W. Patterson	102	103	103	98	36
Edward H. Rollins	67	59	39	16	1
Onslow Stearns	25	25	31	39	
Mason W. Tappan	12	16	19	18	9
Gilman Marston	9	6	7	6	5
Bainbridge Wadleigh	3	8	18	39	152
Aaron F. Stevens	1				
Samuel M. Wheeler		2	3		
Walter Harriman				2	4
Asa Fowler				1	3

caucus. He was a member of this legislature, as he had been of the preceding, where he had attracted the attention of the Republicans of the State by his leadership when his party was in the minority. He was popular with the members, of whom probably one-half had been members of the previous annual session. If a compromise candidate was to be selected, he of all others was the easiest to unite upon. He readily made friends, was a pleasing speaker and skilful in debate. He had avoided in politics all those contests which create antagonisms. His career in the Senate brought him into prominence, and he was recognized by his colleagues in that body as a man of ability and strength. Senator George F. Hoar, of Massachusetts, in his autobiography, commends both Wadleigh's ability and integrity, and condemns the practice of New Hampshire of frequently changing her representation in the Senate. Wadleigh was grievously disappointed at his defeat for reëlection, and an independence of party which he had shown in the Senate led, in 1882, to his bolting the Republican nominee for governor and casting his lot with the Democratic party. After his retirement from the Senate, he removed to Boston, where he practised his profession until his death.

Senator Patterson's defeat was not regarded by himself or his friends as his retirement from politics. He had many admirers in the State. He had occupied a professor's chair at Dartmouth College at the time of his first election to Congress. In that body he had attained distinction. As a scholar he had high rank among public men, and as an orator he was without a rival in New Hampshire and with but few peers in the United States. In the Senate his eloquent speeches had attracted the attention of the country, and the metropolitan press of Boston, New York, and Washington with hardly an exception were earnest advocates of his reëlection. The Credit Mobilier exposure involving so many public men followed soon after his defeat, and from the effect of this he never recovered. He was later made superintendent of public instruction of the State, a position he held until his death. In 1883 he was again a candidate for the Senate, but his support did not extend beyond a few devoted admirers.

The *Dover Enquirer,* which had supported Mr. Rollins's candidacy for the Senatorship, had this to say after election: " E. H. Rollins made a good fight for the Senatorship, receiving sixty-seven votes on the first ballot or nearly one-third of the entire number. It is said this would have been sensibly larger but for the jealousies of some rotationists and the last effective arguments of their opponents, resulting in surprising violations of good faith. Mr. Rollins, in fact, had on hand not only the biggest kind of a contest with Mr. Patterson but several little side encounters with various other gentlemen who were only too willing to relieve Mr. Patterson, provided they did not aid Mr. Rollins. The result is highly creditable to the latter's personal influence and popularity. He comes out of the whole with warmer friends and greater strength than ever.

His efforts for the Republican cause may fail of recognition, but they will never make him false to principle. The Republican party needs just such men and we believe, if it is to endure many years, it can only be by appreciating and sustaining them."

The Senatorial caucus had taken place before it was known what effect the nomination of Horace Greeley by the Liberal Republicans would have upon either the Democratic or the Republican parties. Rollins's defeat was a disappointment to many of the working Republicans of the State. The Democratic newspapers were inclined to regard it as likely to produce a wider breach in the Republican party of New Hampshire. They were, therefore, disposed to sympathize with Rollins and to give prominence to his labors in behalf of the party. The Concord *People,* which was becoming more and more to be recognized as the Democratic organ at the capital, thus refers to the Republican Senatorial caucus.

" Mr. Rollins, in our view of the late Senatorial contest, and it is one of impartial observation, cannot look upon the mode and means of his defeat with much satisfaction. Every man in this State knows that he has been the efficient and successful manager of the political campaigns of his party for years. To him more than any other man the Republican party of this State owes its success for the last fifteen years. As a compensation for signal services he has rendered to his party, he asked the favor of an election to the Senate of the United States. But the very services which he has rendered to his party have been the cause of his defeat. His efficient generalship of the Republican affairs has made him personal enemies and aroused the jealousies of rivals. To those mean sentiments and motives he has been sacrificed."

If by sympathizing with his defeat the Democrats had an idea that they would unsettle Rollins's loyalty to his party, they were soon to find out their mistake.

Rollins's identification with the Union Pacific Railroad as its secretary and treasurer did not help his candidacy. The newspapers were already giving currency to suspicions that the road was not properly managed and they were leading up to the Congressional investigation which took place some months later. The Credit Mobilier of America, an organization within the Union Pacific directory for absorbing the profits of building the road, was known to exist, though the extent of its operation had not been exposed. Enough, however, appeared in the press regarding this company to raise the question of the propriety of electing an officer of the Union Pacific Railroad to the Senate. The opponents of Rollins used this against him. He, however, was never a stockholder either in the Union Pacific Railroad or the Credit Mobilier Company. If his attitude toward the Credit Mobilier Company had been known, it is not impossible that his connection as an officer of the Union Pacific Railroad would have helped rather than injured his canvass. The following memorandum found among his papers, which is confirmed by Henry McFarland, of Concord, then his assistant in the treasury of the Union Pacific Railroad and afterwards his successor in that office, shows that, if his advice had been followed, this great scandal would have been avoided. Mr. McFarland was present when the protest was made by Rollins against the use of a certain note by the Credit Mobilier Company.

" MEMORANDUM

" Mr. Rollins has always said that the note purporting to be that of the Union Pacific Railroad Company to the Credit Mobilier of America, for two million dollars, was given without the authority of the corporation, and without consideration; that it was made and put into the hands of a trustee to be held merely as a sort of indemnity to protect the signers of a certain bond, which bond was given to a Pennsylvania court, to secure the payment of such sum as the court might find to be due in a suit for income tax brought in said court; and that when (after all possibility of liability on said bond had been escaped, the bond itself having been surrendered and cancelled) the said note was finally delivered to the agents of the Credit Mobilier in his presence, he, as representing the Union Pacific Railroad Company, made a most emphatic and vigorous verbal protest against such delivery."

Rollins's connection with the Union Pacific Railroad led to the charges that this road helped the Republicans with contributions of money. This was believed not only by Democrats but even by some Republicans. One prominent Republican of Concord thought he had proof positive of this in the campaign of 1872, and perhaps he still believes the evidence of his eyesight. Rollins, as treasurer of the Union Pacific Railroad, had many checks to sign in payment of the bills of that corporation. Henry McFarland, of Concord, was his confidential clerk at that time. Rollins was at the Republican headquarters during the campaign. It was, therefore, the practice of McFarland to prepare the company's checks and send the check-book to Concord for Rollins's signatures thereto. One day Rollins was busy at headquarters signing these checks when this Republican happened in. His eyes lighted upon the check-book bearing the imprint of the Union Pacific Railroad. He smiled significantly to himself, but asked no questions. After some general conversation he left. That evening he confidentially told a friend that the campaign was all right and the Republicans would win, for the Union Pacific Railroad had given Rollins *carte blanche* to draw on the company's treasury for funds, and he had seen Rollins signing the checks.

That Rollins was disappointed at the outcome of the Senatorial caucus is not to be denied. His service in Congress at a critical time in the history of the party and the country had been most creditable to himself, and his work in the Republican organization in winning victories justified him in feeling that his elevation to the Senate would be a proper recognition of that service and work. In writing immediately after his defeat, he said to his friend, C. W. Rand, of Littleton:

"A partial victory was achieved in the establishment of the doctrine of rotation. Wadleigh is a man of undoubted ability and a good fellow. His election, I think, is generally satisfactory, although it seems to many working men of the party as somewhat unjust. I am bound, however, to accept the result in a proper spirit, for I feel that, if a mistake has been made, it is not my fault. I have done my duty faithfully for seventeen years in the party and have no apologies to make. On the contrary, I feel proud of my Republican record. It may be that I am altogether mistaken in my view, but I honestly think that the men who do the work in the party should receive better treatment than is often given to them."

This letter bears the date of June 25, 1872. In this same spirit he wrote to other friends. It is not improbable that he had at this time a disposition to withdraw from political life, for, in writing under date of July 23d, to Samuel Upton, of Manchester, who had been his supporter, he says:

"I hardly know yet what I can do in connection with the coming campaign. I have taken upon myself additional duties in railroad matters, and it may be impossible for me to devote very much time to the work. I suppose we shall have a meeting of the committee very soon, and I hope by that time to have additional light upon the subject. With proper effort,

I think we can carry our State, but there is some work to be done."

Yet three days later, his interest is quickened, if it ever flagged for a moment, for he writes as follows to William E. Chandler, who was then secretary of the national committee, concerning the coming Presidential election:

"I hope you have made sure of North Carolina. If you have not, the prospects are very dubious. Things are not very prosperous in New Hampshire. There are a good many men who are talking Greeley, but the right turn of affairs in North Carolina would save them. When you have taken care of North Carolina, then concentrate all your energies on Maine and give us a big majority there."

In a letter to John Kimball, of Concord, written while the Senatorial campaign was pending, Rollins had said: "I probably shall not trouble my friends much more politically, as I shall not again be a candidate for office, and I hope a hearty effort will be made for me, especially by my neighbors in Concord, at this time."

This thought of retiring from political activity in case of defeat was strengthened by the additional duties imposed upon him as treasurer of the Union Pacific Railroad. He felt that he could now resign the chairmanship of the State committee with credit to himself and without detriment to the party. Under his leadership the Republicans had won a signal victory and were again in full control of the State. The State had been lost in 1871 because of his enforced absence. It had been redeemed in 1872 under his direction of the political forces. If his leadership had provoked the jealousies and enmities of other prominent Republicans, he would now eliminate them by his retirement. It is quite certain that he thought that his political aspirations were at an end, and that his efforts hereafter would be directed mainly to a business career, for which he had both the taste and the talent. He took his defeat for the Senatorship philosophically and without personal animosity toward any one. Three times he had tried for the Senatorial nomination and failed. Now four years would elapse before another Senatorial vacancy would naturally occur.

None knew better than Rollins how likely new issues are to bring new men into prominence. He would, therefore, remove himself from a position which for years had brought him constant labor even to the exclusion of his personal affairs, and, if his services were needed, give such time as he could to politics and take such recognition as naturally came to him.

CHAPTER XVI.

HAVING reached the conclusion to resign as chairman of the State committee, Rollins called the committee together August 7, 1872, that his resignation might be acted upon and early opportunity given for the choice of his successor and the organization of the party for the approaching campaign. At this meeting Rollins, addressing the committee, said:

"On account of pressing business duties which have arisen since my election as chairman of the committee in January last, and which I could not have foreseen upon the acceptance of the position, but which will prevent me from giving that time and attention to the work of the Presidential campaign which its importance demands, I am compelled to ask you to accept my resignation, so often tendered, as your chairman.

"While doing this I am happy to congratulate the committee upon the union and harmony which prevail in the Republican party throughout the State. Our overwhelming victory in March last, and the united front which we now present to the enemy, whom we have fought and defeated in twenty campaigns, render certain a complete triumph in November over the mongrel force marshalled under the leadership of Greeley and Brown, and the emphatic endorsement by the Granite State of President Grant and that self-made son of New Hampshire, Henry Wilson.

"To such a consummation I shall, in common with you as my associate members of the committee, look forward with profound satisfaction, believing it to be the only result which can assure peace and prosperity to the country."

His resignation was accepted, and Orrin C. Moore, of Nashua, was elected to fill the vacancy. The *Manchester Mirror* in its account of the meeting says: "Mr. Rollins had no sooner resumed his seat than member after member arose to bear testimony to the impartial, faithful, and efficient manner in which he had discharged his various duties as chairman of the committee. His reward is the confidence of the party, and the evidence of his noble work is the record of the brilliant victories that, with the exception of a single year, illumine our political history from 1855 to the present time. Mr. Rollins's resignation was then accepted, and resolutions embodying the above were presented by Austin F. Pike, and unanimously adopted."

The *Statesman* said: "E. H. Rollins, renewing his pledge of devotion to the interests of the party, said that his business relations would not permit him to attend to the duties of the chairmanship during the campaign, for which reason alone he tendered his resignation. The expressions of admiration and thankfulness for the service rendered by Mr. Rollins in this difficult position were so spontaneous, so profuse, and so hearty that any man might justly be proud of them. All the more may Mr. Rollins be proud because the tangible results of his work show so plainly that the praise bestowed upon it is richly deserved."

The Democratic *People,* commenting upon Rollins's resignation, said: "We know nothing of what Mr. Rollins's purposes are, and do not in any way desire to misrepresent him, but we do know that as an organizer and manager of a campaign his equal cannot be found. To him the party is indebted for whatever victories it has won in the last ten years."

Rollins's apparent optimism on the political situation was not shared by Republicans generally. There was a feeling of doubt as to the result of the Presidential election. The *Statesman* of August 8th, the day after Rollins resigned as chairman, in an editorial on "What of New Hampshire," said:

"Whenever and wherever one meets a Republican or a Democrat from any State, almost the first question is: 'Well, what of New Hampshire; is she for Grant or for Greeley?' And strange as it may seem, the answer is not uniformly in one direction. The friends of Greeley claim the State very confidently, and the friends of General Grant do not all and always claim it with the same confidence. There is no use in disguising or denying the fact which must be patent to nearly everybody that there is thus far on the part of many Republicans a lack of enthusiasm for General Grant which accounts for the confidence of his opponents and the doubts of his friends. As little use is there in denying that there are in every county of the State, and perhaps in a majority of the towns, a few Republicans who incline to vote for Greeley and would be greatly in danger of doing so were the voting to be done at this time."

This view was soon brought home to Rollins in letters from active Republicans of the State telling of defections which became more pronounced because of his resignation of the chairmanship of the committee. Among Rollins's admirers at that time was Charles B. Gafney, of Rochester. He was a young lawyer of influence in that section of the State, a sagacious politician, and untiring worker. He had a charming personality, which, united to a ready wit, made him many friends. He continued until his death a potential force in New Hampshire politics. He was disappointed at Rollins's defeat for Senator both on account of his personal attachment to him and because the choice for Senator gave no recognition of those whose work had kept the State Republican. He was not present at the State committee meeting. Rollins, however, wrote him immediately after, to which letter he replied under date of August 12th, as follows:

" MY DEAR ROLLINS: — Your letter of this morning is at hand and contents noted. You have finally concluded to do something for yourself and I am pleased. Hall [Daniel] missed the train on the evening of your meeting. We have sacrificed good men enough in our political warfare of the past few years, and under the present generalship I propose to bushwhack for Greeley. Last year we carried this town and several others for the Republican party by your aid, and this campaign they must go the other way. North Carolina has spoken and her words can give no consolation to the followers of Grant. You have been a devoted Republican for years and we have all been proud of you as a leader. . . . If Dan [Hall] had been running the campaign, out of respect and regard for the chairman, many of us would have remained, but now our way is clear. Shall call on you when in Boston, and you can say to friend Moore [Orrin C.] that I will show him Greeley men in the Republican ranks of this district sufficient to carry the State Democratic."

The tenor of this letter was a surprise to Rollins because it gave a different impression of his resignation than he intended. He found that he must by personal work with his friends correct this misunderstanding. He immediately wrote to Gafney urging him to take no step until he saw him. In subsequent correspondence and by personal appeals, he implored him to stand by the party. His efforts were successful and Gafney not only did not come out for Greeley, but prevented not a few of his friends from so doing.

Soon after a report appeared in the *New York Tribune* that Rollins had declared for Greeley. This was immediately corrected by him, and from this time forward he was at work with his old-time vigor to make

New Hampshire sure for Grant. He was in active coöperation with the new chairman, Orrin C. Moore, as the following letter shows:

"MY DEAR ROLLINS:—Was pleased to hear from you, though I have written Blaine about speakers, including himself. Have also written Dawes and Conkling. We have sent out blanks for a thorough organization, and also to obtain names of leading Republicans and anti-Greeley Democrats. When we get these, we shall dose them with doses specially prepared for them. The meeting must be a success all around.

"What you are doing is just what every live and hearty man should be doing, but I expect few appreciate the situation as you do. Here in Nashua and vicinity things look first-rate. I could not ask for them to look better. Write me often and keep pegging away."

In a letter to Gen. Horace Porter, President Grant's private secretary, Rollins wrote: "I regret that I was obliged to resign the chairmanship of the Republican State committee of New Hampshire on account of pressing business engagements, but I shall still be in the position to be of much service to the cause. I shall render it all the aid in my power. I never felt a stronger inclination to make a hard fight for the cause than now, for it seems to me the best interests of the country require the defeat of this mongrel crew.

"The papers report Senator Wilson as giving up

our State to the enemy. I have not seen him and am not sure that the report is true. It seems to me that, notwithstanding the defection of Senatorial aspirants, we can still carry the State if a proper amount of work is done. Tappan will not carry anybody with him of consequence. Patterson probably will not go over to the enemy because they will not accept him on his terms, while most of the other Senatorial aspirants will either coldly support President Grant or do nothing.

"I returned from New Hampshire this A. M. I am glad to see that Senator Chandler [Zachariah] is to speak there. Our people are decidedly more hopeful, and, in fact, I think the tide is turned and moving in the right direction. If our Pennsylvania troubles are only settled — and W. E. Chandler writes me hopefully about things there — I shall feel that the President's reëlection is certain. Hoping to hear from you when convenient, and trusting for a Grant triumph, I remain," etc.

To this letter General Porter replied: "I was very glad to receive your letter of the 22d ultimo. The manly course pursued by you after the result of the Senatorial fight has won the admiration of all your friends and the respect of your enemies. I hope you will continue to keep your shoulder to the wheel until November. Should the Republicans make New Hampshire and Connecticut sure, we may count upon the whole of New England. I hope the report is not true that Mr. Wilson at any time gave up your State. He certainly will not after the news from Mane."

Viewed solely from the election returns in November, it is difficult to see wherein the Republicans of New Hampshire had cause for apprehension of the result in their State. These figures show nearly six thousand majority for Grant, while Governor Straw had only about twelve hundred majority at the spring election. But the figures tell only the result and not the work which brought about that result. For several months after Greeley's nomination by the Liberal Republicans and endorsement by the Democratic party, there was uncertainty of the extent of Republican disaffection in New Hampshire. Besides Mason W. Tappan, several other well-known Republicans of the State declared for Greeley. Among these was Henry O. Kent, of Lancaster, who had been active in politics since the birth of the Republican party. He had owned and edited a Republican newspaper in Coos County, and had fought the Republican battles in this then Democratic stronghold with courage and persistency under adverse circumstances. He suffered the fate of many another leader who takes upon himself the brunt of the battle in seeing less active and oftentimes less worthy men preferred in the distribution of popular honors. If he chafed under this yoke, the issue presented by the Liberal Republican movement gave him an opportunity, which he early improved, to cut loose from the Republican party. He was warmly welcomed by the Democrats and was afterward their nominee for Congress and governor. During Cleveland's first administration he was appointed naval officer at the port of Boston. During Cleveland's second administration he was offered the position of Assistant Secretary of War, which he was obliged to decline for business and family reasons.

Besides those who actually declared for Greeley, there were a number of Republicans who were at first inclined to support him. Some joined Greeley clubs and afterward withdrew. Others in conversation indicated an inclination to favor Greeley, while, as the *Statesman* said in the article above quoted, there was "a lack of enthusiasm for General Grant which accounts for the confidence of his opponents and the doubts of his friends." To solve these doubts a large amount of personal work was performed by Rollins and other members of the State committee through his direction. The Maine election gave the Republicans much courage, but it was not until the October elections had shown Grant's reëlection to be certain that apprehension as to the Greeley movement in New Hampshire subsided or the extent of Democratic disgust at Greeley's nomination was known. The open campaign was short. Very little speaking occurred. The early returns election night of November, 1872, foreshadowed the result both in State and nation. For a few weeks the political parties in New Hampshire rested on their arms preparatory to the approaching State campaign of 1873.

In the winter of 1872-3, the Union Pacific Railroad was under investigation by Congress. This investigation related to the Credit Mobilier Company of America, to which reference has already been made. Rollins had no connection with this company and was not even a stockholder in the Union Pacific Railroad. As treasurer of that railroad, he was examined as a witness and testified before the committee at Washington and before a sub-committee that visited Boston to further examine the books and accounts of the company. The investigation in no way involved Rollins directly or indirectly with the proceedings which cut short the public career of several distinguished men, but it did occupy his time so that he could give but little attention to politics. His testimony before the committee is thus epitomized in the *Monitor* of February 7, 1873:

"In regard to his employment by the company in Washington, while its secretary and treasurer, Rollins said that he never asked an officer of the government, a member of the Senate or House of Representatives, to do for the company what he would not have done himself had he occupied their positions. He never knew of any money of the company that was expended for political purposes. He furthermore said that he himself never received a dollar from the company which was not earned by hard labor, and that never to his knowledge had a dollar been expended for political purposes since he became treasurer."

The spring campaign opened in New Hampshire in midwinter with the nomination of four candidates for governor. The Republicans renominated Governor Straw, and the Democrats James A. Weston. The

Liberal Republicans, who had coalesced with the Democrats the fall before in a joint electoral ticket, presented, as their candidate for governor, Samuel K. Mason, of Bristol, and nominated candidates for Congress in each of the three districts, endorsing the Democratic candidate in the first district. About fifty people were present at their convention, including Mason W. Tappan, Henry O. Kent, Willard A. Heard, of Sandwich, John H. Goodale, then of Nashua, and Lemuel P. Cooper, of Croydon, the last two being of the late Labor Reform party. Kent was made chairman of their State committee, Goodale secretary, and John Foss, of Concord, treasurer. The Prohibition party, which for two campaigns had polled an inconsequential vote, took on new life in this canvass. Their nominee for governor was John Blackmer, of Sandwich.

In all the Republican Congressional conventions, there was active rivalry for the nomination. In the first district, William B. Small, who was a defeated candidate in 1871, was renominated after a spirited contest. In the second district, Aaron F. Stevens declined to be again a candidate, and Austin F. Pike, of Franklin, was nominated. In the third district, Simon G. Griffin, of Keene, secured a renomination, although meeting with strenuous opposition. In the result of all these conventions Rollins took a deep interest. Mr. Small and Mr. Pike had been his staunch supporters, and his activity in favor of both was apparent. In the third district, rumor of an attempt to bring forward as a candidate Senator Patterson, whose term as Senator expired March 4th, caused Rollins to write some vigorous letters of protest to his friends in that district. The Congressional investigation of the Credit Mobilier Company had involved Senator Patterson, and his nomination for Congress would have made that transaction a direct issue of the campaign. Whatever foundation there may have been for the report, Senator Patterson's candidacy did not materialize.

The Democrats renominated their candidates for Congress in 1871, who comprised the New Hampshire delegation in the House at Washington, Ellery A. Hibbard, Samuel N. Bell, and Hosea W. Parker.

At the meeting of the Republican State committee, Orrin C. Moore, who had succeeded Rollins as chairman when the latter resigned, was reëlected. Benjamin F. Prescott was chosen secretary, and Carlos G. Pressey, of Concord, treasurer. Moore was the editor of the *Nashua Telegraph* and a young man coming into prominence through his editorial writings and his speeches upon the stump. He had none of those qualities which made Rollins successful as a campaign manager. His conception of a political campaign did not extend beyond the public demonstration in the press and upon the platform. He had little capacity for organization and no grasp of details. He was a man of strong convictions and strong prejudices. Opposition intensified his earnestness, but he was apt to look upon that opposition as personal to himself. He was a mere student of theories and unpractical in many things pertaining to politics and public life. He was a forceful speaker, a strong debater, and an able man. He lacked that spirit of conciliation so essential to leaders of men, and was entirely devoid of humor. The political honors he won were in recognition of his ability rather than his popularity. He served with distinction in both branches of the legislature, and was elected one term to Congress, where he made himself felt, although a new member. His defeat for reëlection at a time when the second district was close was due largely to troubles arising from the distribution of patronage, a part of his work which he cordially disliked and for which he had no aptitude. As a political writer, he had few equals, and, as a speaker upon the stump, his services were always in demand. Had his lot been cast in a State of strong Republican majorities, he would have attained a national reputation.

In this campaign, Jacob H. Gallinger and Henry M. Putney, who afterward became potential leaders of the Republican party, first appeared as members of the State committee.

The campaign of 1873 was quiet and uneventful. There was but little public speaking, and no one was heard from outside the State. In response to calls for his services, Rollins was invited by the State committee to speak, and agreed to do so if his assignments were made in such parts of the State as would enable him to return to his office daily. He questioned very much the advisability of his appearing on the stump in view of his connection with the Union Pacific Railroad, then under investigation. Writing Dr. T. E. Hatch, of Keene, under date of February 17th, he said:

" There is a good deal of work to be done in our State to make everything safe, in my judgment. I have just received a telegram from Griffin asking me to speak at Whitefield and Lancaster on the 27th and 28th. They are so far away that I cannot possibly spend the time. I must speak, if at all, at points easy of access from Boston. I suppose if I undertake to speak, everybody will be thinking about Credit Mobilier and the Union Pacific Railroad, and it may be questionable if I can do much good. I shall make no defence of the Credit Mobilier, but shall stand by the Union Pacific Railroad as a Republican measure. Talk this matter over with Griffin and see what he thinks about it. Situated as I am, I cannot escape discussing this matter on the stump."

While Rollins did not speak in the campaign, his interest in the work continued unabated. February 25th he wrote to Chairman Moore as follows: " Your article in a recent issue, on the ' State Tax,' is a capital one. I see that it is copied into the *Monitor,* and I hope it will be published in every Republican paper in the State. The Democrats should be charged with repudiation, and their shortcomings, in this regard, kept before the people. No doubt you are looking after the close towns, for they are the key to the situation. We never fail to carry the State when these are secured."

The chairman of the Democratic State committee was George F. Putnam, of Warren, who conducted the

campaign with more method than some of his predecessors. He had been a member of the legislature,
where he obtained prominence by his knowledge of
parliamentary practice, and his skill in debate. He
was a lawyer, a pleasing speaker, and a man of large
executive ability. Later he aspired to the nomination
for Congress, but was beaten in the Democratic convention by Henry O. Kent. Soon after this he removed
to Kansas City, Missouri, where the remainder of his
life was spent in business pursuits.

Affairs at Washington favored the Democratic party.
The Credit Mobilier investigation involved a large
number of prominent Republican leaders in Congress
and only a few Democrats. The report of the investigating committee, while it exonerated several, reproved
some for indiscreet action, and strongly censured others.
This investigation had been conducted by a committee
of the House of Representatives. No defence could be
made of the Credit Mobilier Company, and the Republicans attempted none. More members of their
party were involved than Democrats, and, being the
party in power, and the Union Pacific Railroad having
been aided by the government, the Republicans had
to bear the odium of the Credit Mobilier scandal of
bribery and illegal profits.

In addition to the Credit Mobilier scandal, a bill
was passed by Congress increasing the salary of the
President, the Vice-President, members of the Cabinet,
Supreme Court judges, Senators, and members of Congress. The bill was known as "the salary grab," be-

cause the increase in
men dared back to
members. The
Ham
afte
a
mea
pre
ver
Ha

"I most heartily congratulate you on your election to the House of Representatives. You had a hard fight and have come off victorious, much to your credit. You had to fight your own fight and I only regret it was not in my power to render you more assistance. I fully appreciate your complimentary remarks concerning myself, and feel grateful for your assurances of consideration hereafter. I shall not hesitate to call upon you whenever I think you can aid a friend or advance the cause. When in Boston, please call and see me and we will talk over the fight. Something should be done at an early date looking to the future of our party in the State. In its present demoralized condition it needs looking after. We must put our best foot forward to secure success."

Although holding no official position in the party, Rollins continued to be consulted on matters of party policy and to be appealed to for assistance by candidates for office.

He never forgot a promise to help a friend, and the persistency with which he urged an appointment gave no peace to the appointing power. In one instance, that of a railway mail appointment, there is continued evidence in his letter-books running through more than two years that he had the applicant constantly in mind. A failure on the part of any one to keep a political promise always roused his indignation, and, whether it was a Cabinet officer or a bureau chief who was the offender, he did not hesitate to remind him that such a promise should be as sacred as a business obligation. This persistency in anything he undertook brought to Rollins many applications for counsel and help from ambitious men within the party, although he held no official position to support his recommendations. Appeals were also made to him for advice whenever there was local political trouble in the State, to which he always responded urging patience, forbearance, and the harmonizing of differences.

Although Rollins secured in his time many positions under the government for young men, for the civil service law was not passed until 1883, he was very much opposed to a young man of character taking one of these places, especially if it were in the departmental service at Washington. His first reply to an applicant was usually a lecture to the young man, in which he assured him that he was better off in a position at home even if it were not so lucrative. In some instances his advice was heeded. In 1871 Henry M. Baker, of Bow, who was then in the Treasury Department, applied to Rollins for assistance in securing a promotion. The letter of reply is characteristic of Rollins.

"My dear misguided Friend: — I have yours of the 10th inst. before me, and note your remarks with reference to the vacancy in the office of commissioner of customs. Agreeably to your request, and to gratify you, though contrary to my best judgment, I enclose you herewith a letter of recommendation to Secretary Boutwell. If you have your heart set upon it, I am willing and perhaps desirous that you should succeed, although I am firmly of the opinion that it will be a calamity to you. I have so much regard for you and for your success in life that, did I not suppose you had considerable feeling in the matter, I should write to Boutwell and urge him to remove you from office at once. What a great blessing it would be if he would kick you out of the Treasury Department before the sun sets! If you will remain where you are you may safely calculate the road to ruin lies wide open before you, and you are bound to pursue it to the end. I hope you will change your views, and turn yourself out into the world. There is enough of you to make a man, but I am very much afraid that we shall never have the evidence of it if you remain where you are."

A little later Baker followed Rollins's advice and resigned to practice his profession of law at Washington. Keeping in close touch with New Hampshire he engaged actively in politics, becoming a prominent political factor in the State. He was elected to the States Senate and afterward a member of Congress for two terms. In 1901 he was a candidate for the United States Senate with considerable support.

CHAPTER XVII.

A DEMOCRATIC TRIUMPH

THE organization of the Grange or "Patrons of Husbandry" in New Hampshire was not without its influence on political parties of the State during this and the succeeding campaign. Politicians expected the Grange to become ultimately a factor in politics, and the leaders of both sides catered for the support of the farmer vote. Long before the conventions the *Manchester Mirror* urged the nomination of a farmer for governor by the Republicans. Governor Straw had had the customary two terms. A new candidate was now to be brought forward by the Republican party. Those most prominently mentioned were Luther McCutchins, of New London, Charles H. Bell, of Exeter, Dexter Richards, of Newport, Benjamin F. Prescott, of Epping, William H. Y. Hackett, of Portsmouth, Natt Head, of Hooksett, David A. Warde, of Concord, Benjamin J. Cole, of Gilford, and Larkin D. Mason, of Tamworth. McCutchins was favored because he was a farmer, the others because they had been active in the party and were worthy of recognition. Mason was especially urged by some because it was thought his activity in behalf of temperance would hold the Prohibition Republicans loyally to the party standard.

The Pearson wing of the Democratic party, whose platform continued to be anti-monopoly, advocated the nomination of a farmer for governor. This brought forward as a candidate Hiram R. Roberts, of Rollinsford.

The Republican State committee met November 20, 1873, to fix the times and places for holding the several conventions. There was a large attendance at the meeting. After the routine work, speeches were made by Rollins, Harriman, and Wadleigh. The *Monitor* said of the meeting:

"Much enthusiasm was manifested and, when Rollins laid down the proposition that something must be done to relieve the country of its burdens and that our Congressional delegation must help repeal the obnoxious salary grab, the applause was loud and prolonged. His suggestion also that the amount of the deficiency complained of by the internal revenue commissioner in his report might better be obtained by reorganizing our banking system and saving the interest than by a tax on tea and coffee, as suggested by the commissioner, seemed also to touch a responsive chord. The assertion with which Mr. Rollins closed, viz., that the best way to succeed in the coming campaign is to let the office seek the man, met with unmistakable approbation."

The Republican convention was held at Concord, January 7, 1874. Rollins was absent in New York on railroad business, but he wrote Daniel Hall making suggestions as to the platform to be adopted by the convention. The resolutions reported by the committee were accepted without debate in the convention, but they were the subject of much discussion and contention in the committee. Rollins's suggestions were not adopted, and there was some apprehension on his part and the part of other leaders that the platform was not as skilfully drawn as it might have been. There were four ballots for governor, a large number of candidates receiving votes on the first ballot, those leading being Luther McCutchins and Charles H. Bell. The former won on the fourth ballot. It was generally regarded by the party as a good nomination, though not a few of the leaders had doubts of its wisdom. These doubts were strengthened when the Democratic convention selected its candidates and presented its platform.

The Democratic State convention was held the next day, January 8th. The Democratic newspapers had advocated making an issue of the liquor question, and in the Democratic platform a plank was inserted favoring license with local option. The contest for the nomination for governor was between Albert R. Hatch, of Portsmouth, Hiram R. Roberts, of Rollinsford, and James A. Weston, of Manchester. The movement in favor of " Farmer " Roberts had gained such headway that the Democratic leaders who were opposed to his nomination had great difficulty in controlling the convention. Two ballots were necessary to effect a choice. On the first ballot Weston received 240 votes, Roberts

230, and Hatch 143. On the second ballot the greater part of Hatch's support was transferred to Weston, who became the nominee.

The Prohibitionists had previously renominated the Rev. John Blackmer, of Sandwich. After the Republican and Democratic conventions were held, the third party adherents were stirred to greater activity. The Republican plank on the liquor question was regarded by them as perfunctory, while the Democrats were arrayed in open opposition to the prohibitory law. The Prohibitionists, therefore, hoped so to increase their strength as to hold the balance of power in the State.

The Republican State committee met for organization January 16th. The *Monitor* in its report of the meeting says: " The chairman, O. C. Moore, of Nashua, called the meeting to order, stated its objects, the first being the election of a chairman, and then called for an expression of opinion by ballot, indicating a cheerful readiness to yield up the chairmanship if it was thought best to make a change. Two ballots were taken without a choice, Mr. Moore leading and Daniel Hall, of Dover, being next in order. On the third ballot Mr. Hall was elected. Benjamin F. Prescott was reëlected secretary and Charles H. Roberts, of Concord, was chosen treasurer. An executive committee consisting of David A. Warde, of Concord, and James A. Wood, of Acworth, was then elected to coöperate with the chairman. Brief but earnest speeches were made by Warde, of Concord, Clarke [John B.], of Manchester, Rollins, of Concord, and J. Horace Kent, of Portsmouth."

Hall reluctantly accepted the chairmanship. The margin of victory the year before had been very narrow, a little more than two hundred majority on the popular vote for governor. The action of the Democrats in thrusting the liquor question into the canvass added to the uncertainty. Realizing that it was to be a doubtful campaign, urgent appeals had been made to both Rollins and Chandler to accept an election to the chairmanship of the committee. In a letter to Rollins January 14th, Congressman Pike said: "Friend Rollins: — You must run the campaign this year or we are gone 'where the woodbine twineth.' Now make up your mind to take it, and wade in."

On the same day Chandler wrote Rollins: "I have an urgent appeal signed by Henry M. Putney, James A. Wood, Cyrus A. Sulloway, and Henry French to come home and act as chairman of the committee. I wish I could go, but do not see how it could be possible even if I were unanimously elected."

The Democrats reëlected George F. Putnam, of Warren, as chairman of their committee, and entered upon the campaign with a spirit of confidence. There were very few political rallies on either side, the Democrats conducting a "still hunt" canvass. A momentary gleam of encouragement came to the Republicans from the bolt of the Democratic nominee for governor by *Foster's Democrat,* a Democratic newspaper in Dover. This newspaper claimed that the party had been betrayed by its leaders in preferring Weston to Roberts as a candidate, and that corporation influence controlled the Democratic party. Roberts, however, came out in a letter endorsing Weston's nomination, and but few Democrats were influenced by the attitude of Foster's paper.

Rollins, in response to Chairman Hall's appeal, wrote from his office in Boston many letters to active Republicans of the State urging activity and the necessity for united effort if the election was to be carried. In the midst of this campaign Congressman Dawes, of Massachusetts, chairman of the appropriations committee, made a speech in Congress similar to the one he made in 1870, which was considered by the Democrats as an attack upon the national administration for its extravagance in appropriations and expenditures. Like his former speech, it was spread broadcast over the State by the Democratic State committee. Rollins was applied to to secure Dawes's services upon the stump. He communicated with Chandler in Washington, but they were unable to get Dawes to speak. Then he telegraphed Dawes as follows:

" The Republicans of New Hampshire unanimously favor rigid economy and sustain the administration of President Grant. Your late speeches have been construed by copperheads, soreheads, and pretended labor reformers into attacks upon the administration and the Republican party, and they say you will refuse to speak for the Republican cause in New Hampshire. Being as sure of your devotion to the Republican party and to the national administration as we are of your determination to reduce appropriations and enforce economy, in behalf of the Republican State committee I have to earnestly request you to visit and canvass New Hampshire before the March election."

Dawes telegraphed this reply: "I regret that my engagements make it impossible for me to speak in New Hampshire before election for a cause never more worthy of support, and never dearer to me than now — retrenchment and reform by and through the Republican party."

As the despatch bore date of Dawes's home in Pittsfield, Mass., the Democrats construed it as an unwillingness on his part to appear in the State and explain the charges he had made against the administration.

The following letter to Rollins from Henry W. Blair, afterward member of Congress and United States Senator, shows the political situation in the State, the dangers to Republican success, and the faith of the party workers in Rollins's ability to bring victory out of defeat.

"The prospect in our vicinity is rather mixed — the general result, I think, cannot be any better than last year. The Prohibition party and the license movement both hurt us, and it will be almost impossible to avoid losses upon State and county, and I fear for one or two Representatives also. Still we shall do the best that can be done. Our standard workers are in the field, and, realizing the danger, will do the best to avert it.

"You make a suggestion as to my personal duty if I expect a certain result. That result I do not seriously expect in any event, although I should be gratified if considered fit for the position and nominated by the general and unsolicited preference of the party, but in these times the prevalence of new ideas and the class prejudices which are being appealed to, and in some sections of the country at least aroused, will be very likely to lay one of my profession upon the shelf, certainly for the present. This, however, is not important, for the State will be perhaps better served by some hard-fisted farmer — although they won't get a man who knows more of the sorrows of the toughest sort of hill-farm husbandry than I did until my twenty-first year. I hope you will not spare your pen during this campaign. Your very extensive acquaintance throughout the State with the working element of the party will enable you to work most effectively in furtherance of our cause. There cannot be a single town where you may not save and perhaps make us votes by a word in season to the right person."

February 24th Rollins wrote Chandler as follows: "I am writing into the State all the letters possible, and have a large correspondence. Our people are being gradually worked up to the importance of the election, but 'free rum' on one side and the ultra temperance men on the other, both fighting the Republicans and playing directly into the hands of the enemy, make the situation critical. However, I hope we shall worry through."

A letter from Ithiel E. Clay, of Chatham, in reply
to one received from Rollins is indicative of the confidence the party had in his management: " It seems
like old times in politics to hear from you, although
I had supposed you were lost to New Hampshire politically. As to our town, we hope to come out all right.
Still many of our men are lukewarm and seem indifferent as to the result of the election. Those moves
at Washington one year ago staggered many of our
thinking laboring men to such a degree that it is difficult to make them believe that our rulers care for
their country as they should. I have never known the
Democrats to be more active in this town than now. I
never have had but small personal acquaintance with
you, but I have received so many communications and
favors from you that you seem like an old friend with
whom I have struggled for principles and success of
which we may well be proud. The Republicans of
New Hampshire are much indebted to you for their
past achievements, and I always shall be glad to hear
from you and hope ever to keep track of you while life
lasts. I hope when you get the returns from Chatham
they will be all right, as well as those from New Hampshire."

The election returns from the earliest reports bore
indications of Democratic victory, and before midnight of the day of the election the Republicans had
given up the State. There was no choice of governor
by the people, the Prohibitionists doubling their vote
of the year previous. The House of Representatives,

upon which depended the control of the State, was Democratic by at least ten majority. The official vote was: Scattering, 40; Blackmer, 2,100; McGutchins, 34,143; Weston, 35,608.

Immediately after election Chairman Hall wrote Rollins: "It seems that we have lost everything — governor, Council, Senate, and House. I cannot express my mortification at this result. If I had had no responsibility beyond that of an ordinary Republican fighting in the ranks I should not feel very badly about it. But the fortunes of the party and of its individual members in office and hoping for office, they will say, go down under my mismanagement, and, of course, I shall never be forgiven. No general is ever forgiven for losing a battle. This is hard to bear, and is about as much as I can bear."

To this Rollins replied: "Yours of the 13th is just at hand. I intended to have written you before, but this has been an exceedingly busy week with me. Annual meeting, directors' meetings, and signing of bonds, with the usual business of the office, have left me no time for private correspondence.

"I feel exceedingly mortified myself, in view of the result in New Hampshire, although in looking back over the past, I do not see anything that I could have done to have changed the result. I have acted each day according to the light I had, and I have nothing to reproach myself with; and what I say of my own conduct, I feel to be equally true of your own.

"You have no occasion to reproach yourself in any

respect. I can bear willing testimony to your earnest efforts for the cause, and think you have labored discreetly and with great ability. The Republicans of New Hampshire owe you a debt of gratitude for the determined efforts you have made to save the State. It doesn't matter what a few disappointed men say. I know, and all must know who have had any opportunity to form a correct opinion, that you have done everything it was in your power to do, even to the sacrifice of your business and personal comfort.

"I am very anxious indeed to see you, and look over the field and see if there is anything that can be done for the cause. We must keep our standard well advanced and continue the fight. We cannot lug Sanborn contracts and this infernal moiety system without suffering."

The *Monitor* in summing up the causes of Republican defeat said: "We charge the repulse we have suffered to the shortcomings, unavoidable in part there is no doubt, of the national government. We were too heavily handicapped with Sanborn contracts, Jayne and Bingham blackmailings, Western inflation schemes, the moiety system, and the failure of Congress to meet the wants of the masses by legislation demanded by the hard times. . . . To be sure, the course of the Prohibitionists in running a third ticket has worked to our injury, but this alone could not have prevented the election of McCutchins."

The *Manchester Mirror,* while admitting that these national issues were not without their influence, attributed defeat to the liquor interests, which it charged with supporting the Democratic party and supplying it with funds.

Whatever the cause that led to Democratic success, the completeness of their triumph was admitted. For the first time in twenty years that party was to be put in full possession of the State government. Moreover, by reorganizing the courts, they would control as well the State judiciary. They could legislate Republicans out of office, appoint Democrats in their places, redistrict the State for Councillors and Senators, change the ward lines of cities, take the initiative in legislation, and avail themselves of every opportunity to fortify their party in power. The outlook for the Republican party in New Hampshire was the most gloomy it had ever been.

Among the steadfast Republicans of the State whom Rollins always relied upon for effective work was Larkin D. Mason, of Tamworth, for many years judge of probate of Carroll County. He was a quaint character. An early abolitionist, a prominent temperance worker, and an agent of the State during the Civil War to look after the soldiers, he had a strong personal influence with these elements of the party. Although he was not an educated man, his fund of common sense and his odd illustrations gave force and pungency to his speeches and writings. He was in constant correspondence with Rollins, and some of his letters are quite frank and amusing. In 1872, replying to Rollins's request for his support for Senator, he said:

"I don't know just when I shall go to Boston or see you. I remain the same 'Senatorially' as formerly. I am quiet. I don't have great advantages of late to associate with the Republican party. A mysterious Providence interposes. There has not been an important meeting of the State committee for a long while but has been on the day of probate court in Carroll County. Don't understand me to complain of Providence. Its ways are mysterious. I have a neighbor who is very jealous of me. When we are before the people, I always win. So his remedy is to have communion with his God and get him to interpose a special Providence. As he is a man of prayer, Providence grants his request and I am not in the ring. I have got the hang of Providence so that I am able to foretell months beforehand when all our conventions will come off. Natt Hubbard will bear me witness that I told him as soon as last March that our convention to choose delegates to the Philadelphia convention would come off May 8th. I will now tell you when our next State convention will occur. It will be the anniversary of the Battle of New Orleans, January 8th. The probate court will be held at Conway on the 7th, so of course I cannot meet with the State committee if invited, and you must excuse me. I hope you will see in this what advantages Providence gives the humble Christian who is a man of prayer, and, as this old friend will not fail to plead, I prepare myself to submit to Providence. I appreciate your past service and hope I will do you no injustice. I will make up my mind by and by what my duty is and then try and perform it. Still Providence shuts me out to prevent my doing mischief. Of course it will not require of me much good. I think I may see you ere this month is out, and I will compare notes with you."

In the campaign of 1874 the Prohibitionists polled the largest vote they had ever polled in the State. It was their defection which was one of the causes of the defeat of McCutchins. Their vote this year exceeded all their other totals by nearly a thousand. Orrin C. Moore in the *Nashua Telegraph,* prior to the Republican convention of 1874, in mentioning candidates for the gubernatorial nomination, had spoken most flatteringly of Larkin D. Mason, whose work among the ultra temperance Republicans of the State had been most effective in holding them in the Republican party. After the election, Mason felt that, if he could have been nominated for governor, the State would have been saved, and, in a letter to Rollins, he attributed his passing as a gubernatorial candidate to the influence of the " clique," namely, Rollins, Chandler, and Ordway. He also expressed the opinion that his nomination would have brought Fogg, Tappan, and other disaffected Republicans into more active support of the party. Neither discouraged nor wavering in his support of the Republican party, he frankly put the case to Rollins that his (Mason's) candidacy for governor in 1875 would bring back the disaffected and restore the party to power. He asked Rollins's advice, and this part of his letter is as follows:

"Now suppose we were just entering upon the new campaign, and suppose the *Nashua Telegraph* should present my name as it did last fall, and then suppose the 'clique' should get together, and, instead of 'cussin'' Moore for his treason, they should say let us try and rally the whole organization and should then let some of their more quiet ones succeed Moore. Then let some soldiers, who would delight to do it, start the ball. Let Fogg, Tappan, and Cogswell, and Gove, and Heard, and finally all that host among the masses who have perfect confidence in me, come into line. Then let the 'clique' or, if you choose, Ordway, Rollins, Harriman, Hall, and all their allies and supporters, quietly, firmly, sincerely, and determinedly put their science, skill, and activity into the campaign. What do you suppose would be the result? Of course, Rollins, you will readily see this is a kind of a feeler. I put it forth with the sincere belief that some such an arrangement promises the only hope of ever developing the full strength of the Republican party again. I do not necessarily feel that I must have any prominent place, but who is more competent? Something must be done first to recover our lost position, and this something must be a recall of all the exiled ones. Please write me, and do not despise the day of small things."

To this letter Rollins replied: "Yours of March 26th is received and has been perused with great care. In looking back over the history of the Republican party from its organization in New Hampshire to the

present moment I can see no reason why I should object to the term 'clique,' and to being reckoned a portion of the 'clique.' The past must stand, and results,
at least in my judgment, vindicate my political course
in New Hampshire.

"Now as to the gubernatorial nomination — I do
not know whom all the members of the 'clique' were
for. Ordway, I believe, was the only member present
at the convention, and he was for Natt White. I was
in New York and can hardly tell what I should have
done had I been present, but have no idea that I should
have supported the man who was nominated. Do not
think the 'clique' had anything to do with making the
nomination. I think it would have been better for the
party had they taken a hand in it and helped shape
things in a different direction. Had I been at the convention, I should have supported some worthy man who
in my judgment would get the most votes. Whether
it would have been Mason, Bell, or somebody else I
cannot tell.

"I notice what you say about Fogg, Tappan, and
others. Some time before the convention I had a talk
with these gentlemen, but did not learn from any of
them that they thought your nomination would be
stronger than that of almost any other Republican.
Tappan seemed always to be friendly to McCutchins,
and talked of him as his candidate. I do not think he
would have taken any more active part had you been
nominated. You speak of a meeting of the 'clique'
at Concord before the convention, attended by Moore,

Durkee, Harriman, Cheney, and others. I do not think any member of the 'clique' attended that meeting. I was not invited. I had heard that there was such a meeting, and, while I know that Mr. Moore did say something in his paper in favor of your nomination, I learned at the time that the judgment of this gathering of leaders was in favor of Prescott for governor. One of the gentlemen present told me it was perfectly evident that the design of the men in getting up this meeting was to shape things for Prescott's benefit. They did not mean Mason at all.

"I was raised an old-fashioned Congregationalist, and am rather inclined to believe in foreordination. In looking back over the past campaign, it rather strikes me that it was foreordained from the beginning that the devil would triumph for a time in New Hampshire in the shape of the free rum Democracy, and I do not think anything could have been done to set aside the decrees of the Almighty. It rather looks so to me now. It is possible that we have done something worthy of stripes and this is our punishment. As to the future, I want to see the State in the hands of an honest Republican party and am willing to do all in my power and to make any and all concessions consistent with principle that may be required. If the success of the good cause can be best secured by nominating the gentleman from Tamworth for governor, he can have my hearty support both before and after the convention, but it isn't worth while to look back and fight our old battles over again.

" What reason have you to believe that your nomination would ensure the active coöperation of the gentlemen you have named, particularly of Mr. Gove? He seems to have gone over into the Democratic camp. What assurance will he give? Heard has been elected by the Democrats. What will he do? I am in search of light and am earnestly seeking a way out of our present difficulties. If you can give us any, I will listen and follow. I shall be glad to hear from you at any time in regard to these matters."

Another correspondent of Rollins at this period, and for years after, was Alfred F. Howard, of Portsmouth, who was formerly collector of customs at New Hampshire's only seaport. Howard is a man of genial personality, clear judgment, and resourceful activity. Early interested in politics, he has never ceased to do his part in political campaigns. For quite a quarter of a century his influence has been felt in the councils of the Republican party of the State. Few men of New Hampshire have so large a circle of devoted friends, and few have had opportunity of declining so many political honors. From 1870 to Rollins's retirement from politics Howard was devoted to his interests from a conviction that Rollins was one of the most useful Representatives New Hampshire ever had in Congress.

CHAPTER XVIII.

ROLLINS AGAIN AT THE HELM

THE Democrats immediately after the election of 1874 began making preparations for taking charge of the State government. Numerous conferences were held to map out the work of the incoming legislature. From March until June their leaders met frequently to discuss the details of their programme. These gatherings were attended not only by the leaders but by many others who looked forward to holding the offices which everybody recognized would be made vacant by expiration of terms or by address of the legislature. Unlike the election of 1871, there was no doubt of the ability of the party immediately to organize the legislature, and much of the work could be anticipated.

Never did a party meet in legislative session with fairer prospects of a long lease of power and with greater confidence in its ability to maintain its hold upon the State. Elected to the legislature were their most prominent and sagacious leaders. Albert R. Hatch, of Portsmouth, an able lawyer, technical in his training and practice, was made Speaker of the House, while Harry Bingham and John G. Sinclair were to lead the party on the floor, assisted by a number of able lieutenants, among whom were Isaac N. Blodgett, of Franklin, afterward chief justice, Daniel Marcy, of Portsmouth, Alvah W. Sulloway and Warren F. Daniell, of Franklin, Edwin C. Bailey, of Hopkinton, Joseph Burrows, of Plymouth, Joseph Roles, of Ossipee, and Edwin P. Jewell, of Laconia.

The leaders on the Republican side were James W. Emery, of Portsmouth, Edward B. S. Sanborn, of Franklin, afterward a Democrat, James F. Briggs, of Manchester, and Joshua G. Hall, of Dover, afterward Congressmen, John D. Lyman, of Exeter, and J. Horace Kent, of Portsmouth.

In this legislature were two young men, friends of Rollins, who were later to come into prominence, Hiram A. Tuttle and Henry E. Burnham, the former becoming governor in 1891, and the latter United States Senator in 1901. Tuttle is a self-made man, successful in business, public-spirited, and an inspiration to every worthy cause. His election as governor came after one of the closest contests in New Hampshire politics, the result not being definitely known until the legislature organized. His administration was during a period of warfare between railroad corporations of the State. Yet, with remarkable tact, he held the respect and confidence of all parties to the controversy, while yielding none of his convictions.

Burnham's career in politics, until his election to the United States Senate, was a generous contribution of his services in campaigns where others were personally interested. An eloquent speaker, he was always in demand upon the stump. Liberal and helpful, his circle of friends constantly enlarged. Frequently urged to become a candidate for office, he persistently declined all political honors until the contest was made in the campaign of 1900 for the seat in the Senate occupied by William E. Chandler. Since his election to the Senate those traits which have made him popular at home have gained for him the esteem of his colleagues in the upper branch of Congress.

The initiative in the legislature was with the Democratic majority, and the Republican minority had naught to do but take advantage of the mistakes of their opponents. Except on the liquor question, there was no change of State policy proposed by the Democrats. The work of the session early developed the purposes of the Democratic leaders to make the most of their victory from a partisan standpoint. First came the addresses for the removal of Republican office-holders, to be followed by the political gerrymander of the State, the reorganization of the courts, a fierce railroad controversy arising out of the consolidation of the Nashua and Lowell and Boston and Lowell Railroads, and an attempt to pass a license law. The session dragged along to the last of July, and, when it had adjourned, the Republicans had an issue for the next campaign.

When they came to sum up their legislative work, the Democratic leaders had little cause for congratulation. The party had pledged itself to substitute license for prohibition, but was defeated in that promise by Democratic votes. A railroad contest had arrayed in personal controversy their two most conspicuous leaders, developing a rivalry between them boding no good to the party and emphasizing more clearly the factional warfare for control of the Democratic organization. The Democrats, however, were in possession of the State offices. The greater part of the session, which was longer than usual, was taken up with partisan work. The courts were reorganized on the basis of having both a trial and a law court, a change commendable in itself, but giving their opponents opportunity to charge partisan interference with the judiciary. The change was made unpopular because it was associated with a referee law passed at that session, which failed to meet the expectations of its authors. The State had been redistricted into Councillor and Senatorial districts, a gerrymander which the Republicans caricatured in maps showing the grotesque shape of the districts. The ward lines of several cities were changed to obtain party advantage, arousing the anger and activity of the Republicans in those localities full more than the gerrymander of the Councillor and Senatorial districts. That the Democrats acted otherwise than the Republicans would have done in like circumstances cannot be charged, but there were nearly two-thirds of a generation of voters then upon the stage to whom partisan work on so grand a scale was both a surprise and a novelty. Then the failure of the Democratic party to carry out its pledges made its partisanship more pronounced. In addition, a clean sweep of officials and the appointment of new men afforded opportunity for criticism of the appointees. Among so many appointments it would be surprising if there were not some incompetent men. Again there were the usual disappointments arising out of the selections made by the governor and Council, where there was earnest rivalry for executive favor. Yet, in spite of all these things, the party in power had the advantage of possession and was really stronger than at any time since its defeat in 1855. It was, moreover, soon to be encouraged by the political tidal wave which swept over the country in the fall of 1874, giving the Democrats victory in many Republican States, and securing to them possession of the national House of Representatives by a two-thirds majority.

Both sides made immediate preparation for the New Hampshire campaign of 1875. Besides the election of a governor and legislature, three Congressmen were to be chosen. Governor Weston had been four times a candidate of the Democratic party, and twice elected. Besides having had the compliment of two terms, although not in succession, he was identified with the mistakes of his own administration, and there was no movement to present him again as a candidate. The farmer candidate of the preceding Democratic convention, Hiram R. Roberts, was now successfully pressed for the nomination. For Congressional nominations Samuel N. Bell, of Manchester, who had defeated Stevens in 1871, and been defeated by Pike in 1873, was once more nominated in the second district. In the third district Henry O. Kent secured the nomination, defeating George F. Putnam, chairman of the Democratic State committee, and Horatio Colony, of Keene, both of whom were candidates. Kent's nomination disaffected some of the old-time Democrats who thought he was too recent a convert to the principles of the party. In the first district the Democrats presented as their candidate Frank Jones, of Portsmouth, who was soon to become the controlling force in the Democratic party.

Jones was a rich brewer with many business interests outside of his brewery. He was a public-spirited citizen who dispensed a large income with a liberal hand, contributing generously in political campaigns. Although of limited education, he was shrewd and sagacious in his knowledge of men. Enjoying the excitement of politics, he made it his diversion from business, and he gradually came to be the dictator of the Democratic party in New Hampshire. Jones was loyal to his personal friends, whom he drew from both political parties. He was active and potential in all State affairs, and he took an interest in all that contributed to the welfare of New Hampshire. His personal influence in politics and legislation was so marked at one time that his Republican friends were classified as "Jones's Republicans." He aspired to be governor of his native State, and his nomination five years later gave the Republicans an arduous campaign. During the Cleveland administration, Jones dispensed federal patronage in New Hampshire, and

it is said was offered a seat in Cleveland's Cabinet.
In 1896, he headed the New Hampshire delegation to
the Democratic national convention at Chicago. Dis-
gusted with the platform there adopted, he immediately bolted the nomination and openly supported
McKinley. Four years later he was a delegate at large
to the Republican national convention at Philadelphia
which renominated McKinley, and for the remainder
of his life gave earnest support to Republican policies.

The Republican leaders were aware of the magnitude of the fight to regain the State, and early began
to discuss candidates for governor and Congress, and
to suggest Rollins for chairman of the State committee. At a meeting of the committee, December 1,
1874, to issue the call for the various conventions,
Austin E. Pike, whose election to Congress two years
before was secured by a very small majority, promptly
told the committee that he would relieve the party of
any embarrassment of renomination to which he was
entitled by usage if any new candidate would strengthen
the ticket. He was followed by Luther McCutchins
and Congressman Small, who made similar declarations. This gave the party opportunity to make nominations without regard to precedent, an encouraging
sign in this emergency.

As to the gubernatorial candidates, there were many
minds. Charles H. Bell and Gilman Marston, of
Exeter, John J. Morrill and Benjamin Cole, of Gilford, Benjamin F. Prescott, of Epping, James W.
Emery, of Portsmouth, and others were suggested.

Earnest appeals were made to Judge Charles Doe, afterward chief justice, to consent to the use of his name, without avail. Finally opinion settled upon Person C. Cheney, then mayor of Manchester, who had shown great popularity in his two candidacies for that office.

Cheney was one of the most lovable characters in public life. His nomination for governor brought him into State prominence, and for a quarter of a century he was a leader in political campaigns in New Hampshire, his influence gradually broadening into national politics. He was governor two terms, minister to Switzerland, United States Senator by appointment, and a member of the national Republican committee from New Hampshire. These positions came to him as the general wish of his party associates without his seeking. He filled them all with credit to himself and his State. He was intensely patriotic, and gave freely of his time and money to promote all public interests. A large part of the financial burden of the campaign of 1875 fell upon him, and he never afterward relieved himself of personal responsibility for the success of the Republican ticket. His kindly manner, his thoughtfulness of others, and his generosity were unfailing. His tactfulness and the absence of self-seeking in his leadership were factors in many an emergency which harmonized differences and promoted victory.

The Republican convention was held January 12th. Gilman Marston, of Exeter, presided, and the resolutions which dealt largely with State affairs were written and reported by Orrin C. Moore. Before a ballot was taken, McCutchins, the candidate for governor in the previous campaign, withdrew his name. The vote was as follows: Scattering, 10; Charles H. Bell, 241; Person C. Cheney, 392; and Cheney's nomination was made unanimous.

The Democratic convention had been held January 5th. The breach between the two Democratic leaders, Bingham and Sinclair, which occurred in the legislature, was still further emphasized in the convention. Bingham was now fully allied with Pearson of the *People* newspaper in opposition to railroad consolidation, and they had as their candidate for governor Hiram R. Roberts, the farmer candidate of the previous convention. Sinclair favored the nomination of Warren F. Daniell, of Franklin, a popular manufacturer, who was by far the most available candidate, and whose selection at that time, it was generally believed, would result in his election. At a later date Daniell was nominated for Congress by the Democrats, and elected, defeating Orrin C. Moore, when the latter was a candidate for reëlection. In the southern part of the State there was a considerable following for Frank A. McKean, then the Democratic mayor of Nashua. The ballot resulted as follows: Scattering, 21; Frank A. McKean, 79; Warren F. Daniell, 240; Hiram R. Roberts, 347.

Roberts's nomination was made unanimous. The resolutions of the convention dealt wholly with national affairs. There was not a word in the platform referring to the State administration, or a single expression of praise in any of the speeches made at the convention of the work of the preceding legislature.

For Congress the Republicans nominated Charles S. Whitehouse, of Rochester, in the first district, Henry W. Blair, of Plymouth, in the third district, and renominated Austin F. Pike in the second.

The Prohibitionists had met as usual in convention earlier than the other parties, and nominated candidates for governor and Congress. Nathaniel White, of Concord, was their nominee for governor. He was a self-made man, who, from driving a stage before the days of railroading, drifted into the express business. In this business he accumulated a fortune. He was philanthropic, and gave liberally to any cause he espoused. He was originally an Abolition Whig, and later a Republican. The cause of temperance had in him a strong advocate. He had not until this year been identified with the Prohibition movement, and his nomination now gave no little embarrassment to the Republicans. The Prohibitionists hoped to force the Republicans to endorse him, and this idea had some encouragement among active Republicans. The Prohibitionists had polled twenty-one hundred votes at the last election. What might they do if White were to authorize a campaign regardless of expense, which his well-known generosity and earnestness might prompt him to do? While the endorsement of the Prohibition candidate by the Republicans would have been suicidal, it was important that White's nomination should be treated with the respect due to so prominent a citizen. The *Monitor,* however, came out with an injudicious personal attack upon White, which its editor, William E. Stevens, afterward retracted. For a time, however, it gave great offence both to White and his friends, and threatened to spur him into an active candidacy.

From the very beginning, appeals had been made to Rollins to return to the State committee and run the campaign. Editor Stevens, in a letter to him dated November 11, 1874, said: "Can't you take charge of the campaign? You can win the fight. I fear no one else can. Winning it, you cannot again be cheated out of your reward."

These appeals were supplemented by the offer of Chairman Hall, of the State committee, to retire in Rollins's favor. The latter, however, was unwilling to supplant Hall, whose work in the previous campaign he believed to have been as efficient as any that could have been given. So strong, however, was the opinion of the party that he should have the direction of the campaign, he did consent to become chairman of the executive committee and to give his whole time to the canvass. With this understanding Hall accepted the chairmanship. In a letter, dated January 16th, Congressman Pike wrote Rollins as follows:

"I see that you are chairman of our executive committee. Good! What do you advise to have done to throw the full vote in our State? I certainly hope you will be able to give some time to our State this spring.

If your hand is in it, it will bring great confidence to our people and be worth a thousand votes to us."

The Republican State committee had organized immediately after the adjournment of the State convention. Benjamin F. Prescott was reëlected secretary, and John Kimball, of Concord, chosen treasurer. The executive committee consisted of Edward H. Rollins, James A. Wood, of Acworth, and George C. Gilmore, of Manchester. Soon after the State committee had organized, the *Monitor* said:

"It will gratify the Republicans of New Hampshire to know that Edward H. Rollins was elected chairman of the executive committee and that he has accepted the position, and, in connection with Daniel Hall, chairman of the State committee, will run the present campaign, a fact which will not be welcome news to the Democracy of this State. Mr. Rollins will put his best work into this campaign, and the Goths and Vandals of the Democracy of this State know what that forebodes."

This was one of the most intense campaigns that ever occurred in New Hampshire. Others have been more demonstrative in campaign oratory and pyrotechnic display, but, for individual work and personal appeal to the voter, no campaign ever excelled it. The following letter from Rollins to John Coburn, of Hollis, is a type of many that he wrote to Republican local leaders, to be supplemented by others as the information called for was supplied.

"Yours is received. I regret that the report from

your town is not more encouraging. Our friends must rouse themselves and save Hollis. Give me the names of the most active Republicans in the town. Let me know who are at work, and who may be relied upon to push the campaign vigorously. We can't afford to spare Hollis. The House will be very close, and we shall have no votes to waste. Confer with our friends. See what can be done, and let me hear from you forthwith."

Republicans were urged to select their strongest candidates for the legislature, as Rollins recognized that the result of the election would hinge on the control of that body. If it was learned at headquarters that any particular Republican could be more easily elected than another, Rollins immediately communicated with him urging him to sacrifice all personal interests by becoming a candidate, and to all aspirants in that town urging them to postpone their ambitions for just this one time that there might be no doubt about the result in the State. To James W. Emery, of Portsmouth, he wrote as follows:

"I have not forgotten what you said to me a few days since in my office, namely, that you can be elected Representative from Ward 1, Portsmouth. Neither have I forgotten what I said in reply that we would take care of the State if you would do it. Now will you pull off your coat, wade in, and take that ward away from Frank Jones? If you should do this, you would be covered all over, forty feet thick, with glory. The fact that you have been Speaker would help you in the race, with the probability of reëlection, and it seems to me that for the credit of the State, and for the glory of Zion, Ward 1 would stand by you. Things are looking well in the State. Our people were never more in earnest or more determined to win the fight than now, and, if you will take hold of this matter earnestly, it would encourage our friends in all the other wards in Portsmouth, and in all the region round where we need every vote, to elect our candidate for State Senator. Now, Emery, ' mount the walls, blow the trumpet till your cheeks crack,' and lead on to victory."

In the same strain he wrote to Congressman Small, urging him to become a candidate for the legislature from Newmarket, and to Nehemiah G. Ordway, who would cease to be sergeant-at-arms of the national House of Representatives as soon as the Democrats attained power, to become a candidate for the legislature from Warner. No event however small, likely to have an influence on the campaign, escaped Rollins's attention. It was reported to him that ex-Governor Straw was to leave for Florida about a week before election on account of his health. He immediately wrote Cheney:

" I think it is perfectly wicked that Straw should go away under the circumstances. You stood by him, and he should not desert you. It looks like giving up the ship for him to go away just at this time. It will be only necessary for him to remain here a little more than a week longer. I want to call your attention beforehand to the disheartening effect which it will have all over the State when it is announced that Mr. Straw has gone to Florida. The Democrats will say that he has given up the fight and expects you to be beaten. You must look this thing squarely in the face. I think it is your duty to state to him frankly what must be the inevitable influence of his departure at this time."

Straw left for the South before election, and the construction put upon his departure by the Democrats was as Rollins predicted. They charged that he went away to avoid voting the Republican ticket.

The Prohibition vote was an important factor in this campaign. It had doubled in the previous campaign and was at that time nearly sufficient to defeat an election of governor by the people. To win some of these back to the Republican fold from which most of them had departed was one of the tasks before the Republican State committee. White, the Prohibition candidate for governor, who was at heart a loyal Republican, was appealed to by Rollins not only to make his canvass perfunctory but also to aid the Republicans by advising his Prohibition friends to support the Republican legislative ticket in the close wards and towns of the State. This with commendable self-sacrifice he did, and so successfully, that his vote at the election was only about one-third that of the Prohibition candidate for governor the year before, while his personal influence saved several close towns to the Republicans.

The campaign was aggressively personal in the

attacks made upon the Democratic candidate for
governor, but it is doubtful if these attacks cost him
any Democratic votes. He polled the full strength
of his party, but, unlike his competitor for the nomination, Warren F. Daniell, he had no personal following among Republicans to draw from. For the
first time in many years the Republicans made their
canvass largely on State issues, dwelling upon the increased cost of Democratic administrations, the extraordinary length of the legislative session, the
character of its work, and the failure of the Democratic party to redeem its pledges. The Democrats
made vigorous defence and attacked the Republicans
on their administration of national affairs, holding
up as a spectre the probability of President Grant seeking a third term, and receiving it at the hands of his
party. The great Democratic victories throughout the
country the fall before gave an impetus to the Democratic campaign that fully offset any party disappointment at the failings of the Democratic State administration. Toward the close of the canvass, the Democratic leaders roused the enthusiasm of their followers
by the character of the campaign speakers they brought
into the State. Among these were Gen. John B. Gordon, of Georgia, Lucius Q. C. Lamar, of Mississippi,
Edgar K. Apgar, of New York, John K. Tarbox and
Augustus O. Brewster, of Massachusetts. Their campaign was well-managed by George F. Putnam, who
was reëlected chairman of the State committee, and
the morning of election they were confident of success.

On the Republican side the local speakers were assisted by Congressman Eugene Hale, of Maine, Julius C. Burrows, of Michigan, Frederick Douglass, of Washington, D. C., and John L. Swift, of Boston.

Not all Republicans of the State were imbued with Rollins's confidence that New Hampshire could be redeemed. Some were for making the best fight possible to keep the organization intact with a view to making the real contest in the Presidential year, 1876. This view was shared by many Republicans outside the State, and it was with the greatest difficulty that speakers and assistance from other States could be obtained. Rollins, in his correspondence, frequently referred to the contest as " desperate," and a large share of his time was given to stimulating by letter and by personal appeal the activity of leading Republicans in the close towns. In the candidate for governor he had a most efficient helper whose arduous labors contributed greatly to the result obtained. Such reports as came from the Democrats reported them as confident of carrying the legislature, the first and third Congressional districts, with the second district and the governor in doubt. In the first district there was strong suspicion that Whitehouse was not being loyally supported by some of the leading Republicans who were openly charged with promoting Jones's election. Some of these men were Rollins's personal friends. As soon as these charges were brought to his attention, he wrote to one of them as follows:

" It is reported to us that Oliver Wyatt, Charles M.

Murphy, and a great many others of our personal friends are going to support Jones. Now it needs no prophet to foretell what will be the result if this course is carried out. If these men living in your city vote for Jones, it will compromise you beyond all question, no matter whether you can influence them or not. Now you must go to all such men yourself at once, lay the case before them and urge them to stand up square to the work. If Whitehouse is defeated by people voting in this way, the effect of it will reach far into the future and come back to plague the inventors. The report that these men are thus going to vote is doing more to lose us the State than anything else. It is demoralizing our forces fearfully, and disaster may come to us all by reason of it. You know I am not needlessly alarmed. I am writing, I think, with a full knowledge of the situation. While I write thus frankly for the good of the cause, I have, as I think, a most sincere desire to promote your personal welfare."

The election returns were awaited at both party headquarters with feverish anxiety. Before the Republican State committee adjourned for the night of election, it was apparent that there was no choice of governor by the people, and that the Republicans had carried the legislature. The Congressional districts remained in doubt for several days. When the complete returns were received, they showed the election of Jones and Bell, Democrats, in the first and second districts, and Blair, Republican, in the third.

The vote for governor was: Scattering, 19; Nathaniel White, 777; Hiram R. Roberts, 39,121; Person C. Cheney, 39,293.

It was a great victory considering all the circumstances surrounding the contest. That it was due to Rollins's genius in marshalling the party is conceded by all who had part in the campaign. The chairman of the committee, Daniel Hall, whose work in this canvass is deserving of the highest praise, with entire self-abnegation pays this tribute to Rollins's management in a letter dated October 12, 1903.

" My first campaign as chairman of the Republican State committee was in 1874 and was lost. The Democrats carried the State and put us in a very bad position for the contest of 1875. I think it was the most desperate fight we ever had in New Hampshire, and Rollins was the Ajax Telamon of the struggle. All his political genius, energy, and resource as a campaigner were freely given, and for whatever was achieved in the campaigns of 1875 and 1876 he is entitled to more credit than anybody else. As chairman of the committee, I was in the closest intimacy with him, and had all the benefit of his experience, skill, advice, and guidance. No extravagance of praise or eulogy can overstate the services of Edward H. Rollins to the Republican party of New Hampshire and the Union."

The campaign did not close with the election. The official returns showed that the Republicans had at least nine majority in the House of Representatives, that five Republican and five Democratic Senators had been elected, and that in two districts, the second and fourth, there was no choice. The Democrats were loth to concede the State, and for several weeks vague rumors were current that a sufficient number of contests would be made over the certificates issued to ·Republican candidates for the House of Representatives to enable the Democratic clerk of the previous legislature, who made up the roll of the incoming legislature, to put a majority of Democrats on that roll.

The Republican suspicions up to this point concerned the organization of the House, but on April 21st, the *Monitor* refers to a story appearing in an associated press despatch from Manchester to the Boston papers that the vote of Natt Head, the Republican candidate for State Senator in District No. 2, is to be rejected by the governor and council because his real name is Nathaniel and not Natt, and that the vote for the Prohibition candidate for Senator in District No. 4, Arthur Deering, is for an ineligible candidate and not to be counted. This was the first intimation the Republicans had of the Democratic programme to control the Senate, and which was afterward known as "The Senate Steal of New Hampshire." The votes in these two Senatorial districts, as shown by the official returns, were as follows:

District No. 2: James Priest, 3,834; Natt Head, 3,771; Joshua C. Merrill, 95; Scattering, 6.

District No. 4: John Proctor, 3,495; George E. Todd, 3,454; Arthur Deering, 46; Scattering, 18.

The ground taken by the Democrats for rejecting the vote cast for Natt Head was a statute of the State which read as follows:

" The full Christian and surname of every person voted for with the initial letter or letters of the middle name and the usual abbreviations for junior, second, third, and the like shall be written or printed upon every ballot, and every ballot not thus prepared and cast shall be regarded as a blank and not counted."

The basis for rejecting the votes cast for Arthur Deering in the fourth district was that he had not been a continuous resident of the State for seven years as provided by the State constitution for State Senators, and therefore ineligible as a candidate. Rejecting the votes for Natt Head in the second, and Arthur Deering in the fourth, would give James Priest and John Proctor, the Democratic candidates, a majority in each district.

It was the duty of the governor and Council to canvass the returns from the towns and issue certificates to those candidates for Senator who appeared on the face of the returns to be elected. Governor Weston and the Democratic majority of the Council would have this duty to perform.

The report that the Democratic leaders would urge the governor and Council to reject the votes cast for Natt Head and Arthur Deering was immediately denounced by the Republicans as an outrage and a usurpation. They took the ground that the governor and Council in canvassing election returns were merely clothed with ministerial duties and must issue certificates to those only who appeared on the face of the returns to be elected. To the Democrats the report came as an escape from total defeat in the State election, for, if the Senate remained Democratic, there could be no removal of Democratic office-holders, no redistricting of the State, and no change of the ward lines in cities. Nothing in the canvass for votes at the election equalled in intensity and feeling the campaign which was now made to secure results, and interest in the outcome soon extended beyond State lines. A dual State government seemed imminent, for the Democrats were determined that these votes should be rejected, and the Republicans were equally determined not to submit to what they considered a usurpation by the governor and Council.

Rollins had been active and vigilant in seeing that the town clerks issued certificates to the Republican Representatives-elect, and in stirring up the Republican leaders to stand firm in demanding their rights so long as there was suspicion of the Democrats attempting to organize the House. Now his attention was turned to the Senate, and he outlined to Hall the course to be followed by the Republicans in resisting the Democratic programme. In a letter to him, May 8th, he said:

"Charles P. Sanborn was here and reports that the impression is gaining ground that the Democrats intend to push through their scheme of villainy. In fact, I think there is no doubt about it, and we must be prepared for them. I think you had better see Doe and have him prepare a proper protest for Councillor Lovell to present and have spread upon the records if they attempt this thing. There is no time to be lost, and Doe can present the case the best of any man in the State, and this protest will form the basis of our discussion hereafter. It is evident that we have got to make a fight, and we must start right. All may depend upon that. I think you should also write to General Marston and have him present, and secure all the legal force advisable and have them at Concord on Wednesday night. I think you had better go to Concord Monday and remain there to engineer matters. Sanborn will be there and, of course, Tappan. See if Doe does not advise that Lovell demand of the governor and Council that the question be submitted to the court."

Judge Doe's views of the situation, and the legal course to be pursued, are set forth in two letters of Hall to Rollins. In the first he says:

"I called on Doe yesterday. He is all right in sentiment, agrees with us on all the legal questions, and is in favor of maintaining our rights at every hazard, even coolly contemplates a double-headed State government. He don't want to be chief justice, says he won't and don't think it best to disturb the courts. He is in favor of Ordway for Speaker, and of decisive action in every respect. Did you know Grant was considering his name for Attorney-General?"

After the decision of the governor and Council, Hall wrote Rollins: " Doe is of opinion that the convention may ascertain vacancies for themselves and legally fill them. This is very important. If it be so, we have only to carry the House to march straight to the control of the Senate."

Charles Doe was not then on the bench, having been legislated off by the Democratic legislature of 1874. He was one of the ablest jurists the State ever produced, and some of his opinions after he became chief justice, in 1876, obtained a world-wide reputation. He simplified the practice of the New Hampshire courts, sweeping ruthlessly aside all technicalities in his endeavor to do justice to litigants. His contempt for formalities was pronounced, whether in court or at hearings outside, and it was no uncommon occurrence for him to give audience to counsel, and hear petitions wherever he happened to be found. Disclaiming all interest or even knowledge in public affairs except as they concerned the court, he, nevertheless, managed to convey his views on important public measures to the political leaders of the State. During his life he wielded a great influence in New Hampshire. His friendship for Rollins dated from their boyhood days, and he watched with interest Rollins's rise in political life. Many efforts were made at various times to induce him to accept nominations for political office, but without avail. During President

Arthur's administration he was urged for appointment to the United States Supreme Bench, a position for which he was preëminently fitted.

When it was necessary for some one to take responsibility, Rollins did not hesitate to take it, and, regardless of the indifference or weakness of others, his attitude always remained firm. Writing Hall, May 11th, he said: " Yours of the 9th inst. came to hand last evening. I sympathize with you fully in your troubles. The fact is, a great many of the Republicans in New Hampshire do nothing but leave the work for a few men. It is getting to be a burden too grievous to be borne. You must stir them up. Write to such lawyers as you want and can reach by letter, and telegraph others. Take the full responsibility yourself. Have everybody there and we will see you through all right. I will stand by you to the end. I am satisfied the Democrats mean mischief. Good pluck must be shown, and a bold front, leaving nothing to chance. Wish I could be with you. Doe is a trump. He has done a big thing."

Both the Republican and Democratic State committees were in frequent consultation, and there were almost daily conferences of leading Republicans with Rollins in Boston. Able counsel was secured on both sides. The governor and Council met Thursday, May 12th, to canvass the vote for Senators. After the arguments had been made, the Republican Councillor moved that the questions raised be referred to the Supreme Court for an opinion. This motion was

amended by a proviso that such opinion must be
obtained before the following Monday at 3 P. M.;
otherwise the governor was instructed to get such advice as the circumstances might admit. As amended
this motion was passed by the vote of the four Democratic Councillors. Although the Supreme Court was
at that time composed of two Democrats and one
Republican, the Republicans felt confident that its
opinion, if given, would sustain their position that the
governor and Council had merely ministerial duties to
perform, and had no right to pass upon the eligibility
of candidates for Senators.

Governor Weston personally consulted the chief justice of the Supreme Court, who took the position that
it was impracticable to convene the court and give an
opinion in the limited time between Friday morning
and Monday afternoon. Therefore, when the governor and Council again convened, they proceeded to
canvass the votes, rejecting those cast for Natt Head
and Arthur Deering, and issuing certificates of election to James Priest and John Proctor. Seven Democrats and five Republicans now held certificates of
election as Senators, giving the Democrats control of
the State Senate. The contest, however, was not
ended. If the Republicans controlled the House, that
body could refuse to recognize the Democratic Senate.
On the other hand, Governor Weston would continue
in the executive chair until the legislature fully organized and chose his successor. Supported by Judge
Doe's opinion, Rollins, Chandler, and others were in

favor of having the five Republican Senators holding certificates of election meet with the Republican House as a convention, canvass the votes for State Senators, declare no election in the two disputed districts as appeared on the face of the returns, and fill the vacancies by the election of Head and Todd. If this course had been followed, a dual State government would, of course, have been the outcome of such action. In addition there was difficulty in carrying out this programme, as the election returns were in the hands of the Democratic Secretary of State.

Party interest increased as the day for the assembling of the legislature approached. Each party determined to maintain its position regardless of consequences. Newspaper utterances were vehement and sometimes incendiary. It was asserted on the Democratic side that Governor Weston as commander-in-chief of the State militia would protect the Democratic seven in their possession of the Senate Chamber. By the Republicans it was contemplated that it might be necessary to appeal to President Grant to recognize their organization as the legal State government. Between the time of the issuing of the certificates by the governor and Council, and the meeting of the legislature, the leaders of both parties were in an anxious frame of mind. Each side waited for the other, but the legislature met without any act on the part of either that would precipitate violence.

At the Republican legislative caucus, Charles P. Sanborn, of Concord, was nominated for Speaker of the House, defeating Nehemiah G. Ordway and John D. Lyman, of Exeter, who were also candidates. Sanborn became the most popular Speaker who ever presided over a New Hampshire legislature, although his tenure of office was in a stormy partisan period. He had a keen mind, a pleasing address, great tact, and a thorough knowledge of parliamentary practice. Nature had generously endowed him, and, had he inclined, he might have led at the bar or in politics. His political ambition, however, did not extend beyond this position, which he filled to the satisfaction of both political parties.

The Republican Senatorial caucus, which included Head and Todd, who had not received certificates of membership, nominated George H. Stowell, of Claremont, for President of the Senate. Stowell is one of the " Old Guard," who is still active and influential in the politics of the State. The Democrats renominated Albert R. Hatch as Speaker of the House, and the seven Democrats with Senatorial certificates nominated John W. Sanborn, of Wakefield, for president of that body.

John W. Sanborn, or " Uncle John," as he was familiarly known in the State, was a born leader of men, and for more than a quarter of a century his influence was marked in the politics of New Hampshire. From being superintendent of the Eastern Railroad of New Hampshire he grew to be the legislative agent, first, of that road, and later, of the consolidated Boston and Maine. He entered politics as a Democrat, and so continued until 1896, when he became a Republican. In protecting the railroad interests with which he was connected he gradually assumed the direction of the Democratic party by his influence over its leaders. Later his power was felt in Republican councils, and for a time his advice was potentially and impartially bestowed upon both. He was a most prominent figure at every political convention assembled at the capital, and no legislative session was complete without his presence. He was a born diplomat, and he maintained his prestige until within a few years of his death. One source of his strength was the fact that he never used his power for his own personal gain. The interest of the railroad with which he was allied was always the primary consideration of all his actions.

The five Democratic Senators with Priest and Proctor organized a Senate in the Senate Chamber, voting for John W. Sanborn as president, who was declared elected. The five Republican Senators protested, and refused to vote. The Democrats then completed their organization, and sent a notification to the House, which the latter body ignored. The five Republican Senators withdrew, and, with Head and Todd, organized a Senate, electing Senator Stowell as president. This body notified the House of its organization as a Senate, which notification the House received. Immediately after the organization of the House a resolution was introduced asking the opinion of the court on the disputed questions. This resolution was passed after some debate. The Democratic Senators also presented the question in dispute to the court, but in another form. Both parties then rested on their arms awaiting the opinion of the court. This opinion came the following week in communications addressed to both the House and the Democratic Senate, and signed by all the judges. In its communication to the Senate, the court said:

" We have, in reply to a resolution of the House of Representatives, declined to express our opinion upon a past and completed act of the executive department of the government, performed in the discharge of a duty expressly required of that department by the constitution, upon the ground that such opinion, if given, would have no greater weight or authority than a criticism of one branch of the government upon the conduct of another coördinate branch, and such official act on the part of the justices of this court would not be consistent with the grave duties imposed upon them by the constitution of the State."

The position taken by the court was a surprise to both sides, but was accepted by the Democrats as a confirmation of their position. It was bitterly denounced by the Republicans as a cowardly evasion of duties imposed upon the court by the constitution, and was regarded by them as an additional justification for reorganizing the courts when they again obtained power. There was nothing, however, for the Republicans to do but submit, unless they were prepared to resort to arbitrary proceedings which would undoubtedly result in the establishment of a dual State government.

CHAPTER XIX.

THE campaign of 1876 began while the legislature of 1875 was in session. To add to its interest, there was a United States Senator to be elected from New Hampshire to succeed Aaron H. Cragin, whose term expired with the sitting Congress. The party carrying the legislature of 1876 would secure this prize. Both parties, therefore, were stimulated to put forth their best efforts, and the leaders were early at work organizing their forces for the conflict. Daniel Hall, the chairman of the Republican State committee, asked to be relieved of the burden of another campaign, and desired to resign at once so that a new chairman might immediately begin his labors. The duties of the chairman had continued almost without interruption for nearly a year, and Hall pleaded that his private affairs needed his attention. Rollins protested, and finally secured from him consent to serve through another campaign.

Hall was well equipped for the position, although inclined to depreciate his own abilities. He is a man of scholarly tastes, and a ready and graceful writer. His public addresses and writings show

352

care in preparation and extensive information. He is recognized as a man of marked ability, and at one time he aspired to a public career, being a candidate for Congress in the first district. Had he succceded in his ambition, the State would have had reason to be proud of him, but he had no taste for the preliminary canvassing so essential where rival ambitions conflict. He was Rollins's friend, and was appointed naval officer of customs at Boston for two terms while Rollins was United States Senator. It was at the time of his first appointment that the final contest was made between the New Hampshire and Massachusetts delegations in Congress for the control of this office. The result was that this position has continued ever since as a part of the federal patronage of New Hampshire.

The story of the campaign of 1876 is but a repetition of that of the previous year. There was the same systematic work and the same anxiety over the outcome. The Republican party, however, was in a better state of discipline, and its members eager for the contest. The party was determined to win such a victory that no disputed question should imperil the result. To this end the most skilful leadership was demanded. Jealousies were put aside, and all united in asking Rollins to take the supervising direction of the campaign.

The Republican State convention was held January 5, 1876. Orrin C. Moore presided, and delivered one of his masterly addresses, which plainly set forth the issues of the campaign. Daniel Hall reported the resolutions, which, after dealing with national affairs, arraigned Governor Weston and his Council, charging them with an open, palpable usurpation of power, and as guilty of an overt encroachment of the executive department upon the legislative branch of the government, and a deliberate subversion of the electoral rights of the qualified voters of the State. Governor Cheney was renominated by acclamation.

The Democratic State convention met January 12, 1876, William W. Bailey, of Nashua, presiding. Hiram R. Roberts having declined a renomination for governor, Daniel Marcy, of Portsmouth, was nominated. The resolutions were reported by William Butterfield, of Concord, former editor of the *Patriot,* a virile writer, whose pen for years had been at the service of the Democratic party. Butterfield never made any half-hearted defence of his party and its principles. He was a man of strong convictions and aggressive action. Through his loyalty to Pierce's successors in control of the party, he suffered both financially and in prestige after the Pearson family established a rival newspaper at the capital. He was one term Secretary of State, being elected when the Democrats secured control in 1874. His resolutions on State matters boldly met the challenge of the Republican party, and both defended the Democratic position and denounced that of the Republicans.

The Prohibition party still kept up its organization, although attracting little interest. Asa S. Kendall, of

Swanzey, was nominated for governor at a convention held November 10, 1875.

The campaign for the most part was conducted along the lines of the resolutions of the Republican and Democratic parties on State matters. The Democrats were in control of the lower branch of Congress, and the session had hardly begun before occurred that celebrated debate between Benjamin H. Hill, of Georgia, and James G. Blaine, of Maine, regarding the conduct of the Civil War and the treatment of prisoners of war by the Union and Confederate forces. Marcy, the Democratic candidate for governor, had been in Congress during the Civil War, and his record there was made a prominent part of the canvass. On the other hand, the Democrats were encouraged just before election by the exposure and impeachment of William W. Belknap, Secretary of War, for his complicity in grave irregularities in that department. Fears were entertained by the Republican leaders of its effect upon the New Hampshire election. At any other time, it would have cost the Republican party some votes, but, overshadowing the intensity of national issues, was the feeling of the Republicans that the action of Governor Weston and his Council must be rebuked, and this was the controlling factor in the campaign, which resulted in the reëlection of Governor Cheney by the people, and the control of both branches of the legislature by the Republicans. The vote for governor was: Scattering, 14; Asa S. Kendall, 411: Daniel Marcy, 38,133; Person C. Cheney, 41,761.

The Democrats held but few political rallies in this campaign, and had no outside speakers. The Republicans were assisted by William P. Frye and Eugene Hale, of Maine, Richard Oglesby, of Illinois, James A. Garfield and Edward F. Noyes, of Ohio, Julius C. Burrows and E. W. Andrews, of Michigan, A. E. King, of Maryland, Henry O. Pratt, of Iowa, and S. W. Tenney, of New York.

After election, the *Monitor* said of Rollins: " Without a superior anywhere as an organizer and leader, he has, as the head of the executive committee, put all his energies, all his thoughts, into this campaign from the outset. Indeed he may be said to have kept up the fight continuously for two years. The outrage of last June, which robbed him of a portion of his well-earned victory, did not discourage him. On the contrary, it gave him new strength, new determination, and he has from that hour to the present brought all his splendid powers of organization, his foresight, his aggressive habit, his pluck, and his great experience to bear on the enemy, and the *Portsmouth Chronicle* is right when it says, ' If any feeling of gratitude for the splendid victory is uppermost in Republican hearts to-day, it is due him for his zealous persistence and untiring efforts to accomplish the grand results.' "

Not all the Republican leaders felt the same as editor William E. Stevens, of the *Monitor,* in regard to the credit for the victory. Orrin C. Moore, in his newspaper, the *Nashua Telegraph,* said: " No one man and no set of men won the victory. We doubt if any one man or set of men was essential to its achievement, although, as we have heretofore said, individuals performed signal, laborious, and valuable service."

The *Manchester Mirror* said: "Great credit is due to Daniel Hall, the efficient, laborious, and untiring chairman of the State committee, to Edward H. Rollins, the skilful and active organizer, and to all their willing helpers in the State and county organizations," etc.; but that paper placed " first and foremost," Person C. Cheney, the candidate for governor, and added: " It is no disparagement to any other to say of him that he eclipsed any leader we ever had in devotion to the cause, in cheerfulness, courage, in the belief that right would triumph, and in the power of imparting the same spirit to his followers."

The Democratic newspapers, while crediting Rollins with the generalship of the victory, fostered all efforts to defeat his candidacy for the Senate. If he were defeated in his ambition at this time, the Democratic party hoped for his elimination from the politics of the State.

The legislature chosen at this election contained a considerable number of prominent Republicans of the State. Three members were candidates for the United States Senate, Aaron F. Stevens and Orrin C. Moore, of Nashua, and Levi Barton, of Newport. Gilman Marston was returned from Exeter, but he does not appear to have sought at this time the Senatorial nomination. One of his colleagues from the town of Exeter, Horace S. Cummings, was a pronounced champion of Rollins. Cummings made a marked impression upon the legislature, and, had he remained in the State, would have attained to political leadership. The city of Manchester sent to the House David Cross, then in the prime of his activity, Elijah M. Topliff, later chairman of the Republican State committee, William P. Newell, Nathan P. Hunt, and George C. Gilmore, all leading and influential men. The Concord delegation, which was a unit for Rollins, was exceptionally strong. Besides the Speaker of the House, Charles P. Sanborn, there were Oliver Pillsbury, for a long time insurance commissioner, Moses Humphrey, Benjamin F. Gale, Horace A. Brown, and Stillman Humphrey, all four honored by elections as mayors of the city, John Ballard, Joseph C. A. Hill, M. W. Dickerman, and John C. Kilburne. At no time were so many leading Republicans friendly to Rollins elected to the legislature as this year. Nehemiah G. Ordway was returned from Warner, while others to be mentioned were David H. Goodell, of Antrim, and Charles H. Sawyer, of Dover, two future governors of the State, William M. Weed, of Sandwich, Charles J. Amidon, of Hinsdale, Edward Gustine, of Keene, Frank P. Brown, of Whitefield, Wyman Pattee, of Enfield, Augustus A. Woolson, of Lisbon, afterward Speaker, Timothy Kaley, of Milford, Charles Scott, of Peterboro, William S. Pillsbury, of Londonderry, John Wheeler, of Salem, O. B. Warren and S. C. Meader, of Rochester, and Edwin G. Eastman, of Grantham, afterward attorney-general of the State.

The Presidential campaign immediately enlisted public attention. The third term spectre had now faded from the public gaze, as President Grant had stated that he was not a candidate for another nomination. Interest, therefore, centred about the various Republican aspirants for the Presidential nomination. Blaine, who was the leading candidate, was at that time the choice of a majority of New Hampshire Republicans, yet, of those who admired him for his transcendent ability, not a few doubted his success at the polls if nominated. When the Republican State convention met May 24, 1876, to elect delegates to the national convention, it was not thought advisable to declare for Blaine. Ossian Ray, of Lancaster, presided. The following were chosen delegates at large: Daniel Hall, of Dover, Charles H. Burns, of Wilton, Nathaniel White, of Concord, and Ira Colby, of Claremont. The district delegates were George W. Marston, of Portsmouth, Alonzo Nute, of Farmington, in the first district, Jesse Gault, of Hookset, and Ezekiel A. Straw, of Manchester, in the second, and Thomas C. Rand, of Keene, and Benjamin F. Whidden, of Lancaster, in the third.

Interest in the Presidential campaign did not obscure the fact that on the incoming Republican legislature devolved the duty of electing a successor to Aaron H. Cragin in the United States Senate. With the rank and file of the Republican party, Rollins was the first choice. He had been a candidate for this position in 1864, withdrawing at that time so as not to prejudice Concord's interest in remaining the capital of the State, and again in 1866, 1870, and 1872. As the directing force of the State committee, he had conducted the campaign for two years, and, under his guidance, the Republicans had regained control of the State. Aside from the fact of his remarkable aptitude for legislative work, as shown in his Congressional career, there was a feeling of gratitude among Republicans of the State and a desire to show appreciation by electing him to the Senate. Yet he was not to attain his ambition without a contest, which at one time threatened his defeat. He was still treasurer of the Union Pacific Railroad. Toward this road there was a strong prejudice in the popular mind. The road was a debtor to the government, and its management had been involved in several scandals. A considerable number of people felt that Rollins's election to the Senate would give the road a special champion in that body. Other leaders of the party were also ambitious of the honor of representing the State in the Senate, and became candidates. The opposition to Rollins did not concentrate on any one candidate, but divided its forces among several. These candidates were: Orrin C. Moore, James F. Briggs, Aaron F. Stevens, Levi Barton, Charles S. Whitehouse, Onslow Stearns, and Jacob Benton. Cragin was not a candidate for reëlection.

The Republican press of the State began at once after election to take sides on the Senatorship. The *Nashua Telegraph,* whose editor was later, as a member of the legislature, to openly oppose Rollins because of his connection with the Union Pacific Railroad, after remarking that the position should seek the man, said: " The times are calling loudly for a type of men in Washington of which we have too few there. We mean men who have no entangling alliance with rings or monopolies. We mean men whose hands are clean, and who will lead lives of simplicity, no matter what glamour and temptations may surround them. We mean men who will have no other ambition or purpose or scheme except to consecrate themselves to the public service. We mean men who can and will stand up and give a reason for the faith that is in them, who can and will master the great public questions that are pressing for solution upon the country, who can and will stand firmly and boldly forth as champions of those principles and reforms that are essential to good government and to the continued ascendency of the Republican party."

It was charged by Rollins's friends that Moore, in thus stating the qualifications of the man who should be elected Senator, was setting out his own fitness for the position, and that his ambition for the place obscured his judgment of Rollins. Moore denied this impeachment of his motives, saying that he had asked no member of the legislature for his support. That Moore had an ambition to go to the Senate he did not disavow, but his opposition to Rollins was undoubtedly promoted by his belief that no man connected with the Union Pacific Railroad should be elected to the Senate.

Rollins's connection with the Union Pacific Railroad disturbed his personal friends as well as his supporters. Judge Doe, then in private life, in a characteristic letter to Rollins expresses both his friendship for Rollins and his apprehension that his being an officer of the Union Pacific Railroad would be embarrassing. Referring to a conversation he had had with one of the members of the legislature, Doe says: " The Pacific Road is the sole trouble with you, as I supposed it would be. Precisely what course you would think advisable to take in Pacific Railroad matters I cannot be sure. I can see that in such matters your position as Senator would be embarrassing. I have merely expressed my opinion about you when I have heard your nomination opposed, and I understand I am put down as a Rollins man, which is a great mistake. The question of nomination, like all political matters, I do not meddle with, but, when I hear you unfairly dealt with, I shall, as a schoolmate and townsman, do my best to see that you have justice, speaking upon an acquaintance of forty years. So far as that goes, I am ready to bear voluntary testimony that I would not hesitate to trust you anywhere. . . . For old acquaintance' sake, I should defend you whenever defence seemed to be called for by declaring that upon my personal knowledge of you I should entrust any duties private or public to you with perfect confidence in the ability and integrity with which they would be performed."

While the canvass for Senator was moving along,

Blaine, as a candidate for the Presidential nomination, was charged with having improper relations with the Pacific Railroads, and Rollins was accused, as treasurer of the Union Pacific Railroad, of trying to shield Blaine. With this assumption as a basis, further accusations followed that Rollins was unfaithful to his trust as treasurer of the Union Pacific Railroad. Rollins's answer to these charges was the publication of letters from each of the directors of the Union Pacific Railroad appointed by the government. These directors were John C. S. Harrison, of Indiana, J. A. Tibbits, of Connecticut, F. B. Brewer, of New York, J. H. Millard, of Nebraska, and James F. Wilson, of Iowa. Their letters expressed the fullest confidence in Rollins's integrity and ability, and his cordial coöperation in the affairs of the company with the government directors. They all united in saying that, while Rollins had always ceaselessly guarded the interests of the Union Pacific Railroad, he had ever been fair and just to the government. Mr. Millard, in closing his letter, indiscreetly said: "I believe I speak the sentiments of all the government directors in saying that New Hampshire will have in you a most worthy Senator, and, while we shall regret to lose you as our secretary and treasurer, we most earnestly hope the Republicans of the State will honor New Hampshire by making you United States Senator."

As has already been implied, the opposition to Rollins fostered in both Republican and Democratic newspapers attempted to secure his defeat on account of his railroad connections On the day preceding the Republican Senatorial caucus, Orrin C. Moore rose to a personal explanation in the House, in the course of which, referring to the letters of the government directors of the Union Pacific Railroad, he said: "What business and what right has the Union Pacific Railroad Corporation to interfere with the election of a United States Senator in New Hampshire, and what kind of a man is he who attempts to get elected by such means? No such man deserves nor can receive my commendation and support."

This attack upon Rollins created a profound sensation and led to the belief that, if Rollins was nominated in the caucus, Moore would bolt the nomination. The caucus assembled that evening amid intense excitement, for it was expected that Moore would be even more explicit in defining his position before his party associates than before both Democrats and Republicans in the House. The caucus, however, proceeded immediately to ballot, and Rollins received the nomination by just the requisite number of votes.[1] After the excitement incident to the declaration of the vote, Moore arose and moved that the nomination be made unanimous. He then spoke as follows:

[1] The ballot was : Charles P. Sanborn, of Concord, 1 ; Aaron H. Cragin, of Lebanon, 1 ; Jacob Benton, of Lancaster, 8 ; Charles S. Whitehouse, of Rochester, 9 ; Levi W. Barton, of Newport, 12 ; Aaron F. Stevens, of Nashua, 16 ; Onslow Stearns, of Concord, 20 ; James F. Briggs, of Manchester, 20 ; Orrin C. Moore, of Nashua, 21 ; Edward H. Rollins, of Concord, 109.

" I need not say, Mr. Chairman, to the gentlemen present, that I have taken a somewhat active part in the present canvass. I have done so from motives that I need not speak of. I have done the best I could to defeat the nomination of Edward H. Rollins. I have done it honestly; I have done it strenuously; I made up my mind at the outset I would do it outside of the caucus. He has received the nomination, and, sir, I move that the nomination be made unanimous.

" In saying that, Mr. Chairman, I wish to add one word further that may disabuse any gentleman of any remarks that I have made elsewhere to-day, — that, in the remark I made in the House, I only intended — if I was not so understood — that my remarks should apply to the nomination; that I could not support the nomination before it was made. But that nomination has been made in this caucus. So far as I know, it has been made fairly, and it is enough for me. The Republican party has a great duty before it in the canvass that is soon to open on the national field, and it will take all the efforts of the united Republican party to win the canvass, and I have no wish, no purpose, to throw anything into the arena that shall militate against a victory next fall in the State as well as in the nation.

" Mr. Chairman, I put the question to Mr. Rollins just before I came in here to-night, which determined my action in regard to this matter. I said to Mr. Rollins: ' Do you propose, upon your honor, if you are nominated and elected, to sever all your connections, direct or indirect, with the Union Pacific Railroad?' and he gave me his word of honor that he would, and upon that I determined to support his nomination."

Rollins appeared in the caucus in response to an invitation, and accepted the nomination. His speech was informal and brief. He expressed his gratitude for the honor conferred upon him, and pledged the State his best efforts in her behalf. He denied that any railroad had sought or labored for his nomination. He accepted the nomination as from the people, whose servant he should be, and not that of any ring, clique, or corporation. After complimenting his rivals, he thanked them for their generous action in making his nomination unanimous. His election by the legislature followed the next week.

The Republican press of the State very generally commended his selection. The *Monitor* said: " We are gratified, not only because we shall have a Senator who can be counted on to vote right on all the great questions of our time, who is able and practical, and always approachable, not only because it is a just and fitting recognition of the services of a matchless leader, but because we believe that no other result could promise so much for the future success of our party, harmonizing all elements, healing all wounds, and giving a new impetus to the cause of good government everywhere."

The *Dover Enquirer* said: " It is a result emphatically in accordance with the popular will, and in it the legislature has only recognized and carried out the preference and expectations of an overwhelming majority of the Republicans of New Hampshire. No other man would have so satisfied public sentiment as Mr. Rollins. In his success, unwearied service and skilful ability have received deserved appreciation."

The *Portsmouth Journal* said: " The very qualities which make successful soldiers against their political enemies often provoke jealousy in their own ranks, and parties, like republics, are proverbially ungrateful. While we have always acknowledged the very great service of Mr. Rollins in the battles which the party has fought in the State with his constant aid, we have advocated his selection as a candidate from other motives. Mr. Rollins has never disappointed his fellow citizens in any of the responsible interests entrusted to him. A' man who, as Speaker of the State legislature, as member of Congress, as chairman of the State committee in a State where campaigns have been conducted against greater odds and with more ability than in any State in the Union, has always ably and successfully carried through all that he has undertaken, is a man who possesses the elements that will make him a good Senator."

The *Boston Journal* said: " The Republicans of New Hampshire are to be congratulated on the prompt and successful manner in which they have finished up their canvass for the office of Senatorship. There is no doubt whatever that Mr. Rollins was the first choice of the party. From the outset, he has had for competitors some of the ablest men of the State, and the canvass has been earnest and general, yet Mr. Rollins has steadily advanced in strength until his nomination was achieved on the first ballot of the caucus. A large part of the triumph is unquestionably due to a feeling of gratitude on the part of the Republicans of New Hampshire for the invaluable service rendered by Mr. Rollins during so many years. Whenever there have been seasons of special trial, when the cause was in peril and the prospects looked dark, Mr. Rollins has never failed to throw in his efforts as an organizer and director of campaigns with the almost invariable result of victory at the polls. No better manager has ever appeared in a State which peculiarly knows what good political management is. In addition, however, is the feeling that Mr. Rollins has the ability and character to make a United States Senator who will promote the interests of his constituents and prove useful to the general principles of sane legislation. In this connection it is no more than was expected of him by those who knew him that he should declare his purpose on his election to the Senatorship to dissolve all his relations with business enterprises which might come before him as a legislator. In this spirit we have no doubt he will meet and ably discharge all the duties of his new position."

The nomination of Rutherford B. Hayes for President followed almost immediately after the Republican Senatorial caucus in New Hampshire. It came as a surprise and a disappointment to the Republicans of the State. Those who were not for Blaine had a par-

tiality for Benjamin F. Bristow, who was a member of
Grant's Cabinet and who had been identified with the
reform movement within the party.   A ratification
meeting, however, was immediately arranged at Concord, at which Rollins and other leaders of the party
spoke.   The selection, a few weeks later, of Samuel J.
Tilden by the Democratic National Convention as the
standard-bearer of that party, infused the Democrats of
New Hampshire with confidence in the general result
and encouraged them to make a contest to carry the
State.   Chandler and Rollins arranged a mass-meeting
at the capital for September 21st, which was addressed
by Blaine, George William Curtis, and Nathaniel P.
Banks.   The October State elections in Ohio and Indiana indicated a close election in the country in November.   While there was little doubt in the minds of
the Republican leaders of New Hampshire regarding
the result in the State, the campaign was conducted, on
their part, with their customary attention to details.
The result was the choice of the Republican electors by
a majority of about three thousand.   Then followed
the disputed Presidential election, its reference to an
electoral commission, and the decision of the commission that Hayes was elected.   While the Presidential
dispute was in progress, the Republicans opened their
campaign of 1877.

The Republican State convention was held January
10, 1877, and Austin F. Pike, of Franklin, was elected
president.   There was a spirited contest for the nomination of governor, although Benjamin F. Prescott, of

Epping, then Secretary of State, and for a long time secretary of the Republican State committee, was the leading candidate. On the second ballot Prescott was nominated, Natt Head, of Hooksett, being his principal opponent.

Prescott proved to be a popular candidate. Through his connection with the State committee and his service as Secretary of State, he was well known to the people of New Hampshire. He was a man of pleasing personality and a public-spirited citizen. The State owes him a debt of gratitude for the excellent collection of portraits of its governors which now adorns the walls of the State Library.

Jacob H. Gallinger, of Concord, reported the platform which brought forth this commendation from the *Boston Journal:*

"For many years it has been the distinctive privilege of the Republicans of New Hampshire to give the key-note of the campaign, the first utterance of an intelligent people for or against any policy, and the first opinion in the great political crises of the past twenty years. On such critical occasions the New Hampshire Republicans have never failed in their duty In the earliest days of the organization, they sustained the champions of freedom in their contest against the slavery propagandists. In the Lincoln campaign the New Hampshire Republicans gave the first indication of the sentiment of the North. When the contest came between union and secession, the sturdy Republicans of New Hampshire in their March election strengthened the purpose of the loyal heart by their declarations for union. Their bugle-blast of victory was full of inspiration, giving courage to men in Congress and in all the States, and so it has ever been since. Other States, with greater majorities and easier fields to fight, have faltered, but New Hampshire never has wavered in a great crisis."

For Congress Henry W. Blair was renominated in the Third District, and Gilman Marston again secured the nomination in the First District. In the Second District James F. Briggs, of Manchester, was nominated on the first ballot, the vote standing: Briggs 137, Orrin C. Moore 46, Austin F. Pike 24, Nehemiah G. Ordway 21, Charles H. Burns 9.

The Republican State committee organized by the choice of Elijah M. Topliff, of Manchester, as chairman, George E. Jenks, of Concord, secretary, and John Kimball, of Concord, treasurer.

The Democratic State convention was held January 17, 1877. John S. H. Frink, of Greenland, was chosen president. Some opposition developed to the renomination of Daniel Marcy as a candidate for governor, his principal opponent being Frank A. McKean, of Nashua. A ballot, however, showed Marcy largely the choice of the convention, 385 votes being cast for him to 127 for McKean and 12 scattering. The Democrats renominated Frank Jones for Congress in the First District and Henry O. Kent in the Third District. In the Second District they brought forward a new candidate, Alvah W. Sulloway, of Franklin.

Briggs and Sulloway, who were opposing candidates for Congress in the Second District, were coming into prominence as leaders in their respective parties. Both were self-made men and both had great personal influence. Briggs was a successful lawyer, Sulloway a successful manufacturer. Briggs had served in both branches of the legislature and was to serve three terms in Congress. His service in the national House of Representatives was contemporaneous with Rollins's service in the Senate, and he became Rollins's leading rival when the latter sought reëlection to the Senate in 1883. Briggs was one of the strong men of the State, a powerful and fearless advocate in debate when aroused, but not inclined to court controversy. He was courageous in his convictions and loyal in his friendships. His last public service was in the Constitutional Convention of 1902. His public career was a credit to himself and the State.

Sulloway became one of the master spirits of the Democratic party of New Hampshire and helped to shape its policies until the campaign of 1896, when, not agreeing with the principles set forth in the Democratic national platform, he withdrew from active participation in politics. Throughout his political career he possessed the confidence of both political supporters and opponents.

The campaign of 1877 was not exciting. The attention of the whole country was riveted on the proceedings in Congress leading up to the electoral count. The Electoral Commission declared Hayes elected President, to the gratification of Republicans and to the disappointment of Democrats. The latter in New Hampshire seemed to lose heart after the Electoral Commission had concluded its labors, and the March election resulted in a Republican victory except in the First Congressional District. The vote for governor was: scattering, 56; Asa S. Kendall, 338; Daniel Marcy, 36,721; Benjamin F. Prescott, 40,755.

Briggs was elected to Congress in the Second District by 1,097 plurality, Blair in the Third District by ·861 plurality, while Jones secured his reëlection in the First District by 43 plurality.

During the decade from 1870 to 1880, the Democratic party brought a number of its young men to the front. Their names are nearly all to be found in the legislative rolls of those years. The House of Representatives was the arena where they secured their introduction to the public, for the fierce political battles waged in that body during a part of this period afforded excellent opportunity for the display of their talents. The reader familiar with that decade will readily recall the following who were then entering upon a political career: Edward K. Mann, of Haverhill, Frank Hiland, of Manchester, George E. Cochrane, of New Boston, John M. Mitchell and Albert S. Batchellor, of Littleton, Herbert F. Norris, of Epping, Charles A. Jewell, of Plymouth, John T., Lewis F., and Charles A. Busiel, of Laconia, Charles H. Smith, of Newmarket, Frank H. Pierce, of Hillsboro, Nathan C. Jameson, of Antrim, John Hatch, of Greenland, and

Clarence E. Carr, of Andover. Two of the foregoing were afterwards candidates of their party for Congress, several held important State positions, and one, Charles A. Busiel, was elected governor in 1894, having then become a Republican.

CHAPTER XX.

ROLLINS took the oath of office as United States Senator March 4, 1877, at the extra session of the Senate called by President Hayes to confirm the Cabinet and other appointments. He was assigned to the Committees on the District of Columbia, Manufactures, and Audit and Control of the Contingent Expenses of the Senate. At the second session of this Congress he became chairman of the Committee on Manufactures. With the work of the other two committees he was familiar, having served on corresponding committees in the House of Representatives. From the beginning of his Congressional career he had taken a deep interest in the affairs of the District of Columbia. The government of the District was now in the hands of commissioners, and it forced much detail work upon the District committees of both branches of Congress. Legislation for the District occupied a large part of Rollins's time during this Congress. He was frequently called to the chair of the Senate, and, during his term as Senator, he probably presided over that body more than any other Senator except the president *pro tem.* of the Senate.

375

His activity was along the lines which gave him prominence in the other branch of Congress. He made no set speeches, but he participated in debate on measures reported by his own and other committees. His reputation for accomplishing results soon gave him a full calendar of personal requests from constituents and others whose interests were affected by legislation or by the action of the departments. The untiring attention he contributed to all matters entrusted to his charge and the persistency with which he advocated a cause in which he was enlisted gave to him success where others failed. When he had a bill in charge, he never lacked support in the Senate from the older and more prominent Senators, for he was helpful to his associates in the same manner that he was helpful to his constituents. The courtesy of the Senate gave him in return an influence not always possessed by those heard more frequently in debate. As a working member of the Senate, attentive to details, skilful in the management of measures, knowing when to press them to conclusion and when to allow them to be set aside, Rollins was unexcelled in his day. New Hampshire has had more brilliant members of that branch of Congress, men who have been conspicuous in shaping party policies, men who were strikingly prominent in debate, but none who as legislators could count more net results to their credit. The State never had a more useful Senator or one who accomplished more for her benefit.

An instance of the character of Rollins's service to the State is his successful effort in this Congress to secure relief for a number of savings banks of New Hampshire, affected by a ruling of the commissioner of internal revenue on the law in force at that time, taxing bank deposits. This law, as previously interpreted, taxed deposits in banks, but exempted deposits in savings banks. The bank most effected by the ruling of the commissioner of internal revenue was the New Hampshire Savings Bank of Concord, and the story of its case will serve to illustrate the hardship imposed upon the savings banks of the State.

The charter of the Merrimack County Bank of Concord expired in 1866. Its directors were men well advanced in years. They did not care to incorporate as a national bank as other State banks of discount were doing, and so they allowed their charter to expire by limitation. These directors and some of the large depositors of this bank transferred their deposits to the New Hampshire Savings Bank under an arrangement which permitted them to check out these deposits, but allowed them no interest on their balances. These business deposits averaged about fifty thousand dollars. The New Hampshire Savings Bank paid the tax on these business deposits to the United States government under rulings made by two successive commissioners of internal revenue that these deposits and not the deposits of savings depositors were subject to taxation. Other savings banks of the State in towns where there was no national bank accepted business deposits subject to check for the accommodation of the business men of the community, but allowed no interest thereon.

These savings banks regularly returned the amount of their business deposits and paid taxes thereon.

About 1874 a new commissioner of internal revenue held that a savings bank to be entitled to the exemption of the law must have no other deposits than those of savings depositors, and that, when a savings bank took business deposits subject to check, all the deposits of the bank were subject to taxation. While this last ruling was undoubtedly correct, the New Hampshire savings banks were entitled in equity to relief, for the reason that previous commissioners of internal revenue had sanctioned the practice by accepting the tax on the business deposits with a full knowledge of what the savings banks were doing. Then again, the burden did not fall upon the business depositors, but upon many new and later savings depositors who were not depositors at the time the practice prevailed. This ruling not only applied to the future, but related back several years. All the savings banks of the State having business deposits at once paid them in full and discontinued the practice of taking them. The back taxes thus assessed upon New Hampshire savings banks became a burden of no small proportions and in some instances threatened the solvency of these institutions. The savings deposits of the New Hampshire Savings Bank at that time were over a million dollars. The tax due from it was thirty thousand dollars or more, or about one-half of its annual dividend. None of the savings banks of New Hampshire then had any considerable surplus. The New Hampshire Savings Bank contested the ruling of the commissioner and suit was brought against it by the United States government. At the first regular session of this Congress, the matter was brought to Rollins's attention.

Senator Davis, of Illinois, had already introduced a bill in the Senate for the relief of insolvent savings banks. This bill was favorably reported to the Senate by the committee on finance. Rollins offered an amendment providing relief for the New Hampshire savings banks. The amendment at once met with strong opposition. The West and South were without savings banks at that time. The Western and Southern Senators not only opposed the relief for the New Hampshire savings banks, but claimed that the general exemption of savings banks from this tax was a discrimination in favor of the East. Their ground of opposition was that savings banks deposits were used just as much for commercial purposes in the loans made by the savings banks as the deposits of national banks. Being unfamiliar with savings banks, they took no account of the fact that the aggregate of these savings deposits was made up of the small savings of wage-earners, or of the further fact that all of the earnings of the savings banks, except the small cost of their management, were divided among the depositors. They argued that both business and savings deposits made up the banking capital of the community, and that, whereas the West and South paid the tax upon all their banking capital, the East was exempt from taxation of a part of its banking capital. In the debate that followed, Rollins had the assistance of Senators Morrill, of Vermont, and Dawes, of Massachusetts, and finally carried his amendment. The vote was close and along sectional lines. The bill as amended went to the House where it was referred to the committee on ways and means, and there it slumbered for the remainder of the session.

At the second session of the forty-fifth Congress, a revenue bill passed the House of Representatives amending the existing internal revenue law granting relief to certain business interests affected by the law. When the bill came up in the Senate, Rollins offered his old amendment for the relief of the New Hampshire savings banks. Opposition to it was renewed by the Western and Southern Senators. After a spirited debate, the Senate voted to incorporate it in the revenue bill. The measure was then returned to the House for concurrence by that body in a number of amendments made by the Senate. The House readily concurred in most of the amendments offered by the Senate, but non-concurred in some, among which was the Rollins amendment. The bill was then sent to a conference committee of the two houses and each house for a time adhered to its position. The session of the forty-fifth Congress was drawing to a close, only three or four working days remaining. The revenue bill was important to the interests affected by it. The Senate as a whole had no special interest in the relief of New Hampshire savings banks, but many Senators and Representatives, especially those from the South

ınd West, represented constituents who were intensely
nterested in the revenue bill. Rollins insisted that
he revenue bill must pass ,as it left the Senate or not
ıt all.   Owing to the fact that the Senate had still
.everal appropriation bills to dispose of, and, as these
ıills had the right of way, any one Senator could defeat
he revenue bill. Rollins was ready to become that
ıne Senator.   In this way, he held the Senate con-
'erees firm in their position, and finally induced the
Iouse conferees to recede.   The bill with the Rollins
ımendment affording relief to the New Hampshire
avings banks was then accepted by the House and
iecame a law by the President's signature.

On all questions of party policy, Rollins stood with
he stalwart wing of the Republican party. As a mem-
ıer of the national House of Representatives from
.861 to 1867, he had favored the vigorous prosecution
ıf the war, the early abolition of slavery, and all meas-
ıres promoting the welfare of the negro race.   The
ıfteenth amendment of the federal constitution,
dopted during the interim of Rollins's Congressional
ervice, met with his cordial approval, and he was a
trong advocate of the exercise by Congress of the
ıowers therein conferred for its enforcement.   Coming
o the Senate at the beginning of President Hayes's
dministration, Rollins had no faith in the President's
onciliatory policy toward the South. He looked upon
hat policy as an abandonment of the negro and a
urrender of the principles for which the Republican
ıarty had contended. With Conkling and Blaine, he

regarded the recognition by the President of the Democratic State government in Louisiana and South Carolina as an impeachment by President Hayes of his own title, but he did not go so far as to make an issue with the administration on this account. As heretofore, he looked ahead to the next campaign and deprecated any action which might defeat the Republican party or contribute to Democratic success. The administration might make mistakes. To his mind, it was better to bear with these patiently than to take the risk of a Democratic national triumph, which would mean the setting aside of all the principles for which the Republican party had so long battled.

On the financial questions of the forty-fifth Congress, Rollins steadfastly voted against all inflation measures and to sustain the President in upholding the financial credit of the country.

During this Congress, two important campaigns occurred in New Hampshire. The constitutional convention of 1876 had submitted amendments to the State constitution providing for biennial elections and biennial sessions of the legislature, which had been ratified by the people. The legislature of 1877 had provided that these amendments should go into effect in the fall of 1878. There were, therefore, two elections that year, the last annual election in the spring of 1878 and the first biennial election in November of that year. No change had been made in the time of the meeting of the legislature, so that the administrative year began and ended in June. The legislature elected in March, 1878, would meet in June following, and the legislature elected in November, 1878, would meet in June, 1879. By providing that the first biennial election should occur in the fall of 1878, State elections came in the years of the national elections for the choice of members of Congress and President. With the advent of the biennial election and the change of time from March to November, New Hampshire elections became more local in their interest. The State no longer occupied the position of holding the first election in the year, and its importance from a national point of view materially lessened.

Two judicial appointments made by Governor Prescott in the summer of 1877 were severely condemned by many active Republicans of the State. To fill vacancies on the supreme bench he had appointed as judges Isaac W. Smith and Lewis W. Clark. Smith was the Republican member of the supreme court in 1875. He had joined his Democratic associates in declining to give an opinion to the legislature on the action of Governor Weston and his Council in the controversy that year for the control of the State Senate. Clark was the Democratic Attorney-General at that time, advising Governor Weston and his Council that they had the right to go behind the returns. When the Republican legislature of 1876 reorganized the courts, partisan feeling was so intense that Smith was not appointed to the new court. The recognition of these two men by a Republican administration seemed to many Republicans to condone an offence which the people of the State only a year before had condemned. For a time this action of Governor Prescott threatened his renomination. It, however, appeared that many leading Republicans of the State, including Rollins and the chairman of the State committee, had endorsed Smith, and that both he and Clark had the unqualified endorsement of the bar of the State. After several weeks of agitation in the press of the State, the controversy gradually subsided as it became apparent that the rank and file of the party favored Prescott's renomination.

This was not the only difficulty which beset the Republican party of New Hampshire at this time. There was a marked difference of opinion regarding the Southern policy of President Hayes. Many Republicans of the State looked upon his recognition of the Democratic State governments in South Carolina and Louisiana as a capitulation to the Democrats and as an abandonment of the political rights of the negroes of the South. At the Republican State convention to be held in January, the question of the endorsement of President Hayes's policy was sure to arise. There was determined opposition to this policy, and this opposition was disclosed at the meeting of the Republican State committee held the night before the convention to arrange for the organization of that body. Newspaper representatives were excluded from the meeting, so that no verbatim report of the proceedings survives. Such accounts as are given in the press agree that the meeting was a stormy one, the debate becoming at times personal and acrimonious. The outcome, however, was a compromise. Both sides were represented on the committee of resolutions, and the platform carefully avoided the question in controversy. The convention met January 9, 1878. Charles H. Bell, of Exeter, presided, and Governor Prescott was renominated by acclamation. The platform as reported was adopted without dissent. In spite of the harmony of the convention, there was a lack of enthusiasm among the stalwart Republicans of the State, and strenuous efforts on the part of the State committee were necessary to arouse them to activity. While sympathizing with the feelings of those who opposed "the surrender of the President," as it was called, Rollins was urgent in his appeals to them not to make the situation worse by contributing to Democratic success.

The Democratic State convention met January 16, 1878. Henry O. Kent, of Lancaster, presided. John H. George, of Concord, reported the resolutions. A new candidate for governor was looked for, as Daniel Marcy, of Portsmouth, had received the customary two nominations. Among the names canvassed were those of Frank A. McKean, who had been twice elected mayor of Nashua, Warren F. Daniell, of Franklin, and Horatio Colony, of Keene. Sentiment crystallized about McKean, and he was nominated on the first ballot without opposition. McKean was a young man, and his selection was regarded by the party as a new departure. The elections in the fall of 1877 had resulted in Democratic victories, largely owing to dissatisfaction of Republicans with President Hayes's policy. The Democratic leaders of New Hampshire looked for a similar apathy among Republicans of the State. Thus for a time they were somewhat sanguine of McKean's election.

The campaign which followed these conventions was a remarkably quiet one for New Hampshire. Democratic efforts were confined to perfecting the organization of the party. There was but very little campaign speaking, no man of national prominence being brought into the State by either side. The Labor Reformers and the Prohibitionists each made nominations, Samuel Flint, of Lyme, being the candidate for governor of the former, and Asa S. Kendall, of Swansey, the candidate of the Prohibitionists. These nominations were merely perfunctory and the contest was really between the Democratic and Republican parties. The election resulted in the choice of Prescott by the people, but by a reduced majority. The vote was: Scattering, 80; Asa Kendall, 225; Samuel Flint, 269; Frank A. McKean, 37,860; Benjamin F. Prescott, 39,372.

The election was no sooner over than a question arose for discussion growing out of the change from annual to biennial elections and the change in the time of holding the elections. This question and its final outcome had an important bearing upon Rollins's political future and therefore should be considered in detail.

It had not occurred to the constitutional convention

of 1876 that these changes, without altering the time of the meeting of the legislature, would create a hiatus in the succession of the State in the United States Senate. The constitution of the United States gives to Congress the power to prescribe the times and manner of holding elections for United States Senators, and, in the exercise of this power, Congress, in a statute passed July 25, 1866, directed that:

" The legislature of each State which is chosen next preceding the expiration of the term for which any Senator was elected to represent such State in Congress shall, on the second Tuesday after the meeting and organization thereof, proceed to elect a Senator in Congress."

The amendments of the constitution of New Hampshire making elections biennial instead of annual, and changing the time of the election from spring to fall, were to go into effect October 1, 1878. Consequently, a second State election would occur this year, being the first under the biennial system. The legislature chosen in November, 1878, would not meet and organize until June, 1879. The legislature which had been elected in March, 1878, would not go out of existence until June, 1879. The term in the United States Senate of Senator Wadleigh expired March 4, 1879. Which legislature had the right to elect his successor, the one elected in March, 1878, organizing in June, 1878, and expiring in June, 1879, or the one elected in November, 1878, organizing in June, 1879, and expiring two years later? Which was the legislature " chosen next preceding the expiration of the term," etc., the one in existence when the term expired, or the one whose members were elected prior to the expiration of the Senatorial term but who did not qualify as legislators until three months after the term expired? This question now arose for the first time, and did not cease to be a question until after Rollins's defeat for reëlection in 1883. In 1881 it caused a bolt of the Republican Senatorial caucus on the constitutional interpretation of the United States statute, and this bolt paved the way for the bolt two years later on the action of the Republican Senatorial caucus in renominating Rollins.

Senator Wadleigh, who was the individual most interested, opened the discussion in a letter to the Republican newspapers of the State. He took the ground that the legislature to be elected in November, 1878, and organizing in June, 1879, was the legislature which had the undoubted right to elect his successor. He cited as a precedent the unanimous action of the United States Senate in the Blodgett-Norwood case, of Georgia. Foster Blodgett, a Republican, was elected by the legislature of Georgia, February 15, 1870, for the Senatorial term beginning March 4, 1871. Another legislature was chosen in November, 1870, but did not meet and organize until November, 1871. This legislature elected Thomas Norwood, a Democrat, to the same vacancy. The committee on privileges and elections of the Senate to whom the question was referred reported unanimously in favor of Norwood, and he was seated by the unanimous vote of the Senate, then

Republican. On the committee of privileges and elections at that time were Charles Sumner, of Massachusetts, Oliver P. Morton, of Indiana, Benjamin F. Rice, of Arkansas, Matthew H. Carpenter, of Wisconsin, John A. Logan, of Illinois, Joshua Hill, of Georgia, and Allan G. Thurman, of Ohio.

William E. Stevens, editor of the *Monitor,* took up the discussion, stating the arguments in favor of and against the position taken by Senator Wadleigh, and came to the conclusion that it was the right and duty of the legislature convening in June, 1878, to elect Senator Wadleigh's successor. In addition to the legal argument made in favor of this course, a political reason was urged in its favor. The spring election of 1878 had been very close. The Republicans had elected their governor and a majority of the legislature. There was a possibility that the Democrats might carry the State in the fall election. It could do no harm for the Republicans to elect a Senator by the legislature convening in June, 1878, even if the action of that body had to be ratified by the legislature to be elected in November, 1878. The Democrats generally took the view of Wadleigh, as, with the postponement of the election to the legislature organized in June, 1879, they had another opportunity to carry the State and win the Senatorial prize. Harry Bingham, however, was quoted by Wadleigh as affirming that the legislature meeting in June, 1878, had the right to elect a Senator. The Blodgett-Norwood case seemed to show what action the United States

Senate would take in the event of a Senator elected by the legislature which convened in June, 1878, applying for admission, until this case was dissected by William E. Chandler in a personal letter to Jonathan E. Sargent, a member-elect of the incoming legislature, which was soon after published in the *Monitor*.

Chandler said: " My first impression was against the right (of the legislature convening in June, 1878, to elect), owing to the Blodgett-Norwood case, but an examination of the facts there removed it as a precedent. Blodgett was elected February 15, 1870, to fill a term to commence March 4, 1871, but, when he was elected, there was to be a legislature elected in November, 1870, to meet January, 1871. Of course Blodgett's election was illegal, and was so held by the Senate. To cure its illegality, the legislature which elected him postponed the meeting of the next legislature from January, 1871, to November, 1871. But this subsequent subterfuge did not save the election, particularly as the legislature after postponing the meeting of its successor did not ratify Blodgett's election by a new declaration. It was a trick, and void when made and not cured by subsequent action. This case would be a precedent if the New Hampshire legislature to be chosen next November were to meet January 1st, not otherwise.

" The whole intention of the statute of July 25, 1866, was to prevent vacancies in the Senate, not to determine which was the proper legislature to elect, and to prevent one branch thereof from defeating an election. . . . My own opinion on this whole subject is not wholly fixed. I do not ask a reply from you, but only that you will investigate a question of some difficulty and of too great importance to the Republican party to be decided by any one man or according to the personal interest of any individual, but as may be for the best good of the whole."

Henry W. Blair, then a member of the national House and a candidate for Senator Wadleigh's seat, secured an opinion on this question from Matthew H. Carpenter, who was chairman of the Senate committee on privileges and elections when the Blodgett-Norwood case was decided. Carpenter agreed with Chandler that this case was not parallel to that of New Hampshire. He also took the ground that the legislature meeting in June, 1878, being the last legislature organized before the expiration of the term, should elect a Senator.

Another argument for an election by the legislature meeting in June, 1878, was that, if the legislature in being at the time the Senatorial term expired did not fill the vacancy, New Hampshire for the space of three months, at the close of every Senatorial term, would not have her equal representation in the Senate with other States, an equality guaranteed by the federal constitution. While this discussion was going on, an attempt was made to have Congress pass some declaratory or enabling act to cover the New Hampshire situation. Rollins in the Senate and Blair in the House appear to have been earnest and active to secure such a declaration. The time, however, was short in which to secure such a result. The New Hampshire legislature met while this discussion was going on, but, before the time came for it to act, a report was made by the committee on privileges and elections of the Senate affirming that the right to elect a Senator vested in the legislature which would meet in June, 1879. The legislature of New Hampshire, therefore, took no action, for it was apparently useless to elect a Senator if he was not to be admitted by the Senate. This decision of the Senate was not accepted as final, for some Republicans, and especially those opposed to Wadleigh's reëlection, believed that his position as chairman of the committee on privileges and elections had some influence with the committee in securing from it the report made to the Senate.

Immediately after the adjournment of the legislature of 1878, the Republican State committee convened to fix the times and places of meeting of the conventions for the fall campaign. The Republican State convention met September 10, 1878. It was presided over by Charles H. Burns, of Wilton, and James W. Patterson, of Hanover, reported the resolutions. There was an earnest rivalry between the friends of Natt Head, of Hooksett, and Charles H. Bell, of Exeter, to secure the gubernatorial nomination. The contest was settled on the first ballot by a vote of 412 for Head, 282 for Bell, and 6 scattering.

For Congress, the Republicans renominated James

F. Briggs in the second district, while Joshua G. Hall, of Dover, was selected on the first ballot in the first district. In the third district, three ballots were necessary to effect a nomination. The leading candidates were Ossian Ray, of Lancaster, Levi W. Barton, of Newport, Chester Pike, of Cornish, and Evarts W. Farr, of Littleton, the latter leading on the first ballot and winning on the third.

Evarts W. Farr was a young man of great promise. At the outbreak of the Civil War, he left Dartmouth College to enlist as a soldier when the call came for volunteers, and he was the first man to sign the muster roll at Littleton. Commissioned as lieutenant, he was successively promoted until he was in command of his regiment. He was dangerously wounded at the battle of Williamsburg, Virginia, and had his arm amputated on the field of battle. Refusing to resign on account o his disability, he continued in the service until the close of the war. Elected to Congress, he rapidly attained distinction when his public career was cut short by his untimely death after his second election to that body.

Joshua G. Hall was a lawyer in good standing in his section of the State. He had served in both branches of the legislature and had been mayor of Dover for two terms. At the time of his nomination for Congress, he was serving as United States district attorney by appointment of President Hayes.

The Democratic State convention met September 12, 1878. Hosea W. Parker, of Claremont, presided.

Frank A. McKean was renominated by acclamation. At the Democratic Congressional conventions Alvah W. Sulloway, of Franklin, was renominated in the second district, and Henry O. Kent, of Lancaster, in the third district. In the first district, Herbert F. Norris, of Epping, was nominated on the first ballot.

Norris was one of the young Democrats of the State who had come into prominence through his service as a member of the legislatures of 1877 and 1878. A ready debater, a good parliamentarian, he had already developed strong qualities of leadership. He had a good legal mind and would have made a success at the bar, for which he was educated. Drifting into journalism, he was for a time editorial writer on the *Manchester Union*. Taking up his residence in Boston not long after this service to the politics of New Hampshire, he has since been identified with the newspapers of that city.

The Greenback movement, which had made itself felt in other States, came into prominence in New Hampshire during this campaign. A State convention at which 362 delegates were present was held at Manchester. Cyrus A. Sulloway, of Manchester, presided. Warren G. Brown, of Whitefield, was nominated as a candidate for governor. The Greenback party nominated candidates for Congress in all three districts, Lafayette Chesley, of Nottingham, in the first, Cyrus A. Sulloway, of Manchester, in the second, and James W. Johnson in the third.

Cyrus A. Sulloway's career in New Hampshire politics is unique. His political mistakes in early life, due to an impulsive and generous temperament, retarded his advancement. They were overlooked, however, by reason of his frankness in admitting them. Of commanding stature, original expression, and strong mental equipment, he is popular in campaigns. He served many terms in the New Hampshire legislature. Returning to full accord with the Republican party in the campaign of 1892, he was elected to the fifty-fourth Congress, and has since been reëlected four times. For the last three Congresses he has been chairman of the Committee on Invalid Pensions.

There was a large number of Republican rallies during the fall campaign of 1878. In addition to his work in the State committee, Rollins was active upon the stump. William P. Frye, of Maine, opened the campaign at Manchester. With the exception of Frye, there were no outside speakers of national reputation, and the people of the State realized for the first time that the New Hampshire election, by its transfer from March to November, had lost its national importance. From this time forward both New Hampshire Republicans and Democrats had to depend largely upon local talent for campaign speaking.

The election resulted in a complete victory for the Republican party. The vote for governor was: Scattering, 129; Warren G. Brown, 6,385; Frank A. McKean, 31,083; Natt Head, 38,085. The Republican plurality in the first Congressional district was 2,502, in the second 2,941, and in the third, 952. The Republicans had a very large majority in the legislature.

CHAPTER XXI.

ROLLINS IN THE FORTY-SIXTH CONGRESS

THE forty-sixth Congress was convened in extra session March 18, 1879. There was a vacancy in the Senate from New Hampshire because of the expiration of Senator Wadleigh's term, no successor having been chosen by the legislature. Governor Prescott appointed Charles H. Bell, of Exeter, to fill the vacancy, and Senator Rollins presented his credentials. Objection was made to receiving the credentials on the ground that this was not such a vacancy as the executive of the State could fill by appointment. The constitution provides that "if vacancies happen by resignation or otherwise during the recess of the legislature of any State, the executive thereof may make temporary appointments until the next meeting of the legislature, which shall then fill such vacancies." Did this vacancy so happen within the meaning of the constitution that the governor of New Hampshire could fill it by appointment? If the governor of a State could fill any vacancy occurring during a recess of the legislature, why had not the constitution so provided in express terms? It was generally admitted that the legislature could so far fail of its duty that

397

the executive of the State could not fill the vacancy by appointment. Was the New Hampshire vacancy such a case?

The situation in New Hampshire was exceptional, as has already been explained. A doubt existed as to which of two legislatures had the right to elect Senator Wadleigh's successor. The question had been brought to the attention of the previous Senate, and that body had permitted it to be understood that, without an enabling act, the legislature of June, 1878, could not fill the vacancy. The Senate had passed an enabling act which failed of becoming a law in conference of the two Houses of Congress. The State of New Hampshire had acted upon the best light it could obtain, for the Senate was the "judge of the election, returns, and qualifications of its members." Of what use was it for the legislature of 1878 to elect a Senator if he was not likely to be admitted? Should New Hampshire be deprived of her equal representation in the Senate because there was no legislature qualified to continue her Senatorial succession in that body? All of these questions entered into the discussion which followed the presenting of Bell's credentials, and the equities of the case had something to do with settling it in Bell's favor. Replying to the objection made to Bell's credentials, Senator Rollins said:

"Mr. President, before action is taken on the pending question I desire to submit for the consideration of the Senate such precedents as I find which in my judgment are entitled to weight in the consideration of this case. After a most careful and diligent scrutiny of the records of the Senate from the foundation of the government down to the present time, I have found the following cases only of appointments made to fill a vacancy occasioned by the expiration of a term of office:

"William Cocke, a Senator from the State of Tennessee, whose term of service expired March 3, 1797, was on the 22d of April, 1797, appointed by the governor to fill the vacancy occasioned by the expiration of his term. His credentials were presented May 15, 1797, and he was admitted without objection.

"Uriah Tracy, a Senator from the State of Connecticut, whose term expired March 3, 1801, was admitted as a member of the Senate at the special session called March 4, 1801, under the appointment of the governor. Exceptions being taken to his credentials, he was admitted by a vote of thirteen yeas to ten nays, and held his seat until he was elected by the legislature in May following.

"William Hindman, a Senator from the State of Maryland, whose term of office expired March 3, 1801, was appointed by the governor March 4, 1801, and was admitted as a member of the Senate March 5, 1801, without objection. He served until the election of his successor.

"John Condit was appointed Senator from the State of New Jersey, September 1, 1803, in place of Aaron Ogden, whose term expired March 3, 1803. He was admitted as a member of the Senate October 17,

1803, without objection, and held his seat until his election by the legislature in November following. In this case the appointment does not seem to have been made until a vacancy actually existed, which is identical with the case under consideration.

" Joseph Anderson, a Senator from the State of Tennessee, whose term expired March 3, 1809, was admitted as a member of the Senate at the extra session convened March 4, 1809, without question, under an appointment from the governor of his State. He served until he was elected by the legislature.

" Samuel Smith, a Senator from the State of Maryland, whose term expired March 3, 1809, was admitted as a member of the Senate at the special session March 4, 1809, under an appointment by the executive. He was admitted without objection and held his seat until elected by the legislature in November following.

" Charles Cutts, a Senator from the State of New Hampshire, whose term expired March 3, 1813, was admitted as a member of the Senate at the special session on May 24, 1813, without question, under the appointment of the governor of his State, and served until the election of Jeremiah Mason in June following.

" John Williams, a Senator from the State of Tennessee, whose term expired March 3, 1817, was admitted as a member of the Senate at the extra session called March 4, 1817, without objection, under an appointment by the executive, — his credentials having been read and filed during the previous session, —

and held his seat until reëlected by the legislature in October following.

"James Lanman, a Senator from the State of Connecticut, whose term expired March 3, 1825, was appointed by the governor February 8, 1825, to fill the vacancy which would occur at the expiration of his term. His credentials were presented at the called session March 4, 1825, and question being raised, the decision of the Senate was adverse to his right. The Senate in this case, as is shown by the report of the committee, decided that a vacancy could not be filled by a governor until it actually existed. The Lanman case also differs from that of Mr. Bell in this: that the legislature of Connecticut which had held its annual session the May previous, notwithstanding it had a legal right to elect a Senator, failed to fill the vacancy.

"Ambrose H. Sevier, a Senator from the State of Arkansas, whose term expired March 3, 1837, was appointed by the governor January 17, 1837, to fill the vacancy which would occur at the expiration of his term. At the called session March 4, 1837, objection was made, but he was admitted.

"In both cases of Lanman and Sevier, the appointments were made in anticipation of a vacancy which would occur at some future time. Such was the fact in the cases of Messrs. Tracy, Anderson, and Williams, and the decision in the Lanman case stands alone against all the others.

"The appointments of Messrs. Cocke, Hindman,

Condit, Smith, and Cutts appear to have been made after the vacancy actually occurred, and they were admitted without question.

" These are all the cases found in the records where an appointment has been made by the executive of any State to fill a vacancy occurring by the expiration of a term of office.

" In three cases, — those of Messrs. Tracy, Lanman, and Sevier, — appointments made in anticipation of a vacancy about to occur, question was made; and in two of these cases, Tracy and Sevier, the appointees were admitted. In the other case he was rejected. In five cases, where the appointment was made after the vacancy actually occurred, the appointees were admitted without question.

" In the case under consideration the appointment was made after the vacancy actually occurred, the credentials bearing date of March 13, 1879, the appointment having been made by the executive of New Hampshire after the expiration of the term of Senator Wadleigh, and subsequent to the call of the President of the United States for an extra session of Congress.

" The act of Congress of July 25, 1866, requires that Senators shall be elected by the legislature ' chosen next preceding the expiration ' of any term. By reason of a change in the constitution of New Hampshire which took effect October 1, 1878, two legislatures were chosen in the year 1878, one in March under the old constitution, whose term of office commenced in June, 1878, and will continue to June, 1879, and the other in November, whose term of office will not commence until June, 1879, and will continue to June, 1881.

" Upon a bill being introduced into the Senate of the United States in June, 1878, to define which of these two legislatures had the power to elect a successor to Mr. Wadleigh, the committee on privileges and elections made a report (No. 485) that only the legislature chosen in November, 1878, had the power, which report was adopted by the Senate. The legislature chosen in March, therefore, took no steps to elect a successor to Mr. Wadleigh. But the legislature chosen in November, 1878, cannot be assembled until June, 1879. Therefore, in March, 1879, when the vacancy occurred, there was no legislature in being or capable of being assembled with power to elect a Senator. On the principle of the Sevier case, therefore, the governor had the right of appointment.

" In these circumstances, with these precedents, I hope the oath of office will be administered to Mr. Bell. Then, if it is desirable to make any inquiry, the credentials may be referred to the committee on privileges and elections."

Objection still being made to the acceptance of Bell's credentials, they were referred to the committee on privileges and elections, before whom Rollins appeared in advocacy of Bell's admission. The committee reported its findings to the Senate, April 2d, in majority and minority reports, the division of the committee being along party lines. The Democratic majority reported against Bell's admission and the Republican minority in favor of it. The debate which followed covered all the points at issue and was participated in by some of the ablest lawyers of the Senate. Although the committee divided on party lines, this was not the case with the Senate, the strongest argument against Bell's admission being made by Senator Matthew H. Carpenter, of Wisconsin, Republican, and the most effective in his favor by Senator Thomas F. Bayard, of Delaware, Democrat. The Democrats had eight majority in the Senate, so the admission of Bell would not affect their supremacy in that body. The discussion was entirely free from partisan references. The opponents of Bell's admission claimed that the Lanman case did more than settle the point made by Rollins, that the governor could not appoint until after a vacancy actually occurred, that it really determined that the executive could not appoint when the legislature had an opportunity to act and failed to do its duty. They also asserted that the precedent established in the Lanman case had not been departed from by the Senate since that time, as the Sevier case, which occurred later, differed from the Lanman case in that Sevier and his colleague from Arkansas were Senators chosen prior to the admission of the State, and had to determine between themselves by lot the length of their terms as required by the constitution, and that the legislature could not know in advance which would draw the short term expiring while the legislature was not in session.

In the course of the debate, the action of the previous Senate in declaring that the legislature of June, 1878, had not the right to choose Wadleigh's successor came up for consideration and criticism. Senators Conkling and Kernan, of New York, Blaine, of Maine, Carpenter, of Wisconsin, Davis, of Illinois, McDonald, of Indiana, Hill, of Georgia, Beck, of Kentucky, and Eaton, of Connecticut, repudiated it, Senator Eaton going so far as to intimate that the opinion of the Senate was secured by a trick. Cameron, of Wisconsin, defended the McMillan report, and his view that the legislature of 1878 had not the right to elect Wadleigh's successor received the support of Bayard, Dawes, and other Senators. So far as disclosed, the opposition of most of Bell's opponents was that the legislature of June, 1878, had the right to elect a Senator and had failed to do its duty. Rollins, who was championing Bell's admission, wisely refrained from discussing the question which legislature of New Hampshire had the right to elect Wadleigh's successor, but based his reply to the objections raised to Bell's admission on the equities of the case as shown by the facts presented in their relation to the precedents of the Senate. In his second speech in this debate, he said:

"As we understand the Lanman case, Mr. Bell's application does not conflict with it at all. It may be summed up in a few words. In that case a legislature competent to elect had met and failed to elect a Senator. In this case no legislature met prior to his appointment that was competent to elect. The Senate of the United States had so decided. In the case of Mr. Lanman, the appointment was made in anticipation of a vacancy. In this case, the appointment was not made until after the vacancy happened, so that it makes no difference whatever for the present purpose how you construe the Lanman case. If you say that it turned upon the question of the appointment of the governor prior to the happening of the vacancy, then it is not a precedent to govern in this case. If you say that it turned upon the other point (and that I am inclined to think is the true state of the case), if it turned upon the point made by the Senator from Tennessee that a legislature competent to fill the vacancy having once been in session and that legislature having failed to perform its clear duty, the power of the governor was exhausted and the Senate of the United States did right in rejecting Mr. Lanman. Still that is not this case. No legislature of New Hampshire has ever been in session nor could any legislature have been convened prior to the vacancy that could elect a Senator to fill the vacancy, if the decision of the Senate of the United States upon that question last June is the correct decision. A single suggestion further, Mr. President, as to one other point. There may be some who believe that the legislature of New Hampshire which held its session in June, 1878, should have elected a Senator to succeed Senator Wadleigh, whose term was then about to expire. There was some conflict of opinion about this among lawyers, and the matter was referred to a committee of the Senate, and, upon their report, the Senate (the final tribunal for the decision of such questions) denied the right of that legislature to elect. This construction of the law made by the only tribunal authorized to act thereon was accepted as binding. The legislature could not be expected to elect in the face of that decision, and, if that decision was wrong and a vacancy happened thereby, the State ought not to suffer."

It is apparent that a number of the Senators who voted in favor of Bell's admission were influenced to do so by the situation in which New Hampshire had been placed by the action of the previous Senate. Bell's cause was ably championed by Senators Hoar, of Massachusetts, Blaine, of Maine, Cameron, of Wisconsin, McMillan, of Michigan, Republicans, and Bayard, of Delaware, McDonald, of Indiana, Jones, of Florida, and Groome, of Maryland, Democrats. He also had the support of Thurman, of Ohio, although the latter was absent when the vote was taken. The vote stood 35 in favor to 29 against, and Bell was sworn in as a Senator. Senators Carpenter and Conkling, Republicans, and Davis, Independent, voted against Bell's admission, while ten Democrats voted in his favor.

Rollins was entitled to, and received credit for, the skill with which he handled the Bell case. Very few people in New Hampshire had confidence in Bell's admission to the Senate. The Democratic party had come into control of that body for the first time since 1861, and the extra session opened with political debates in both houses. The Lanman case was generally regarded as an adverse and well-established precedent. The Senate which gave the opinion that prevented the legislature of June, 1878, from electing a Senator had a Republican majority. Of that Senate some twenty or more had been retired to private life and new men had taken their places. It was a good deal to expect that even the equities of the case would prevail with the new Democratic majority. New Hampshire had changed her constitution with the full knowledge of the United States statute of 1866. The Republican party had controlled the constitutional convention of 1876. The Republican party in the legislature of 1877 had fixed the time for the constitutional amendment to go into effect. The Republican party again in 1878 had appealed to a Republican Senate to interpret the work of the constitutional convention. If the opinion of the previous Senate had been obtained by a trick, as Senator Eaton intimated in the debate, there was no obligation resting upon the Democratic majority of this Senate to set the matter right. No just complaint could have been made if the Democratic Senators had stood together in refusing to admit Bell as a Senator. The decision of the Senate, therefore, came as a surprise to both Republicans and Democrats of New Hampshire. The *Exeter News Letter,* whose editor was in Washington at the time, and who was intensely interested in Bell's case, had this to say of Rollins's part in the contest:

"To Senator Rollins of New Hampshire must be accredited the work of preparing the case for presentation to the Senate. From first to last he steadfastly maintained and contended for the right of his State to full representation in the Senate, all hair-splitting objections to the contrary notwithstanding. He produced an overwhelming array of precedent cases, all of which sustained the demand for admission. These cases he submitted in an argument before the Senate, and the minority of the committee embodied them in its report. Mr. Rollins also spoke in a long debate that followed the report, making one of the strongest speeches of that discussion."

The Democrats being in control of the Senate, Rollins, with other members of the minority party, took lower places on committees. Rollins was assigned to the committees on manufactures, District of Columbia, civil service and entrenchment and enrolled bills. Later, he was made a member of two special committees, one on the Yorktown centennial celebration, and the other, contagious diseases among cattle. His principal committee work was on that of the District of Columbia, the record showing him reporting a large number of measures for the benefit of the District, debating their provisions, and working to secure legislative action.

At this date and for some years after, all appropriation bills were in the control of the committee on appropriations of the Senate. There existed opposition to the rule that referred all these bills to that committee, for the reason that it placed large power in the hands of a very few men. Rollins, early in the session, introduced a resolution to amend the rules so as to divide the work of the appropriation committee. His resolution left the committee on appropriations the legislative, deficiency, and sundry civil appropriation bills, but gave to the committees on military affairs, naval affairs, foreign relations, Indian affairs, post-offices, commerce, District of Columbia, pensions, public buildings and grounds, and agriculture the appropriation bills relating to the subjects usually referred to these committees. This was a most radical change of rules, and the resolution was referred to the committee on rules, where it was kept for the remainder of the Congress. Within a few years a division of the appropriation bills among the various committees of the Senate has taken place along the lines suggested by Rollins, but the present practice is not so sweeping a change as was indicated by his resolution.

The time of this Congress was taken up largely with the consideration of political matters, the Democrats devoting much time through their control of the committees of both Houses to investigating the departments of government and elections in some of the Northern States. Some of these investigations were the work of the committee on civil service and retrenchment, of which Rollins was a member and Butler, of South Carolina, chairman. Toward the close of the second session Rollins made a political speech reviewing the work of these investigating committees. Like all of his political speeches, it was not only pointed but exasperating to the Democrats. Fortified by the facts presented to the committee of which he was a member, he made comparison of election methods North and South, which was especially provoking to Senators Butler, of South Carolina, and Lamar, of Mississippi. Both resented the imputations put upon their States by Rollins's exhibits and gave notice of intention to reply formally. Congress, however, adjourned *sine die* within a short time without either Senator making specific answer to the charges. The debate on the questions raised by these investigations continued to the close of the session.

Rollins also made a speech in opposition to a bill providing for the promotion of certain naval officers. This was one of those measures intended to give advance rank to certain officers of the navy who, it was claimed, had been slighted by the Navy Department in its general provisions for promotions. After showing by the records that no injustice had been done them, he objected to the practice of Congress interfering in such matters as demoralizing to the efficiency of the service. This was the beginning of some very effective work on his part in behalf of the navy, for in the next Congress he became a member of the committee on naval affairs.

CHAPTER XXII.

EVENTS IN NEW HAMPSHIRE

IT had been foreshadowed for some time that Senator Wadleigh was to have opposition to his return to the Senate. As soon as the fall election of 1878 was over, the contest for a seat in the Senate began. Wadleigh's leading opponent was Henry W. Blair, whose second term as Congressman expired with the forty-fifth Congress. Blair developed a remarkable personal following, which he successfully held for many years. All of his campaigns were directed by himself and he was without an equal in New Hampshire politics in the art of attaching men to his political fortunes. Loyal to his supporters and the principles of the party, accepting criticism without complaint, a philosopher in every emergency, he triumphed over varied opposition. He had the courage of his convictions and did not hesitate to champion an unpopular cause. His obliging disposition and readiness to give every subject a hearing attached his name to projects for which he was in no wise responsible and which never received his direct approval. The obloquy he incurred on this account at no time drew from him explanation or apology, although it affected contempo-

412

rancous judgment of his ability. His educational bill, a national measure for the benefit of the South, which just failed of success, would have been the solution of some of the present problems of that section of the country. After serving two terms in the Senate, he was again returned to the national House of Representatives, redeeming a district which had been twice lost by the Republican party. His service in both Houses of Congress covered a period of eighteen years, a record made by only one of his predecessors in New Hampshire.

Other avowed candidates for Wadleigh's seat were Orrin C. Moore, Gilman Marston, and Aaron F. Stevens, the last two being members of the incoming legislature. Marston was a gallant soldier of the Civil War, an able lawyer, and had served three terms in Congress. During his service in the New Hampshire legislature, he invariably held the position of chairman of the judiciary committee. In this place he was of unquestioned service to the State in preventing crude and unnecessary legislation. He did not often participate in debate, but, when he did, the House was frequently carried by the strength of his argument and his eloquence. He had a gruff exterior, but underneath the surface lay a disposition susceptible of emotion and sympathy. His ambition, gratified only by executive appointment later to fill a vacancy, was to go to the United States Senate. He had been a candidate with considerable support as early as 1864, and he continued to hope for an election until the close of his active life.

This ambition was not without its influence on his public career and caused him to bend frequently before clouds threatening popular disfavor. It was his weakness, yet to the last there was a profound admiration for his ability, which ranked him as one of the intellectually great men of the State.

Stevens was the Republican party leader on the floor for many legislative sessions. He, too, had served with distinction in the Civil War, while in civil life he had attained national distinction. He was twice elected to Congress, where his ability was recognized, but he failed of a third election by just a few votes. In all the political contests of the legislatures of which he was a member, the burden of defending the Republican cause against the assaults of such Democratic leaders as Harry Bingham and John G. Sinclair devolved upon him. In debate and parliamentary procedure he demonstrated again and again his capacity for leadership. The party was undoubtedly indebted to him for many of its legislative triumphs. Stevens was a man of commanding presence, and to those who did not enjoy his intimate acquaintance his manner sometimes seemed haughty and repelling, but his friends were devoted and loyal. He, too, had been an aspirant for the United States Senate, having entered the lists in 1870 as a candidate against Aaron H. Cragin when the latter was seeking reëlection. His canvass at this time was conducted with great shrewdness. Being the first choice of only a small number of members, he secured a large number of pledges as second choice. His vote grew after the first ballot, and the contest finally narrowed to a choice between him and Blair. Had Stevens been nominated it might have had an important bearing on the election of Rollins's successor two years later. Certainly it would have removed from the arena one of the leading opponents to Rollins's reëlection.

The Republican legislative caucus was held the week preceding the time for the election of a Senator by the legislature. Nine ballots were necessary to a choice, which resulted in Blair's favor.[1]

The campaign of 1880, in New Hampshire, early gave promise of being closely contested. The Democrats fixed upon Frank Jones, of Portsmouth, as their candidate for governor. He had twice carried the first Congressional district as a candidate for Congress, and his party had strong hopes of electing him as its gubernatorial candidate. The party also made special efforts to strengthen the ticket in its Congres-

	1st	2d	3d	4th	5th	6th	7th	8th	9th
[1] Chandler	1								
Bell	1	1	1	1	1	1	1	1	
Harriman					1				
Tappan								2	
Doe	2	1	1						
Briggs		2	2	5	2	2			
Prescott				2	4	3			
Patterson	6	3	4	3			1		
Stevens	20	22	30	49	58	60	79	91	92
Marston	22	23	23	26	26	20	4		
Moore	23	28	28	28	32	32	25	2	
Wadleigh	45	40	32	9	1		1		
Blair	68	67	66	64	64	70	76	91	94

sional nominations. The Republican nomination for governor was settled in advance of the convention. Charles H. Bell, of Exeter, who had been a candidate for the nomination in the previous convention and who had served for three months in the Senate by executive appointment, was the choice of the entire party. He was a man of scholarly attainments and acknowledged ability. He had served in both branches of the legislature and had been Speaker of the House and president of the Senate. Prior to his appointment to the United States Senate, he had for several years retired from active politics. He proved to be an exceptionally strong candidate.

The Republican State convention was held September 7, 1880, being called to order by the chairman of the Republican State committee, Henry H. Huse. Daniel Barnard, of Franklin, presided, and Ossian Ray, of Lancaster, reported the resolutions. Bell was nominated by acclamation. In the first Congressional district Joshua G. Hall was renominated, as was Evarts W. Farr in the third district. In the second district there was opposition to giving James F. Briggs a third nomination, but through Rollins's influence he was renominated. The Republican State committee reorganized by the reëlection of Henry H. Huse as chairman, George E. Jenks as secretary, and John Kimball as treasurer, with Rollins still chairman of the executive committee.

The Democratic State convention met September 15, 1880, being called to order by the chairman of the

State committee, George F. Putnam, of Haverhill. John H. George, of Concord, presided. Harry Bingham, of Littleton, placed Frank Jones in nomination for governor, and he received 600 of the 601 votes cast. The Democratic Congressional candidates were John W. Sanborn, of Wakefield, in the first district, Alvah W. Sulloway, of Franklin, in the second, and George A. Bingham, of Littleton, in the third, the latter resigning from the Supreme Court to accept the nomination.

Entire harmony marked the action of the Democrats in this campaign. They were made especially enthusiastic by the result of the Maine election, which occurred just before their convention assembled. The first returns from that State chronicled a Democratic victory, and the result was a great disappointment to the Republicans. It, however, stirred them to greater activity. Rollins threw himself into the campaign with his accustomed vigor and was at headquarters directing affairs until the campaign closed. The result was a great surprise to the Democrats. Bell was elected governor by a popular majority of 3,500, and the Republicans carried the legislature by a large majority. They also carried all of the Congressional districts and had a majority of four thousand for their electoral ticket. Both the Prohibitionists and the Greenbackers made nominations in this campaign, but the vote of these two parties was insignificant.

The election was no sooner over than the old question of which legislature should elect a Senator was revived. Senator Bell, during his brief term in the

Senate, had introduced a bill in relation to the election of a Senator from New Hampshire which was referred to the committee on privileges and elections, to be subsequently reported adversely by that committee and indefinitely postponed by the Senate without debate. Senator Rollins's term would expire March 4, 1883. The legislature to be chosen in November, 1882, would not meet until June, 1883, and the legislature just chosen would be the last legislature elected and organized before the expiration of Rollins's term. The opinion of some of the ablest lawyers of the Senate was that the legislature elected and organized was the legislature "chosen next preceding the expiration of the term." There were two ways of preventing a hiatus in the Senatorial terms of New Hampshire. One was for the legislature in being at the time the term expired to elect a Senator and let the Senate decide the question of his admission. The other was to get the people of New Hampshire to call a constitutional convention to change the time of the meeting of the legislature. The latter course had its difficulties, for a majority of the people must be convinced of the necessity of calling a convention. The convention when assembled must vote for the amendment, and, when the amendment was submitted to the people, two-thirds of the votes cast must be cast in its favor. Rollins determined to bring the question before the incoming legislature as the short and direct cut to the solution of the problem. Out of this appeal of Rollins to the legislature of June, 1881, came another constitutional convention in New Hampshire, but eight years elapsed before it was called.

The Democratic party, which had nothing to lose and everything to gain by preventing an election by the legislature to meet in June, 1881, naturally lined up in opposition to Rollins's effort. The Republicans of the State looked at his proposition from different points of view. Coming as it did from a candidate for reëlection, the aspirants for Rollins's seat regarded it as giving him an unfair advantage over themselves. The question had not entered into the preceding campaign, and it was asserted by those who were opposed to Rollins that he had quietly secured the election of his friends and supporters as members of this legislature, while the other aspirants for Senatorial honors had refrained from effort in the belief that the question of the election of a Senator would not come to the front until two years later. There is no evidence that Rollins had interested himself in the selection of Republican members of the legislature, but his opponents believed, and were, therefore, firm in the opinion, that his connection at Republican headquarters with the preceding campaign had given him this opportunity. Again, there were Republicans who thought that, whatever the legal aspects of the case, a Senator should not be elected so long in advance of the beginning of his term. If the legislature of June, 1881, were to choose a Senator, it would be a year and nine months before his term began, and, unless there was an extra session of the Senate or of Congress, he would not be called upon to perform any legislative duties for two years and a half. When, therefore, the question came before the Republican members of the legislature, the legal proposition was mixed with political and personal considerations, and these considerations were controlling factors in defeating an election of Senator.

The legislature of June, 1881, was one of the ablest legislatures ever assembled in New Hampshire. The Republican leaders included William E. Chandler, Gilman Marston, Aaron F. Stevens, Walter Harriman, and Ira Colby, while the Democrats were led by Harry Bingham, Edward B. S. Sanborn, Joseph D. Weeks, of Canaan, George E. Cochrane, of Farmington, and Joseph Q. Roles, of Ossipee. Other members who were then prominent or who have since come into prominence were Chester B. Jordan, of Lancaster, Alonzo H. Quint and George S. Frost, of Dover, Henry Robinson, of Concord, Edmund E. Truesdale, of Pembroke, Adam S. Ballantyne, of Northfield, Albert A. Rotch, of Amherst, Albert M. Shaw and Charles A. Dole, of Lebanon, Elihu T. Quimby, of Hanover, Christopher H. Wells, of Somersworth, John Hatch, of Greenland, Alson L. Brown, of Whitefield, Albert L. Eastman, of Hampstead, Herman W. Greene, of Hopkinton, Isaac L. Heath, Waterman Smith, John C. Ray, and John C. Bickford, of Manchester, Frank K. Hobbs, of Ossipee, George W. Mann, of Benton, Irving W. Watson, of Northumberland, and Ithiel E. Clay, of Chatham.

The Senate was also exceptionally strong, as its roster shows. The Senators were: Amos C. Chase, of Kingston, Joseph H. Clough, of New London, Cornelius Cooledge, of Hillsboro, Alfred A. Cox, of Enfield, George W. Cummings, of Francestown, Grovenor A. Curtis, of Hopkinton, George H. Fairbanks, of Newport, Virgil C. Gilman, of Nashua, George C. Gilmore, of Manchester, Richard Gove, of Laconia, Edward Gustine, of Keene, Lafayette Hall, of Newmarket, Timothy Kaley, of Milford, John Kimball, of Concord, Silas F. Learnard, of Chester, Edward F. Mann, of Benton, Sherburne R. Merrill, of Colebrook, Joseph C. Moore, of Gilford, John M. Parker, of Fitzwilliam, J. F. Seavey, of Dover, Charles W. Talpey, of Farmington, George H. Towle, of Deerfield, John S. Treat, of Portsmouth, and David B. Varney, of Manchester.

The State Senate organized by the choice of John Kimball as president. He was one of Rollins's staunchest supporters, and was for many years treasurer of the Republican State committee. A man of probity, he has the confidence of the entire State. Frank and outspoken, of clear judgment, fearless in the discharge of public or private duties, John Kimball is a representative of the highest ideals in citizenship. Four times mayor of Concord, he gave the city business administrations unexcelled in its history. He could have been governor of the State if he had consented to consider the nomination at the hands of his party.

Chester B. Jordan was elected Speaker without opposition. He was a popular presiding officer, his unconventionality and good humor contributing much to softening the asperities arising out of the discussion of the Senatorial question. Jordan had been active in politics in the Democratic stronghold of Coos County. His coming to the legislature enlarged his acquaintance in the State and paved the way for his election as governor of the State, a position he filled with credit to himself and with advantage to the State.

The legislature met June 1, 1881. In his message, Governor Bell referred to the Senatorial question as follows:

" One of the earliest questions which will call for your decision is whether you will elect a United States Senator to hold office for the term of six years beginning on the 4th day of March, 1883. The law of the United States provides in substance that a Senator shall be elected by the legislature which is chosen next before the vacancy is to occur. It is contended that this should be construed so as to mean the legislature which is chosen and organized next before the occurrence of the vacancy. It is for you to determine whether or not you will act upon this construction of the law. If you decide to do so, the choice of Senator is to be made in the manner and at the period of the session presented by the law of the United States."

Both houses of the legislature took action the same day upon this part of the governor's message. The Senate upon motion of Senator Seavey, a lifelong friend of Rollins, submitted this question to the Supreme Court of the State:

" Has the existing legislature the power and right to elect a Senator to represent the State in the Senate of the United States for the term beginning March 4, 1883 ? "

The House on motion of Walter Harriman referred this part of the governor's message to the judiciary committee for an opinion, requesting an early report. Thereupon there arose a contest between those favoring an election of Senator and those opposed, to see which could be first submitted and acted upon, the opinion of the Supreme Court or the opinion of the judiciary committee. All of the prominent lawyers of the House were opposed to an election and the judiciary committee was not long in reaching a conclusion. Only one member of the committee favored an election, and he was Henry Robinson, Rollins's son-in-law.

The committee reported through Chandler its conclusions, a minority report being presented by Robinson. The majority report, after reciting the provisions of the constitution of the United States regarding the election of Senators, said: " The effect of these provisions clearly is to give the legislatures of the States respectively the right to choose Senators in Congress and to give to Congress the paramount right at any time by law to make or alter regulations as to the times and manner of choosing Senators by the legislature of each State. In the exercise of the power thus given by the constitution of the United States,

Congress passed the act regulating the election of Senators, July 25, 1866. Prior to this act of 1866, each State regulated the times and manner of electing Senators as well as the place of holding the election. Abuses sprang up under this system which the act of Congress was intended to avoid. In some cases partisan members, having control of a State legislature, elected without reference to the choice of a Senator, anticipating the expiration of a Senatorial term, and that an intervening legislature chosen, or to be chosen, would be composed of a majority of members of adverse politics to their own, elected a Senator long before the term for which he was elected began. In other instances, when the two houses of the legislature were of adverse politics, the election of Senators was obstructed. To avoid these and other abuses and to secure the latest expression of the people through its legislature, Congress passed the act of 1866 regulating both the time and manner of the election of Senators by the legislature of each State."

The report then gave a résumé of the attempts made to secure from the United States Senate a construction of this statute as applied to the New Hampshire case, and asserted that the McMillan report of the Senate committee on privileges and elections had never been reversed, " although several Senators had expressed their individual opinions in favor of the right of the legislature of 1878 to elect Wadleigh's successor." Continuing, the report said: " At the time of the election of the present legislature in November, 1880, it

is indisputable that the people of the State of both
political parties rested upon the determination of 1878,
and had expectation that the legislature elected in 1882
would choose a Senator. The single question now before the House is whether it will regard the law of
1866, conform to the precedent of 1878, and remit the
next election of Senator to the legislature of 1883, or
will disregard the law, reverse the precedent, and elect
a Senator two and a half years before he will be called
upon to take his seat."

The minority report reviewed the action of the Senate on the McMillan report and the debate on the question of the admission of Senator Bell, and quoted the
opinions of Senators Conkling, Eaton, Kernan, Blaine,
Carpenter, Davis, Beck, Wallace, and McDonald as
declaring that the legislature of 1878 should have
elected Wadleigh's successor. The conclusion of this
report was that the express purpose of the act of
1866 was to facilitate elections, secure an unbroken
representation for every State and not to create vacancies, that it was the manifest intent of Congress to vest
the power of electing a Senate in a legislature in existence and having official powers at the time the term
expires, that the State has a constitutional right to
continuous representation in the Senate by the choice
of its legislature which cannot be infringed, impaired,
or taken away by any act of Congress, that, if the law
cannot be so construed, it is clearly unconstitutional,
null, and void.

The Senate received the opinion of the Supreme

Court before the judiciary committee's report could be acted upon by the House, so that, in the discussion which ensued in the House, both the opinion of the court and the opinion of the committee were considered. The opinion of the court was signed by Chief Justice Doe and Judges Foster, Stanley, Allen, Smith, and Clark, four Republicans and two Democrats. Judge Blodgett declined to give an opinion on the ground that he had not had time to consider the question. The court said:

"The primary right of the State is not to be represented five years and nine months, or any other part of each Senatorial term, by two Senators chosen by the legislature, but to be represented during the whole of each term by two Senators so chosen; and the manifest constitutional duty of the legislature is to elect Senators at such times, that the State may be represented by two Senators, chosen by the legislature thereof for six years.

"The constitution of the United States is the supreme law of the land, and so long as it remains in force in its present form there can be no power, State or federal, legally capable of depriving a State of the right which the constitution has conferred upon it, or of relieving the legislature from the duty which the constitution has imposed upon it, and there is no more power legally to suspend the right and duty for a day than for six years, or forever.

"The next legislature, having no official existence until June, 1883, cannot elect a Senator for the full

term of six years, beginning March 4, 1883. Therefore, the refusal of the present legislature to elect a
Senator for that term would be a violation of the constitutional right of the State to be represented by two
Senators — 'chosen by the legislature thereof for six
years.' Such a refusal, leaving the State for three
months represented by only one Senator chosen by its
legislature, would be as plainly unconstitutional as
similar refusals leaving the State for all time without
any Senator so chosen.

.   .   .   .

"As Congress cannot legally violate the constitutional right of the State to be represented by two Senators chosen by the legislature, and as that right would
be violated by the refusal of the present legislature to
elect, it is not necessary to inquire into the validity
of the act of Congress. But, having examined the act,
it may not be out of place to express the opinion that
it is constitutional because it cannot be fairly construed to be a denial of the constitutional electoral
duty of the present legislature. Section 15, prescribing
the manner of election, has no bearing on the present
question, which is a question of the time only. Section
14 fixes the time. It provides, in substance, that a
Senator shall be elected by the legislature which is
chosen next preceding the beginning of a Senatorial
term.

"The legislature here intended is a body of men
who are the legislature before the beginning of the
Senatorial term, and not a body of men who will be

the legislature if they are alive, three months after the beginning of the term."

An attempt was made to have the Republicans caucus on this question, but, when the caucus met, the leaders who were opposed to an election of Senator stated that they would not be bound by caucus action, so the attempt was abandoned.

Upon the receipt of the opinion of the supreme court, the State Senate proceeded on the day appointed by the United States statute to vote for United States Senator and notified the House that it was ready to meet it in joint convention to complete the legislative action. In the House several days of interesting and spicy debate followed the report of the judiciary committee. Prior to the vote in the House, the Democrats met in caucus and voted to support the majority report of the judiciary committee, being brought into line for attendance and action by their leader, Harry Bingham.

Few men leading a minority party in the legislature through successive sessions of bitter partisan contest have won the generous confidence and affection that was accorded to Harry Bingham in the State of New Hampshire. On all matters not partisan his influence in the legislature was unrivalled. He had a comprehensive knowledge of the State and its needs, and, as a member of the judiciary committee of the House, he was ever helpful in shaping legislation. When thoroughly aroused in debate, he was a veritable lion, and his speech, ordinarily deliberate, poured forth in strong and eloquent periods. Fear he knew not, and, regardless of the passions and prejudices of the hour, he stood by his convictions even if he stood alone. Session after session, from the time of the stormy Civil War period to 1891, he fought in the lower branch of the legislature the battles of the Democratic party with a vigor that knew no thought of surrender. The latter session closed his legislative service. During President Cleveland's second administration he took issue with him on the Hawaiian question, and later opposed the election of Bryan to the Presidency. Frequently he was the candidate of his party for United States Senator. Had he been elected to that body, he would have taken rank with Edmunds and Thurman as a constitutional lawyer and a constructive statesman. Between him and Gilman Marston there existed a warm and intimate friendship. There was much of similarity in the two, but Bingham was the stronger and more positive force.

Another able member of the minority party at this session was Edward B. S. Sanborn, of Franklin. He was a sound lawyer and an accomplished advocate. His legislative triumphs were numerous. He had the rare faculty of knowing when a speech would be most effective. His participation in debate was generally confined to two or three occasions during the session. Near the close of some interesting and protracted discussion, when it seemed as if the last word had been spoken, Sanborn would rise and address the House with a freshness of treatment of the subject and a power of statement rarely equalled.

In the debate in the House, Bingham, who had been quoted by Wadleigh two years previous as giving an opinion that the legislature of 1878 should elect a Senator, put his opposition to an election at this time solely on the ground that the question had been determined by the legislature of 1878, and by the United States Senate in its action on the McMillan report.

When the vote was taken in the House, 118 Republicans favored an election and 119 Democrats and 63 Republicans voted against it. This ended the controversy so far as the legislature of 1881 was concerned. It was to recur again two years later when Blair brought it before the Republican legislative caucus to determine which legislature should elect his successor. The legal aspect of the case was no more determined by the legislature of New Hampshire than it had been by the Senate of the United States, for expediency had largely controlled the votes of members of the legislature. The letters from the capital of Henry M. Putney, the editor of the *Mirror*, to his paper, sets out this view as follows:

" After the caucus of last week, Mr. Chandler for the majority of the judiciary committee, made a report that it is inexpedient to elect a Senator this year, which was followed by a minority report with an opposite conclusion. The debates in the House have been upon the adoption of these reports, Generals Marston, Stevens, and Harriman, Mr. Chandler, and Professor

Quimby, of Hanover, doing the talking for the inexpe-
diency doctrine, and Doctor Quint, Greene, of Hopkinton, Robinson, of Concord, and Dole, of Lebanon, for
the other. It has not escaped attention that neither the
majority report nor its advocates, with the exception
of General Marston, have declared that an election at
this time would be illegal, it being deemed sufficient,
and much safer, to oppose it as inexpedient."

CHAPTER XXIII.

THE Senate of the Forty-seventh Congress was convened in extra session March 4, 1881. The elections of 1880 had increased the Republican representation in that body, but neither side had a distinct majority of its members. There were two Senators who were classed as independent, David Davis, of Illinois, and William Mahone, of Virginia. If both acted with either party they would give that party control of the Senate. If the two divided in their party support, there would be an equal division of the Senate, and Vice-President Arthur would have the casting vote. Davis, after his election to the Senate, two years before, had generally acted with the Democrats, and there was no reason to think that his course would be different in this Congress. The organization of the Senate committees and the election of the Senate officers, therefore, depended upon the position taken by Senator Mahone.

In Virginia politics toward the close of the reconstruction period the State had been wrested from the control of the Republicans by what was known as the Conservative party, local issues predominating in the campaigns. The Conservative party did not take the

432

name of Democrat until about 1880. In the meantime, the absorbing question in Virginian politics came to be the settlement of the State debt, which divided the Democratic or Conservative party. A new party came into existence, led by Mahone, known as the Readjuster party. This party favored one settlement of the State debt, and the Democratic or Conservative party another. Mahone, standing for the protection of the negroes of Virginia in the exercise of the right of suffrage, secured the support of the Republicans of the State, and most of that party was gradually merged into the Readjuster party. The Democratic party of Virginia was represented at the Democratic National Convention of 1880, while the Readjuster party was not. Yet national issues had little bearing upon the State election of that year, many Readjusters of Democratic antecedents supporting the Democratic nominee for President. The Readjusters elected their candidate for governor and carried the legislature, while the Democrats secured the Presidential electors. Mahone was elected to the United States Senate by the legislature. The Democrats of Virginia were very bitter toward him, and he was socially ostracized by their leaders.

When the United States Senate met in extra session, there were rumors that Mahone would act with the Republicans in the organization of that body. This was soon confirmed by his own declarations and by the nomination, as sergeant-at-arms of the Senate, by the Republican caucus, of Harrison H. Riddleberger, of

Virginia, one of Mahone's supporters and afterward his colleague in the Senate. The contest was precipitated by a resolution offered by the Republicans, giving them the chairmanships of the Senate committees. A long debate followed this resolution, in which Mahone was accused by the Democrats with deserting the Democratic party, and the Republicans charged with allying themselves with repudiators, as the Democrats called the Readjusters of Virginia. This last accusation was somewhat ludicrous, because neither the Democratic nor Readjuster party in Virginia proposed to pay the entire State debt, while in a number of Southern States repudiation of State debts had followed the accession to power of the Democrats in those States. Mahone defended his position with force and clearness, repelling the insinuations made against him by Democratic Senators. All the charges of the Democrats were answered by the Republican Senators. The trend of the discussion is shown by a speech made by Rollins during the debate. He said in his direct way:

" I did not propose at this time and I do not propose now to detain the Senate with a discussion of this question, but there is one feature to which I wish to call the attention of the Senate and the country. While Senators on the other side, the Senators from North Carolina, for instance, are shocked at the idea that we upon this side of the chamber should dare under any circumstances to give a vote for a Readjuster of Virginia, they have supported on that side for any and every office of the government, no matter how large or how small, the strongest and boldest repudiators in the land, and not even my friend from Delaware, Mr. Bayard, is shocked. You Senators are disturbed in your nightly dreams, you are horrified because we upon this side determined to vote for a Readjuster of Virginia who proposes to readjust in some way the debt of that great State, when we find he is with us upon the question of a free ballot and an honest count; but you are not disturbed by repudiation in Louisiana. You are not disturbed by repudiation in North Carolina. You are not disturbed by the repudiation of your friends all through the South. You are not disturbed by the repudiation which has taken place in this country in Democratic States and in Democratic States alone. You are only disturbed when we, under some circumstances, dare to vote or to indicate a purpose to vote for Riddleberger of Virginia.

The Republicans succeeded by the vote of the Vice-President in organizing the committees of the Senate, but not in electing their candidates for Senate offices. Rollins's assignments to committees were as follows: chairman of the committee on public buildings and grounds, chairman of the committee on enrolled bills, and a member of the committees on naval affairs, District of Columbia, and civil service and retrenchment. He was also appointed on the select committee to examine the several branches of the civil service and on a committee to investigate the subject of heavy ordnance, but was later excused at his own request from service on the committee on enrolled bills and the select committee on civil service. The chairmanship of the committee on public buildings and grounds was selected by him for the sole purpose of securing a public building for Concord, New Hampshire, a purpose he had had in mind since his election to the Senate. He had already paved the way for a public building at the capital of New Hampshire by having the United States courts transferred from Exeter to Concord. The bill authorizing this building and making appropriation for it passed at the first session of this Congress. This building, pronounced by President Harrison one of the handsomest public buildings in the country, stands as a memorial of Rollins's industry in behalf of his native State.

The Republican party was soon split into two hostile factions by the action of President Garfield in appointing William H. Robertson to the collectorship of the port of New York. This appointment was extremely obnoxious to Senator Conkling of that State, as it put into the most important federal position in New York the leader of the Republican forces in that State antagonistic to Conkling. He regarded it as the beginning of a warfare by the administration on his supremacy in New York. The courtesy of the Senate was invoked to induce the President to withdraw the appointment, and, failing in this, to secure the defeat of Robertson's confirmation. Rollins's relations with Conkling were most agreeable. He regarded the appointment as a mistake on the part of the administration, in that it precipitated a contest which ought to have been avoided.

He joined with other Republican Senators in an effort to have the President withdraw the nomination and recognize that element of the Republican party of which Robertson was a representative by giving him some other appointment. Rollins was a member of the committee of Senators who waited upon the President, but he left no record of the conferences which took place at the White House. The nomination was not withdrawn, and, failing to secure the defeat of the confirmation, Conkling and his colleague from New York resigned. The sequel of this contest is well known.

The death of Garfield a few months later transferred Vice-President Arthur from the Senate to the White House, and, when the Senate met again, a question confronting it was the election of a president *pro tempore* of that body. At that time the president of the Senate was in direct line of succession to the Presidency and, in case of the death or disability of President Arthur, would have become acting President of the United States. The Republicans had not a majority of the Senate, even with the vote of Mahone. To prevent a Democrat from becoming president of the Senate, the Republicans nominated David Davis, of Illinois, the only independent Senator of that body, for that position, and elected him. The committees of the Senate remained in the control of the Republicans, but Davis refused to join them in changing the officers of the Senate.

With President Arthur, Rollins was on very intimate

terms. The former gradually reorganized the Cabinet appointed by President Garfield, filling the positions with men of his own choice. The Navy portfolio went to William E. Chandler, of New Hampshire. Chandler had been nominated by President Garfield for Solicitor General of the United States, but the Democrats defeated his confirmation. They were apprehensive of his activity in this position in prosecuting the violation of the election laws in the South, and bent every energy to secure his defeat. In this they were aided by Senator J. Donald Cameron, of Pennsylvania, who, as chairman of the Republican National Committee, was defeated by Chandler at the Chicago Convention of 1880, in his attempt to enforce the unit rule in the interest of General Grant's nomination for the Presidency. When it became apparent that President Arthur was considering Chandler for the position of Secretary of the Navy, the question naturally arose whether he could be confirmed by the Senate. In addition to the fact that the Republicans had not a majority in that body, Cameron's influence, still hostile, might be sufficient to prevent a confirmation. The appointment would be especially pleasing to New Hampshire, being a recognition of the State she had not received since Levi Woodbury held the positions of Secretary of the Navy and Secretary of the Treasury in Jackson's administration. Rollins canvassed the Senate in Chandler's behalf, bringing to bear all of his personal influence upon Republican Senators unfriendly to Chandler. He also sought and secured Democratic support. His efforts were crowned with success, although the vote was close. It is not too much to say that Rollins's masterly management of the case in the Senate secured Chandler's confirmation.

Throughout this Congress Rollins was most actively employed. His committee assignments were important, and he mastered the details of all the work coming before them. The old antagonism between the leading committees of the Senate and the appropriation committee, which controlled all appropriations, was brought into prominence by the efforts of Rollins to secure reforms in the navy. The naval committee and the appropriation committee were in frequent conflict, and the debates over the naval appropriation bill, in which Rollins took conspicuous part, were spicy and instructive. He succeeded in laying before the Senate and the public the methods by which increased pay and promotions on the retired list of the navy had been secured, and led the way to later reforms. A large share of the work of the District of Columbia committee fell on him, because of his familiarity with the affairs of the District. His work, however, was by no means confined to measures coming before committees of which he was a member.

The question of the revision of the tariff, which had been agitated for some time, came up for action at the second session of this Congress. The fall elections of 1882 had been disastrous to the Republican party, and the next Congress would be Democratic. A Democratic victory in the next Presidential election seemed probable. There remained only three months for the Republicans in Congress to do anything to strengthen their party. A tariff commission had been appointed by President Arthur, and had made its report, recommending changes in the existing rates of duty. There was a strong feeling in the Republican party that the Forty-seventh Congress should revise the tariff before it adjourned. Otherwise it might devolve upon a Democratic Congress to do this work, while the failure of the Republicans to revise the tariff might contribute to their defeat in the next campaign. The time between the first Monday of December, 1882, and the 4th of March following was too short for both houses to fully consider a measure of the magnitude of a tariff bill. The House was not then operating under the Reed rules, and a minority could easily defeat a new measure by filibustering. Even if such a measure passed the House, it would be at so late a date that it could be talked to death in the Senate. Fortunately for the party, there had been passed by the House at its previous session a revenue bill which was then before the Senate. By taking up this bill and striking out all but the enacting clause, the Senate could, under the guise of an amendment, incorporate under this title a tariff measure which, when received by the House, could be sent to conference, thus limiting debate and preventing filibustering tactics. The Republican leaders in Congress determined to take this course, although great doubt existed of their ability to succeed. In the time intervening before the 4th of March were

the Christmas holidays, which usually afforded an excuse for a recess of two or three weeks.

When the Republican plan was decided upon, Senator Rollins went to work with his accustomed energy
and watchfulness of details to make it a success. The
first thing essential was to prevent the usual holiday
recess. This undertaking he took upon himself, seeing
every Republican Senator and securing his written
pledge to vote against a holiday adjournment. When
the customary resolution to adjourn over the holidays
was offered, it was defeated by a solid Republican vote.
This accomplished, he then familiarized himself with
the changes proposed by the tariff bill and the effect
they would have upon New England interests, and he
took a considerable part in shaping the tariff bill that
was finally passed in the closing hours of this Congress.
After the adjournment, his work as a Senator was reviewed by Ben Perley Poore, the long-time Washington correspondent of the *Boston Journal.* Poore said:

" Senator Rollins takes rank second to none in the
influence he exerts in the Senate. A practical business
man, of clear head and sound judgment, he accom-
plishes more work and makes less fuss about it than
almost any other member of that branch of Congress.
He has that push and determination about him that
gives success to any measure he undertakes, as, for
instance, his efforts in behalf of the knit goods bill last
summer, when he and Senator Hawley rescued it from
what seemed to be irretrievable defeat. He is entitled
to the credit of keeping the Senate in session during

the last Christmas holidays — a two weeks' work that enabled the Senate to pass the civil service and tariff bills, and had a healthy influence over the House in expediting its business. Although not frequently engaging in debate, he showed himself at home on the floor of the Senate during the contest a year ago between the appropriation and naval committees, over the action of the former in tacking general legislation upon the naval appropriation bill, and he has had the satisfaction at this session of seeing, not only the appropriation committee, but the whole Senate, put its foot upon the vicious practice of smuggling legislation into amendments of appropriation bills that should properly come before Congress as separate measures.

"Mr. Rollins's attention to the wants of his State and the demands of his constituents is proverbial, and it is said that the smallest request receives the same attention from him as the largest. His service to his State is attested by such accomplished facts as a liberal appropriation for a public building at Concord; the removal of the United States courts to a more convenient section of the State; appropriations for the improvement of the Exeter and Cocheco Rivers; the relief of the New Hampshire savings banks of $100,000 unjust taxes, and numerous other matters of local importance. No Senator is recorded as in attendance and voting more days of a session than he, and his votes have invariably been on the right side. He has kept clear of Credit Mobilier and other jobs, and his State never had occasion to fear that a Congressional investigation would smirch him. His first term in the Senate is creditable to him and his State, and his reëlection should follow, as his six years of experience can but enable him to take even higher rank than he has already occupied."

CHAPTER XXIV.

ROLLINS'S LAST CAMPAIGN

THE Republican campaign of 1882 opened early. There were rival candidates for the gubernatorial nomination. From April to September there was a canvass for delegates unprecedented in the history of the party in the methods employed to secure them, and in the bitterness of strife engendered thereby. Manchester presented one of her distinguished citizens, Moody Currier, as a candidate for the nomination. He had been mayor of the city, a State Senator, and a member of the governor's Council. He was a man of ability and learning, successful in business, everywhere respected, but advanced in years. The other candidate was Samuel W. Hale, of Keene, who was just past middle life. He had been voted for in previous State conventions, and he came from a section of the State that had not furnished a governor for a quarter of a century. The claim of locality was advanced in Hale's behalf, and it was met by the counter-claim that one longer in the service of the party and of better known fitness should be given the nomination. If events had taken their natural course, no danger or harm would have come to the party. The contest, however, increased in intensity as it progressed, and very soon charges and countercharges were made of sharp practices in securing delegates, until the feeling between the friends of the two candidates was wrought to that degree of hostility that it threatened to wreck the Republican party beyond resurrection.

It soon appeared that Hale was not the general choice of his own section of the State. The building of the Manchester and Keene Railroad, with which he had been connected, had caused losses to stockholders, and consequent resentment toward all those who had induced investment or conducted the enterprise. To offset this and the claim that Mr. Currier should be first considered, the charge was made that Mr. Currier was too old to stand the strain of a political campaign, and that, if he did not succumb during the canvass, he would not live out his term. The Republican party was split wide open into hostile camps. There was a contest in almost every town and ward to secure delegates to the State convention. Each candidate had headquarters from which was directed his campaign for the nomination. These headquarters furnished the Democratic party with abundant material to be used against the successful nominee in the subsequent election. The returns of the caucuses indicated that the vote of the convention would be close. A few unpledged delegates were elected. Toward these the friends of the two candidates directed their efforts. It was now or never with each side. The bitterness between the contending factions was such

that there seemed little prospect of electing the nominee, whoever he might be. Efforts to secure the
withdrawal of both candidates and the substitution
of some compromise candidate failed. The contest was
carried into the convention and there fought to the
finish. After several ballots, Hale won by a small
majority, and was declared the candidate of the party.

The Republican State convention met September
12, 1882. It was presided over by Chester B. Jordan,
of Lancaster, and the platform was reported by Alonzo
H. Quint, of Dover. Four ballots were necessary for
the choice of a candidate for governor, Hale's vote
increasing on each ballot.

The Democratic State convention met the next day,
being called to order by Arthur L. Meserve, of Bartlett, chairman of the State committee. Stilson
Hutchins, of Laconia, who had returned to his native
State for a brief residence, from Washington, where
he had achieved marked success in the newspaper
field, presided, and Charles F. Stone, of Laconia,
reported the resolutions. Only one ballot was necessary to select a candidate for governor, Martin V. B.
Edgerly, of Manchester, receiving 296 of the 444 votes
cast. Edgerly was in the insurance business and had
a large acquaintance and personal following in the
State. The convention adjourned with the Democrats
sanguine of Edgerly's election by the people.

The Republican nominees for Congress were Martin
A. Haynes, of Gilford, in the first district, and Ossian
Ray, of Lancaster, in the second, the State's represen-

tation being now reduced to two members. " Private " Haynes had as active competitors for the nomination Benjamin F. Prescott, of Epping, and Andrew H. Young, of Dover, the latter having just resigned as collector of internal revenue for the New Hampshire district. Haynes was a veteran of the civil war, a jovial comrade, and a popular candidate. As a newspaper editor he wielded a ready pen. His nomination was fortunate at this time, as it added strength to the ticket. He served two terms in Congress.

Ray was a lawyer of marked ability, who had been nominated and elected to fill out the unexpired term of Evarts W. Farr at the time of the latter's death. He was a man of forceful character and an earnest advocate.

The Democratic nominees for Congress were George B. Chandler, of Manchester, in the first district, and Jewett B. Hosley, of Lebanon, in the second. Chandler was one of the leading bankers of the State, who with other leading Democrats of New Hampshire supported McKinley for President in 1896.

Charles F. Stone, of Laconia, was elected chairman of the Democratic State committee, and Herbert F. Norris, of Concord, secretary. Stone had been identified with the Republican party until the campaign of 1880. He was subsequently the nominee of the Democratic party for Congress in the first district, and still later its candidate for governor. During Cleveland's second term as President, he was appointed naval officer at the port of Boston. After retiring from this position, he was appointed a judge of the superior court, a position he now holds.

Never had the Republican party of New Hampshire stood in such peril as it did when the State Convention adjourned. The Manchester delegates returned to their home disappointed and threatening a bolt. Cheshire County, the home of Hale, was in open revolt over the nomination. The hostility to his election was nowhere more pronounced than in his own locality. It looked as though a Democratic governor was a certainty by the popular vote, and it was feared that a Democratic legislature would accompany a Democratic governor to the State House the following June.

The term of Rollins as United States Senator expired March 4, 1883. Besides the control of the State government, there was dangling before the eyes of the now confident Democratic party the prize of one senatorship, and possibly two. The United States Senate at that time, as has been shown, was evenly divided, David Davis, the Independent, generally voting with the Democratic party, and William Mahone, of Virginia, with the Republicans. The opposition of the Democratic party to the election of a United States Senator in 1881, to succeed Rollins, had been political rather than legal, and, if they secured control of the legislature of 1883, there was no reason to believe that their action in the legislature of 1881 would preclude them from attempting to elect both Rollins's and Blair's successors. A question of one or two Senators from New Hampshire enlisted the interest of the national Democracy, and New Hampshire Democrats received encouragement from outside the State.

The Republicans began their campaign against the Democratic party under the most discouraging circumstances. It was known that Manchester, the largest city in the State, was likely to give a majority for the Democratic candidate for governor. Cheshire County, the Western Reserve of the Republican party of New Hampshire, which had never before failed the party in returning a good majority, would probably follow suit. The Republican State committee met amid gloom and despair to complete its organization. Jacob H. Gallinger, who had shown capacity as a political organizer, was chosen chairman, as the representative of the Hale forces. Frank D. Currier, of Canaan, as representing the Currier supporters, was chosen secretary.

Gallinger had been active in politics for ten years or more. His beginning was at the printer's case, from which he graduated to enter upon the study of medicine. After several years of successful practice as a physician, he entered the public service, to be ever after identified with State and national interests. At the time of his election as chairman of the State committee, he had served in both branches of the legislature, where he had shown himself a ready debater and parliamentary leader. He was also known to the public as a brilliant speaker and versatile writer. He was soon to embark on a career in national politics distancing all records in the number of his elections and the hold he has had on the affectionate regard of the people of the State. His public life has been a constant growth. As chairman of the State committee, as Congressman, and as Senator, his achievements have been large and his success adequate to any ambition. Of untiring industry, pleasing address, ready adaptability, he has secured triumphs where others have failed. Three times elected to the United States Senate, he now stands number ten in seniority of service in that body, and among the first in the importance of his committee assignments.

Frank D. Currier, the new secretary of the State committee, first came into prominence in the legislature of 1879 through his activities and familiarity with parliamentary procedure. Subsequent to his service on the State committee, he served as naval officer of customs at Boston, and later was elected Speaker of the New Hampshire legislature and member of Congress. As Speaker, he showed remarkable aptitude for the position, and he has attained prominence in the national House as its most popular presiding officer in committee of the whole, where most of the business is transacted. He has entered upon his third term as a Congressman.

It was in a situation such as already outlined that Rollins entered headquarters to conduct his last campaign. If the State were lost, he would not be returned to the Senate. If the State were saved, the party was so broken by this gubernatorial contest that factional quarrels might reach into the Senatorial caucus. In a number of Western and Middle States there had been successful bolting of Senatorial caucuses and prolonged deadlocks. Old leaders had been retired and new men chosen to the Senate. President Arthur was endeavoring to harmonize the party in the country at large divided by the Blaine-Conkling antagonism. No help could be expected from the Republican national committee. Its efforts must be directed to larger States. New Hampshire must depend upon herself. Had the end come to Republican victories in the Granite State? Many thought so. A Democratic Congress was expected as the result of the fall elections. Was New Hampshire to contribute to the probable Democratic victory? Was the Democratic party to have a Senator from this State for the first time in thirty years? The political atmosphere foreboded disaster. What, if anything, could be done to dispel the apathy, arouse the courage of New Hampshire Republicans, and bring peace to the discordant factions?

Rollins at once saw that the fight must be fought on national, rather than State, issues. A Republican President and an equally divided Senate stood between the country and a Democratic assault on the tariff and an attempt to reverse the fruits of the war. The removal of the political disabilities of Jefferson Davis had just been prevented in the Senate by one vote. The feeling was still strong in New Hampshire against the ascendency in the nation of those who had participated in the War of the Rebellion. The next Presidential election might be lost, as proved to be the case. The United

States Senate alone was the sheet-anchor of the Republican party. New Hampshire Republicans were still loyal to the principles of the party. If they could be aroused to the dangers that menaced the party in the nation, even if the governor were lost, the legislature of New Hampshire might be saved, and thereby a United States Senator.

The importance of one vote was again brought home to the voters, and the bearing of that one vote on national affairs. One vote in the town might save Republican ascendency in the legislature. One vote in the legislature might save the United States Senatorship. One Senator from New Hampshire might stand in the way of a complete national triumph of the Democratic party. This was the issue forced to the front in the press, on the stump, and in the correspondence of the State committee. Never was a campaign in New Hampshire conducted with greater skill and greater success. Gallinger, the chairman of the committee, entered heart and soul into the suggestions of Rollins, and developed at that time those remarkable qualities for organization that have kept him for so many years at the head of the State committee by the unanimous voice of the party. He was in touch with the younger element of the party, who had never fought under the personal direction of Rollins. In the nearly six years the latter had been in the Senate, he had been removed from intimate intercourse with the generation coming upon the stage. These young men were superseding the contemporaries of Rollins in all parts of the State. They were brought by Gallinger into more prominent activity.

Little could be hoped from the disaffected districts, yet they were not neglected. Probably more personal letters were written to local Republicans by the committee in this campaign than in any other in the history of the party. They contained appeals for harmony and for party loyalty. Republicans were particularly urged to see that disaffection did not extend beyond the head of the ticket. The best that the committee hoped was to prevent a choice of governor by the people, relying upon a Republican majority in the legislature to elect the governor. Two other State tickets were in the field, a Temperance and a Greenback ticket. The total third party and scattering vote in the election of 1880 was less than a thousand. There was no prospect that this would be increased. Bolting Republicans either would not vote for governor or would cast their ballots for Edgerly, so intense was their hostility to Hale. The danger lay in the latter course. To prevent the defeat of the Republican nominee for governor by the popular vote, the energies of the committee were enlisted to bringing out the full Republican vote in strong Republican and strong Democratic towns, a new experiment in New Hampshire politics, where the fight was mainly made in the close towns. Its success was the turning-point in the campaign.

In few campaigns did Rollins appear to better advantage as a political manager. He was then in his sixtieth year. His intense application to all matters that enlisted his attention had not perceptibly impaired either his mental or physical strength. Of wiry constitution, he responded to the exactions of the campaign with remarkable staying and recuperative powers. The tension, however, was great. The daily reports coming to headquarters were all of the same discouraging character. Both Rollins and Gallinger had not only to show courage and confidence, but to infuse them into others. Both had reputations at stake. With Rollins, it was his prestige to maintain. With Gallinger, it was his reputation to make. With Rollins, who had led to so many victories, it might prove his Waterloo. The association of these two men, the one just entering upon what was to be a distinguished career, and the other with his large experience, both in State and national politics, was most fortunate for the party, and the party had need of both men in this trying campaign.

The night of the election there was little confidence among Republicans in the result. For the first time in the history of the Republican party in New Hampshire, its canvass was uncertain. It foretold nothing with accuracy, except losses in the disaffected sections. Anxious leaders of the party crowded the Republican headquarters. The early returns confirmed their worst fears. Town after town, and ward after ward reported Republican losses and Democratic gains on the governor vote. The election of Edgerly seemed a foregone conclusion, and the legislature hung in doubt. It was well into the night before returns were received from the strong Republican and strong Democratic towns, where the committee had done its effective work. Then, to the consternation of the Democrats and to the joy of the Republicans, the tide began to turn. It was soon apparent that the legislature was Republican, and that Edgerly had not received a majority of the popular vote. The Democratic leaders had been outgeneraled and the State was saved. The next day the committee was able to give out returns that Hale was elected by the people. His majority was only a little over five hundred. It was a victory snatched from the very jaws of defeat. None who participated in that remarkable campaign can forget its struggles, its anxieties, its doubts, and its fears, or the feeling of relief that came after midnight of the day of election. It was Rollins's last campaign. He had fought it with an intensity which subordinated even his personal interests to the welfare of the party. He had completed his record of continuous victory where he had personally directed or advised in the campaigns. He was soon to enter upon the last stage of his political career. He was to fail of a reëlection to the Senate, as the Republican leaders in other States had failed, after a Senatorial caucus had recorded that a majority of the Republicans of the State, through their chosen representatives, desired to reward his services and fidelity by a reëlection.

The vote for governor was: Scattering, 168; Josiah

M. Fletcher, 357; John F. Woodbury, 444; Martin V. B. Edgerly, 36,916; Samuel W. Hale, 38,402.

Both Republican candidates for Congress were elected by large majorities, and the legislature was safely Republican.

CHAPTER XXV.

THERE were seven months to intervene between the election and the meeting of the legislature Three months of this time Rollins spent in Washington, at the short session of the Forty-seventh Congress. He began his campaign for a renomination soon after the election was over, but it was not until after March 4, 1883, that he could give his undivided attention to his canvass. Yet, on his return to New Hampshire, he knew quite accurately the individual choice of the Republican members of the legislature. He felt satisfied that he would secure a majority of the Republican Senatorial caucus, if not on the first, at least on the second ballot. As early as April, the impression became general that, if a Republican caucus were to determine the result, Rollins would be his own successor. The air, however, was pregnant with forebodings of disaster. Bolting of Republican caucuses in other States had become quite common. The bolt two years before in New Hampshire, on the question of the right of the legislature of 1881 to elect a Senator, was still fresh in men's minds, and, the step having been once taken, it was easier to repeat it. The bitterness of the late strife

457

for the gubernatorial nomination was by no means allayed. Both Rollins and Chandler had been accused
of using their influence to defeat Currier and nominate
Hale, a charge which both emphatically denied. The
denial availed nothing. Especially bitter towards Rollins were the opponents of Hale in Cheshire County,
while there was but little friendship for him in Manchester. From April to June, the question of bolting
the result of the Republican Senatorial caucus forged
its way into the foreground.

The legislature met June 6, 1883. The Senate organized by the choice of Charles H. Bartlett, of Manchester, as president, and Frank D. Currier, of Canaan,
as clerk. Bartlett had been mayor of Manchester. He
was a man of attainments and popular as a speaker
at public gatherings. A prominent member of the Senate was Harry Bingham, who appeared for the first
time in the upper branch of the legislature. Another
representative Democrat in this body was Irving W.
Drew, of Lancaster, one of the most brilliant advocates
of the State, and later to become identified with the Republican party. Other well-known members of the
Senate were Chester Pike, of Cornish, J. F. Seavey,
of Dover, Charles H. Amsden, of Concord, afterwards
Democratic candidate for governor, Henry Robinson,
of Concord, later mayor of that city, and postmaster of
the capital for two terms, George W. Cummings, of
Francestown, George A. Wason, of New Boston, Benjamin R. Wheeler, of Salem, and Benjamin F. Perkins, of Bristol.

The House organized with the choice of Samuel C. Eastman, of Concord, as Speaker. Eastman was the best parliamentarian in the State, and at this session enunciated the principle of counting a quorum, although the House did not adopt his views. This was some six years before Speaker Thomas B. Reed counted a quorum in the national House of Representatives. In 1893, Eastman, as a member of the New Hampshire House of Representatives, and temporarily in the chair, counted a quorum, with the approval of the majority of the House and without formal objection from the minority.

Three candidates for the United States Senate were members of the House, Gilman Marston, Aaron F. Stevens, and James F. Briggs. Other prominent Republican members of the House were William C. Todd, of Atkinson, William H. Sise, of Portsmouth, John J. Bell, of Exeter, Alonzo H. Quint and Thomas M. Pray, of Dover, Eugene P. Nute, of Farmington, Edwin Wallace, Charles S. Whitehouse, and John E. Meader, of Rochester, Christopher H. Wells and James A. Edgerly, of Somersworth, Allen J. Hackett, of Belmont, Benjamin F. Drake, of Gilford, Ithiel E. Clay, of Chatham, Charles R. Corning, of Concord, John S. Kimball, of Hopkinton, Jeremiah E. Smith, of Northfield, David A. Taggart, of Goffstown, Charles T. Means and Walter M. Parker, of Manchester, Charles H. Campbell and George E. Gage, of Nashua, Charles J. Amidon, of Hinsdale, Ira Colby and George L. Balcom, of Claremont, William F. Westgate, of Haverhill, and George H. Adams, of Plymouth.

The prominent Democratic members were Henry O. Kent and William S. Ladd, of Lancaster, Edward B. S. Sanborn, of Franklin, David Urch, of Portsmouth, John T. Busiel and Charles F. Stone, of Laconia, Joseph Q. Roles, of Ossipee, Edwin Snow, of Eaton, Jacob B. Whittemore, of Hillsboro, Fred A. Barker, of Keene, and William H. Cummings, of Lisbon.

With the assembling of the legislature, all the influential Republicans of the State were drawn to the capital by their interest in the Senatorial contest. The election or defeat of Rollins was soon the only question under consideration, the following of other candidates being only a factor so far as it might affect caucus action. It was not long before the alignment was of two forces, caucus and anti-caucus Republicans. Marston and Stevens were outspoken against a caucus, and for a time Briggs occupied a non-committal position. The two former had nothing to lose by refusing to attend a caucus, for it was not likely that either would figure in another senatorial canvass. Neither could secure a caucus nomination. A free voting in the legislature did offer a chance for Marston, for it was possible that the Democrats would support him, if he could muster enough Republican votes to make with the Democrats a majority of the legislature. With both Marston and Stevens, however, there was a pronounced hostility to Rollins's reëlection, overshadowing all other feelings.

The situation of Briggs was different. He had

served three terms in Congress, with credit to himself, and, representing the largest centre of the State, could reasonably hope for an election to the Senate in the near future, if not at this time. He and Rollins had drifted apart while serving the State the past six years, the one in the House and the other in the Senate. Their differences had arisen mainly over the control of the federal patronage. One misunderstanding had followed another, and their rival Senatorial ambitions had promoted their estrangements. Briggs had asked for a change in the office of the internal revenue collector for New Hampshire, and brought forward as a candidate Henry M. Putney, of Manchester, to succeed Andrew H. Young, of Dover, who then held the office.

Putney at that time was one of the younger leaders of the party. For a number of years he has been editor of the *Manchester Mirror*. He has a racy style of presenting facts to the public, which fascinates his readers. His letters from the capital during the sessions of the legislature, then a feature of the *Mirror,* gave the people an entertaining insight into the work of their representatives and of public men of the State. Optimistic in temperament, at that time, he drew the young men to him as a leader, and for a decade or more the editorial sanctum of the *Mirror* was the inspiration of much of the politics of the State.

Young was a man of activity and ability. He had been prominent in politics since the birth of the Republican party. With a genial personality which disarmed hostility, he was on terms of intimate friendship

with most of the leaders. Not an original Rollins supporter, he had within recent years become identified
with Rollins's interests. The latter regarded Putney
as Briggs's lieutenant, and, while consenting to Young's
resignation and Putney's appointment, sought to prevent the change from accruing to his own detriment.
It was soon publicly known that Young was ready to
resign, but privately he had asked Rollins to delay the
date. Responding to this request, Rollins held up Putney's appointment. Lack of frankness between Rollins and Briggs led to their suspicion of each other
over an appointment to which they were in many re-
spects agreed. Rollins suffered because of the delay
in making the change, for the public interpreted his
attitude as that of trying to keep Young in office when
the latter was willing to retire. When Putney's appointment finally came, it inured wholly to Briggs's
advantage.

During the administrations of Garfield and Arthur,
changes had been asked in several important post-
offices in the State. The occupants were Rollins's supporters. They had befriended him in various canvasses for Congress and the Senate, but some of them
had survived their days of influence, and had been
superseded by younger men in the control of the party
in their respective localities. Rollins, however, never
deserted a friend, and he steadfastly opposed their removal. As the senior Senator in the Senate, he had
the larger influence of members of the delegation in
bestowing the federal patronage, and so carried his

point. His control of the patronage was to him, as it has been to others, a. source of weakness, and contributed to his defeat. The office-holders he saved were powerless to aid him, while those who were disappointed in their ambitions became his active and potential opponents.

In addition to the opposition arising out of personal grievances and the opposition of rival ambitions, Rollins had to face his own shibboleth in previous campaigns, " rotation in office." Patterson had been retired after one term in the Senate, and so had Wadleigh. Except Hale and Cragin, no Republican Senator from New Hampshire had received two full terms. If Rollins were given a second term, then Blair might claim a reëlection. If both were reëlected, the rotation principle was likely to be set aside. Then, again, the old question, which legislature should fill a Senatorial term, the one elected, or the one elected and organized, before its expiration, arose for consideration. Both Rollins and Blair believed that the duty devolved upon the legislature organized before the expiration of the term. If their view prevailed, the legislature then in session would elect both Rollins's and Blair's successors. That it might prevail seemed probable, for Blair and his friends were openly advocating it, while Briggs was known to be committed to that view.

A call for a Senatorial caucus was issued, but, prior to the assembling of the caucus, another call was sent out by the anti-caucus representatives for a conference of Republican members of the legislature, to be held the night previous to the date set for the Senatorial caucus. This conference was attended by all of the opponents and most of the friends of Rollins. The former took charge of the meeting, and did most of the talking. Marston and Stevens declared their hostility to Rollins's reëlection. They absolutely refused to be bound by caucus action. Briggs announced his unwillingness to abide by a decision of a caucus unless all Republicans participated. The caucus principle was advocated by Quint and Whitehouse. No attempt was made to secure a vote on the question of holding a caucus, each side being uncertain what that vote would disclose. The question of the election of two Senators also came up for consideration. Briggs declared himself in favor of such an election. Stevens and Marston said that, while on record against it, they would make no factious opposition thereto if a majority of the Republican members of the legislature favored it. The conference then adjourned.

This conference surprised and alarmed a very large majority of the Republicans of the State. Whether favoring Rollins's reëlection or not, they foresaw peril to the party, and feared for its integrity. Their apprehension and feelings are well expressed by the following extract from two Republican newspapers, whose editors were representative Republicans. The first is from the *Lebanon Free Press,* edited by Elias H. Cheney, long active in party work. Cheney had shown his preference for Rollins's renomination and represented the views of Rollins's supporters.

The other extract is from the *Nashua Telegraph,* whose editor was Orrin C. Moore. It will be recalled that Moore dramatically opposed Rollins's election to the Senate of 1876. In this canvass his position was neutral, as to candidates, while urging caucus action. His views, therefore, were those of a considerable number of Republicans in the State who could not be counted as Rollins's supporters, but who would have been satisfied with Rollins or any other candidate nominated by a Republican caucus.

The *Lebanon Free Press* said:

"If anybody can give a decent reason why the Speaker of the House, the president of the Senate, the secretary of State, the State treasurer, and the State printer should be nominated by a Republican caucus, and the Republican members of the legislature be bound by the action of the caucus, and yet those same members not be bound by a nomination made in precisely the same manner, for U. S. Senator, we should be glad to have him do it. It can't be done, and every man of sense knows it can't be done. If a regular nomination for any one of these offices may be ignored consistently with party fealty, so may any other. But then there is an end of all party efficiency. It is just as well to look this thing right in the face. We care very little for men; we would as cheerfully support any one of the gentlemen who have been named for the office if he had commanded a majority of the caucus vote. But we do care a great deal for the integrity of the Republican party, and by that we propose to stand. That is safe ground. It is ground upon which any man can safely stand, and time will vindicate the wisdom of his action. It will stand the test of time, when the passions of the hour have cooled. But it will be said that it was not a full caucus; that large numbers were absent. Very well, they had no business to be absent. They were not elected for any such purpose. They were elected as Republicans, to go into a Republican caucus and abide by the action of that caucus. If they did not betray their constituents when they failed to do so, we do not know how they could go to work to betray them. The Republicans of New Hampshire have not won their victories in this way; they will win no more victories, and deserve to win none, till they come back to the old paths."

The *Telegraph* said:

"We listened on Wednesday night with much interest to the statements made by the several speakers who opposed the usual method of selecting a Republican candidate for Senator. We expected to hear some overpowering reasons why Republicans should discard the majority rule in settling their difficulties. For ourselves we have been unable to see any way by which the rule can be discarded and the Republican party held together. Here are four or five distinguished Republicans, who heretofore have held to the rule in all their political relations. They have never before indicated, by word or act, that it could be safely discarded. Now, just as they are about to lay off the political harness, they tell the men who are to succeed them that the rule has a dangerous flaw. This is a late, a very late discovery. It comes in a heated moment, when the fountains of ambition are broken up, and personal stake is greater than party interest.

"The majority rule is a principle. There is none more fundamental. It underlies the whole Republican system. Its counterpart in the State and nation is anarchy. It is the same in a party. When the choice of men and measures cannot be determined by the majority rule, nothing remains but disintegration and defeat. There is not an officer, from fence-viewer to President, that is not settled by the constitution on this principle, and for all purposes a majority of one is as good as a majority of a thousand. If the purpose be to send the Republican party of New Hampshire into a hopeless minority for ten or twenty years, a short, swift, and certain way to accomplish it is to stamp out the principle of the rule of the majority.

"We can see no reason whatever why this principle should not apply to Senators as well as to Representatives, governors, and Presidents. If the office of Senator is high, as it is, then it is all the more important for a party to dispose of it by the principle of the rule of the majority than by a throw of the dice. If any one of the candidates before the legislature felt that he had a majority, would he not insist on the rule? Every one. Then what is good for one is good for all."

The day following the conference was devoted by each side to consolidating its forces. The opponents of a caucus circulated for signature a paper pledging its signers to stay out of the caucus and not be bound by its action. Before the close of the day, they knew that they had secured enough signatures to prevent Rollins's election in the legislature if all who signed the paper adhered to their pledges. This was made manifest to all when the caucus assembled in the evening. Of the 206 Republican members of the legislature only 130 voted in the caucus. The members attending proceeded immediately to business, on motion to ballot for a Senator to succeed Rollins. This ballot gave Rollins 98 of the 130 votes cast.[1] The motion to make the nomination unanimous was carried with only seven dissenting votes. Rollins appeared before the caucus, and accepted the nomination in a brief speech, expressing his appreciation and gratitude for the honors he had received at the hands of the Republican party of New Hampshire, and pointing to his record as an earnest of his future service if elected. He made no direct reference to the prospective bolt of his nomination.

The caucus then voted, with some opposition, to proceed to the nomination of a candidate for Senator Blair's seat in the Senate. Blair received 74 of the 97 votes cast.[2] Nothing came of this effort to elect a second Senator, the question being entirely overshadowed

[1] Mason W. Tappan, 1; William E. Chandler, 1; Ossian Ray, 1; Aaron F. Stevens, 4; James F. Briggs, 7; James W. Patterson, 18; Edward H. Rollins, 98.

[2] Aaron F. Stevens, 1; James F. Briggs, 2; Ossian Ray, 3; Mason W. Tappan, 3; Gilman Marston, 4; James W. Patterson, 10; Henry W. Blair, 74.

by the larger one of the bolt of caucus action in the nomination of Rollins.

The caucus disclosed that a considerable majority of the Republican representatives favored caucus action. It also showed that on the ballot taken to nominate his successor, Rollins lacked six votes of a majority of the Republican members of the legislature. The contention made somewhat later by some of the anti-caucus men was that Rollins, not having received in the caucus a majority of the whole Republican membership of the legislature, was not entitled to their support. The answer to this was that, if they could have prevented Rollins's receiving a majority on the first or subsequent ballots by attending the caucus, they were not justified in remaining outside. Patterson, in 1872, had come within seven votes on one ballot of a renomination in caucus, and failed to secure a majority. There was no certainty that Rollins might not likewise fall just short of the necessary majority of a full caucus. This justification of the anti-caucus men was an afterthought, for the leaders of the anti-caucus movement were determined to defeat Rollins's reëlection, and they felt surer of doing this by staying out of the caucus than by attending, and by repudiating later the action of its majority.

Five days were now to elapse before the legislature would vote for Senator. The time was employed by each side in attempting to create sentiment in the State. When the legislature met the following week, Concord was crowded with influential Republicans from every part of New Hampshire. The first test of strength came on Tuesday, June 19th, when the two houses of the legislature voted separately. With the exception of the joint ballot the next day, this was the largest vote cast in the legislature during the protracted contest which followed. Combining the vote of the two houses for each candidate, their strength June 19th is shown below.[1]

The two houses met in convention the next day with very slight change in the relative vote. They continued to meet in convention each legislative day until August 2d, when a choice was effected. Rollins's strength fell off after the first vote, but part of his loss was due to absenteeism, when it became apparent that the deadlock was to be prolonged. No material gain was made by any of the other original candidates. After the legislature had voted twenty-two times, covering a period from June 19th to July 12th, it became evident to Rollins that no good to the party was to be subserved by his remaining a candidate. The opposition to his reëlection continued intact in its support of

[1] Whole number of votes 328
Necessary for a choice 165
Edward H. Rollins 127
Harry Bingham, Democrat 121
James F. Briggs 28
James W. Patterson 22
Aaron F. Stevens 17
Gilman Marston 10
William S. Ladd, Democrat 1
Mason W. Tappan 1
Charles H. Bell 1

various candidates, and his remaining in the field might prevent an election of Senator. Disappointed as he was at the result, so far as it effected his personal interest, his party loyalty led him to consider the future welfare of the Republican organization. The party needed the additional vote of New Hampshire in the United States Senate. It might be disastrous to the Republicans in the nation, as well as in the State, if the legislature adjourned without choosing a Senator. So, after first proposing to withdraw in the interest of party harmony, if the other candidates would do the same, and failing to receive from them any response, he addressed the following letter to the Republican members of the legislature:

"As your candidate for United States Senator, regularly nominated in accordance with the time-honored usages of the party, I have for several weeks, and at nearly every vote taken, been supported by a majority of you with entire fidelity. From the beginning of the canvass, however, my election has been opposed by several gentlemen of prominence in the party, who have received honors at its hands and always by the agency of caucuses and conventions, and they have succeeded thus far in thwarting the election of a Senator in the legislature, containing ninety Republican majority. Convinced at length that the interests of the Republican party require a speedy termination of this condition of things, I have proposed to the four gentlemen who have from the outset repudiated their party obligations and stood as candidates for the Senate, in defiance of the will of the organization, that we all retire from the field and leave it open to the further consideration of the party. This proposal has not been accepted, and I leave the gentlemen to settle their account in this transaction with their constituents and the Republican party of New Hampshire. In my view of public affairs I am thus brought to face an important personal responsibility. In an active membership of the Republican party ever since its birth, in seasons of victory and defeat, sometimes in a position of leadership and sometimes as a private in its ranks, I have never faltered in supporting its principles, its nominations, and its accredited modes of action. Nor have I hesitated to make any sacrifice of my personal feelings or ambitions which the expressed will of my party associates seemed to demand. It costs me no heart-burnings to tread the path of duty again, and, therefore, in the further interests of harmony and the peace of the party, in whose continued ascendency in the State and nation I believe the best interests of our time are bound up, and for which I am as solicitous to-day as ever before, and especially in view of the approaching Presidential election, the closeness of the U. S. Senate, and the absolute importance of choosing a Republican Senator at this session, I desire to withdraw my name as your nominee for Senator, and leave you free to select another.

" Profoundly grateful to you, and through you, to the Republicans of the State, for the honors and opportunities for service I have already enjoyed, and particularly thanking my friends for their generous support in this protracted struggle, I am, with great respect, your obedient servant."

Rollins's withdrawal, however, afforded no immediate solution of the difficulty. The anti-caucus Republicans could no more agree upon a candidate than they would assent to Rollins's election. Various Republicans were brought forward by their friends and received the votes of the caucus Republicans, but one after another they disappeared as candidates. The contest dragged along until the third month of the session and the forty-third vote before a Senator was elected. Briggs and Stevens in the meantime had dropped out. Apprehension that Marston might finally secure enough votes with Democratic support to elect him, and weariness of the prolonged voting finally led to a concentration of Republican strength on Austin F. Pike, of Franklin, who had not received any considerable votes until the thirty-fifth ballot.

The election of Pike was generally satisfactory to the party. He was a tried and true Republican, a lawyer of the first rank, and a man of marked ability. He had served one term in Congress and been defeated for reëlection. In the early days of the party he had been an active worker, serving in two campaigns as chairman of the State committee. Since his defeat for Congress in 1875, he had devoted himself to his profession. Taking no part in the Senatorial struggle, he was free from its animosities. When Rollins was struggling for political preferment, Pike had been his friend and supporter. His election to the Senate was as gratifying to Rollins as that of any Republican of the State. The anti-caucus Republicans, with the exception of the Marston contingent, readily accepted Pike as a compromise candidate.

A number of Rollins's supporters would have preferred no election of Senator by the legislature of 1883, thereby referring again the question of his successor to the people at the next election. These men regarded Rollins as the candidate of the party, fairly nominated in a caucus held in accordance with its usages for nearly a generation. They were indignant at the bolt of leaders who had been frequently honored by the party, and always as the result of caucus action. They desired the Republicans of the State to pass upon the action of those who had repudiated its most cherished custom.

Rollins, however, foresaw the danger in such a course. It would thrust into the next State campaign an issue which would divide the organization in many towns and imperil Republican ascendency in the State. The Republican majority in the legislature might be entirely wiped out by such local divisions, and the Democrats carry the State. In any event, the Republican majority in the legislature would be reduced and a still smaller number of bolters be able to control the election of a Senator. Whether viewed from the standpoint of party interest or his own future, Rollins regarded his withdrawal from the contest as the only practical solution of the difficulty. His advice, therefore, to those who regretted his withdrawal was to unite upon some loyal Republican and thereby elect a Senator.

The sharp antagonisms which had arisen out of this Senatorial election, antagonisms that at one time threatened to wreck the party, were overshadowed by new issues before another election. Happily for the Republican party in New Hampshire, the elections were now biennial, and more than a year would elapse before the party would be called upon to act in its organized capacity. The feeling engendered by the struggle for the gubernatorial nomination in 1882 was allayed by the nomination of Moody Currier in 1884, while Blair was reëlected to the Senate without formidable opposition.

CHAPTER XXVI.

ROLLINS'S LAST YEARS

THE winter of 1883-4 Mr. Rollins passed in Washington, having the same rooms at the hotel he had occupied while a Senator. During his Congressional and Senatorial career he had had little opportunity to participate in the social life of the capital. Thoroughly enjoying society, he could now gratify his tastes in this direction. He entertained liberally, and freely accepted the many invitations that came to him. The season was one of unalloyed pleasure to both Mrs. Rollins and himself.

He still had calls made upon him by friends in New Hampshire for assistance in measures pending before Congress and the departments, to which he cheerfully responded as of old. A Presidential campaign was approaching, and this engaged his interest and attention. Regarding President Arthur as one of the best executives who had occupied the White House, and believing that the Republican party was indebted to him for a reunion of its factional elements, Rollins entered enthusiastically into the canvass for Arthur's nomination for President. He wrote his friends in New Hampshire urging their support, and, when spring

476

opened, he returned home to assist in securing a delegation from the State in Arthur's favor. He became a candidate for delegate at large and was elected. His associates in the delegation were Charles H. Sawyer, of Dover, George H. Stowell, of Claremont, Joseph B. Clark and Charles D. McDuffee, of Manchester, Warren Brown, of Hampton Falls, Frank D. Currier, of Canaan, and Henry B. Atherton, of Nashua, all his personal friends.

Sawyer was a broad-minded and public-spirited citizen of winning personality. Generous and unassuming, his interest in politics was without desire for political preferment. His election as governor of the State, which followed two years later, was a testimonial of the confidence of his fellow citizens. Brown, Stowell, and Clark were long-time and intimate political associates of Rollins, lieutenants upon whom he had relied in many campaigns. All these had been elected to positions of importance and trust. Atherton was a lawyer who had been active in politics at an earlier period, while McDuffee was a manufacturer whose recognition was particularly appropriate. Currier, as hitherto stated, was at this time secretary of the Republican State committee. Rollins was chosen chairman of the delegation, and later elected a member of the national committee. These were the last political positions he ever held.

The defeat of Arthur and the nomination of Blaine were disappointing to Rollins, for he believed Arthur to be the stronger candidate. Although doubting the wisdom of Blaine's nomination, he engaged energetically in the campaign, making a large number of speeches, and, as a member of the national committee, giving much attention to the work of that committee. His activity gave public assurance that his defeat for Senator was not to interfere with his interest in the success of the party and the principles with which he had been identified for nearly thirty years. The manner of his defeat, however, grieved him. He had at all times and on all occasions respected the integrity of the Republican organization. When at its caucuses the party had preferred another to him, he had accepted in good spirit their decrees. Three times he had been defeated in his canvass for Senator before he was elected, and each time found him urging the party to renewed activity, and working with unabated zeal for its success. It was, therefore, not unnatural that he should dwell upon the methods pursued to prevent his reëlection, and that in private conversation with friends he should give vent to his feelings. Yet, when the peril of the party was mentioned, he laid aside all thoughts of himself in his interest to have the party succeed.

Rollins's enmities in politics were few and short-lived. With Marston he appears to have kept up a social intimacy until death separated them. Even after Marston had bolted the Senatorial caucus, each was invited by the other to visit him. Whatever thoughts those visits awakened, they did not interfere with the hospitality of either. With Stevens and

Briggs his relations were wholly political, but other party associates who worked against his reëlection were frequently among his callers and enjoyed his social entertainments.

After the campaign of 1884, Rollins gradually retired from politics. He continued on the national committee until the next Presidential election, and his name appeared on the State committee for one more campaign. Business interests soon absorbed his time. December 25, 1879, the banking-house of Minot and Company, of Concord, was incorporated as a national bank, and named the Mechanicks National Bank. Rollins was chosen a director. Associated with him in the management of this bank were two men who were prominent in the affairs of the city and the State, Josiah Minot and Benjamin A. Kimball. Minot was the founder of the bank. He was an eminent lawyer and an able financier. At one time he was a law partner of Franklin Pierce. Upon the election of the latter to the Presidency, Minot was appointed to the bench of the State courts. Resigning from this position after a few years' service, he returned to the practice of his profession, also engaging in railroad and banking business. In politics a Democrat, Minot was for a long time a guiding spirit in Democratic councils. He was several times pitted against Rollins in the management of political campaigns in New Hampshire. In whatever enlisted his attention he was a dominant force among his associates, although of a modest and retiring nature.

Benjamin A. Kimball, brother of John Kimball, was associated with Rollins in both banking and railroad matters during the latter years of Rollins's life. With no ambition for political honors, Kimball nevertheless became a prominent factor in the politics of the State. An ardent Republican, he took an active part in the management of the party, wielding a large influence. A long-time resident of Concord, the city has been his pride, and its welfare his concern. He has contributed materially to its development and growth, and in all that pertains to civic betterment he has been a leader.

In addition to his connection with the national bank, in the affairs of which he took a more active part after his retirement from the Senate, Rollins, in 1884, formed a partnership with his son Frank in the bond business. Out of this partnership grew the incorporated banking-house of E. H. Rollins & Sons, with offices at Concord, and later at Boston. In this establishment all three of his sons were at one time interested.

Railroad matters were now becoming more acute in their relation to the politics of the State. The control of the Concord Railroad, the link connecting the northern and southern railroads of the State at Concord and Nashua, and in a position to exact tribute of all, had been for years a bone of contention among the managers of these several railroads. The Boston and Maine Railroad had absorbed the Lowell Railroad on the south and was endeavoring to lease the railroads to the north of Concord. If successful in controlling these northern roads, the absorption of the Concord Railroad by the Boston and Maine was only a question of time. To create a New Hampshire system of railroads, owned and controlled in the State, was the desire of Benjamin A. Kimball, John H. Pearson, and others interested in the Concord Road. Kimball enlisted Rollins in this enterprise and with others they secured control of the Boston, Concord and Montreal Railroad, one of the roads running north from Concord. Rollins was elected a director and president of this road in 1886, positions he held until his death in 1889. Controlling the Boston, Concord and Montreal Railroad, they purposed to unite it with the Concord Railroad, hoping ultimately to secure connections with Boston. The consolidation with the Boston, Concord and Montreal Railroad did not take place until after Rollins's death, however, although authorized by the legislature at its June session in 1889. The consolidated railroad was to be called the New Hampshire Railroad, but, objections being raised by some of the stockholders of the Concord Railroad, the name was changed to the Concord and Montreal Railroad. In the legal and political struggles incident to the railroad warfare of the State from 1886 to the time of his death Rollins was conspicuously active. He was strenuously opposed to the absorption of the Concord Railroad by the Boston and Maine, and he entered the contest to preserve the integrity of this road with his old-time vigor.

Amid all this business activity Rollins found time

for matters of social and local interest. He became a charter member of Capital Grange, at Concord, and gave considerable attention to the work of the Patrons of Husbandry. The organization of Shakespeare clubs at Concord about this time secured his hearty coöperation. As a member of the Warwick Club, he was a constant attendant upon its meetings. Shakespeare had been a favorite study of his hours of relaxation all through life. The winters he spent at Concord subsequent to 1883 were pleasant to him. After his first election to Congress in 1861, his public service and his connection with the Union Pacific Railroad had kept him away from his home city a large part of the time. Friends and neighbors who had been associated with him in the early years of his life at Concord seldom saw him. He had unintentionally grown apart from them. A renewal of the old ties was to him a constant pleasure. His spirits brightened and he found satisfaction in the quieter life he was leading. In summer at the farm at Rollinsford, in winter at Concord, he had equal enjoyment. His children, now grown to manhood and womanhood, engrossed a large share of his thoughts, and he took just pride in their success.

The end, however, was nearer than any had reason to suspect. His sixty-four years had nearly all of them been years of intense application, a continual drain upon his vitality. In 1888 he was prostrated by a shock of paralysis while in Boston on business. He recovered from this after a long illness, but another followed a day or two after the annual meeting of the Boston, Concord and Montreal Railroad, in May, 1889. He again rallied, and, as soon as he was able to travel, he was taken to the Isles of Shoals, where he appeared to be regaining health and strength. A third attack came soon after, and from this he did not rally. He passed away July 31, 1889, aged sixty-four years, four months, and twenty-eight days. His funeral occurred two days later at St. Paul's Episcopal Church, of Concord.

Prominent men, representatives of the State and national governments, and of the railroad and banking interests gave evidence by their presence of the high appreciation of Mr. Rollins's public service. The funeral services were conducted by the Masonic fraternity. He was laid at rest in Blossom Hill Cemetery at the capital of the State, which had been so long his home.

The day of his funeral the following tribute to his memory appeared in the Concord *Monitor:*

"MR. ROLLINS AS A REPUBLICAN AND AS A PUBLIC SERVANT

" Mr. Rollins came upon the stage of political action at the birth of the Republican party, and for a generation he gave to its cause fealty undoubted, and service unsurpassed. He had an unfaltering faith in its principles, and he never hesitated in the support he gave to them. No personal disappointment ever detracted from his fidelity and no defeat ever weakened his belief that the Republican party was best fitted to govern the country. He had a prominent part in the creation of the Republican organization of the State, the most thoroughly equipped political organization of any State in the Union, as its unprecedented line of victories abundantly prove.

"As chairman of the State committee Mr. Rollins became its central figure. He had a mind that readily grasped all the details of party management, and his incisive methods always forced the enemy upon the defensive. He brought the organization to that degree of perfection where the State committee could predict its success and find in the election returns a verification of its prophecies. His repeated triumphs as the leader of political campaigns inspired unbounded confidence in his generalship, and, after one year of absence during which the party lost the State, his return to the chairmanship of the State committee gave an éclat to the canvass that made victory certain.

"Rollins saw the weak points in his opponents' campaign and quickly concentrated his attacking columns at those points. He knew the political history of the towns of the State by heart. He had a good knowledge of men. He placed every man where he would be most effective. Nothing was left to chance. The press, the stump speakers, the town canvassers, every one, received inspiration from headquarters. The times were propitious for party discipline, and the organization worked with the directness and force of a well-drilled army. Rollins's name became a household word in politics. It was associated with every move upon the political checker-board.

"When the battle was won, Rollins was equally efficient in harmonizing rival claims for recognition. Beginning with the Republican party he desired to perpetuate it. Proud of its stand for human rights, he was a radical in all its advance movements. The history of the Republican party of New Hampshire is a biography of the personal work of Edward H. Rollins. The party never had a more intrepid leader or more devoted follower than he.

"Few men have filled so large a space in the public affairs of New Hampshire as Senator Rollins. Six years a Congressman, six years a United States Senator, and for more than thirty years a leader of a great political party, his whole life was one of publicity. No man ever gave more untiring service to the State and nation. Because of his conception of public duty, his ceaseless industry, his constant regard for the wishes of his constituents, it can be truly said of him that he earned the honors that were conferred upon him. His official career was without spot or blemish. The constant target for partisan attacks, no one ever questioned his personal or political integrity.

"He loved his native State and anything that concerned the welfare of New Hampshire always found in him a zealous and effective advocate. In the excitement of a political campaign he was a party man. As a public servant, all New Hampshire men were his constituents. The cause of every citizen of the State was made his own. Whether it was a bill for relief before Congress, a call for a hearing before a department, or a measure that would aid New Hampshire's prosperity, he pushed it with a persistency that seldom failed of success.

"Now that the sad announcement of his death reaches all parts of the State, many an humble individual will recall, to the credit and honor of Mr. Rollins, some incident of the many in his life when the red tape of official routine was rudely brushed aside that some needy or suffering applicant might secure his rights. Mr. Rollins took pride in saying to the people of New Hampshire that, when he failed in being of service to his constituents, he hoped they would demand his resignation. He felt all this saying implied, and he never left Washington at the close of a session until after every request from New Hampshire had received consideration.

"In this city is a handsome public building. It is the post-office of the city, and is for the use of every citizen. Senator Rollins secured the passage of the bill through Congress authorizing its construction. When the Senate committees of the forty-seventh Congress, the last of which Rollins was a member, were made up, he asked for the chairmanship of the committee on public buildings and grounds. Other more important and influential chairmanships were at his disposal, but he declined them all that he might secure for the capital city of his State a public building at once ornamental and useful. No subject ever interested him more, and, when the bill received the signature of President Arthur, it was a proud moment of Senator Rollins's life. He lived to witness the completion of the structure and see it put to public use. In that it was due to his untiring exertions, it was his tribute to the city that had so generously honored him. If he has no other monument erected to his memory, this building speaks more eloquently than granite shaft or statue of the public service of one of New Hampshire's most useful citizens."

CHAPTER XXVII.

ROLLINS'S FAMILY LIFE AND PERSONAL TRAITS

NOTWITHSTANDING his intensely active life in politics and business, Mr. Rollins was a thoroughly domestic man. The old home at Concord and the farm at Rollinsford were ever in his thoughts. He turned to either place with a feeling of relief from all anxiety. Family life seemed to soothe and charm him. Whatever shadows clouded his public career, they never fell upon his household. Here all must be sunshine and laughter. The home-life of his children is the pleasantest of their recollections. The boisterousness of youth never disturbed him. He used to say to his children: "Have all the company you want. Invite your friends to the house at any time. I would rather that your friends visited you than that you visited them." The result was that the Rollins home at Concord and the Rollins house at Rollinsford frequently resembled a school at recess with its babel of voices and romping plays. Whatever the turmoil, Mr. Rollins sat with entire composure reading or writing, apparently oblivious of the noise and confusion. An incident related by his son, Montgomery Rollins, illustrates this characteristic.

"I remember one day when the house was full of my boy and girl friends. Father was reading in the living-room. We were playing very noisy games, dashing in and out of the room he was occupying. All of a sudden we took up some new game which kept us absolutely quiet. In a few minutes father laid down his paper, looked around in a surprised way, and said, 'What's the matter?' The absence of commotion and noise was the only thing which arrested his attention."

In the old house at Concord, the sleeping-room of Mr. and Mrs. Rollins was situated with entrances to both the front and back halls. An old custom in that city ushered in May Day with the blowing of horns. One May morning, about three o'clock, Frank W. Rollins, the second son, then a lad of ten years, led a troop of his boy friends quietly into the house and up the front stairs to the door of his parents' sleeping apartment. At a given signal the door was swung open and some twenty boys blowing horns with the full strength of their lungs marched through the room, by the foot of the bed, out into the back hall, and down the back stairs. Mr. and Mrs. Rollins sat up in bed, rubbed their eyes, and simply smiled on the passing procession.

Yet Mr. Rollins could be a stern though indulgent parent. His punishments of his children were few, but they were never forgotten. As a rule, a look or a quickly spoken word of command were enough to correct any misdemeanor. Those who remember him will readily recall the penetration of his keen black eyes.

They seemed to read the motive of the offender brought up for discipline. When angry, his eyes would flash fire and his voice ring out like a clarion note. Many a politician has quailed before his glance without a word being spoken. Yet to the young his countenance invariably lighted up with a smile of encouragement. Making companions of his children, Mr. Rollins's admonitions and advice were rather those of an elder brother than a parent. He fully appreciated the natural ways of boys and girls, and he had a humane way of dealing with their failings. Speaking again of his father, Montgomery Rollins says: "It was not his custom to scold us at length, but in some quiet way to enforce upon our minds our waywardness and teach us the necessity of obedience. The fact that he did not harp upon our shortcomings made him stand a great deal higher in our estimation, and his system of correction was, therefore, more effective."

While providing generously for his children in all that contributed to their education, comfort, and enjoyment, he did not believe in indulging them in the luxury of too much spending money. He feared that such indulgence would spoil them. From necessity, he had, in youth, passed through the rigid school of economy, and he sought to instil precepts of thrift and self-reliance in the minds of his children. He encouraged travel and all other means of broadening their lives, but enforced habits of industry and independence of parental support. After he had tested them and found them competent, they ever afterward had his confidence

and assistance. He gave to his sons the best education obtainable, but they were made to understand that they must depend upon themselves the day their education was finished. This last injunction was literally enforced, for, from the day that they left school, he cut off their supplies of money, and each was obliged to shift for himself.

The Rollins home was conducted upon broad lines. Supplies for the household were purchased in large quantities and at wholesale. In the autumn the larder was stocked much in the same manner as summer hotels, for the season. There was a big room on the north side of the house at Concord which was never heated. Around this room were hung late in the fall quarters of beef, halves of hogs, hams, etc., while stored within it were barrels of apples, potatoes, sugar, and flour, with bags of coffee and chests of tea. Thus there was never any lack of supplies when unexpected visitors arrived. It was a rare occurrence for the family to sit down to a meal without the presence of some expected or unexpected guest. Sunday was a day when company was most numerous.

The old house at Concord, in which Mrs. Rollins's family, the Wests, had resided for generations, was a curiously constructed building. It had been added to from time to time when more room was needed, until it branched out in all directions without plan or symmetry. One might lose himself in the dark halls which led to outlying rooms. It was a famous house for children's sports, and many a game of hide and seek was played within it. One room, the library, lives in the memory of those who were accustomed to call or visit there. It was a long, narrow room across one end of the house, heated by an air-tight stove. Shelves lined its four sides from floor to ceiling, and these were filled to overflowing with books and pamphlets. This room, when the door was closed, was entirely separated from the main part of the house. It not only served as a retreat for those who were studious and desired quiet, but was also a great resort for the children on stormy days. Here many a successful political campaign was planned and its details carefully worked out. There is hardly a politician of note of the old guard of New Hampshire who has not been there.

The dining-room of this house was large and ample. While a low-studded building, the generous size of all the rooms gave to this dwelling the appearance of extensive proportions. It was simply but adequately furnished, although every piece of furniture bore the marks of constant usage. Not a nook or a corner of the house but served some useful purpose. It was not an uncommon happening to have cots put up in the parlors, for even the accommodations of the sleeping apartments were at times overtaxed. Mr. Rollins's family was ever a large one, for, in addition to his own children, he always had with him some of his nephews or nieces, who made his house their home, and were educated and cared for by him.

At the farm in Rollinsford, it was not unusual for twenty-five people to gather at the dinner-table, with the addition of from seven to ten in the servants' din-ing-room. Mr. Rollins sat at the head of the board and carved for this large family with the greatest satis-faction.   The house had much the appearance of the famous Southern homes in the patriarchal days before the war. When Mr. Rollins, after their destruction by fire, rebuilt the farm buildings, he planned them with the expectation of having all his children and their families with him during the summer season.   He could never understand why it was not perfectly simple for every one of the children and grandchildren to come to the farm the first of June and remain until October. Indeed, if they did not come with " bag and baggage " for a long visit, he felt somewhat hurt and neglected.

Such a family could not have been reared, and such hospitality could not have been dispensed, without the presence of a broad-minded wife and mother.   Most helpful to her husband was Mrs. Rollins. Of cheer-ful disposition, devoted to her family, fertile in re-sources, charming as a hostess, she endeared the Rol-lins home to all who came within its portals. It made little difference to Mr. and Mrs. Rollins whether the company were old or young, their own friends and acquaintances or those of the children, a cordial wel-come awaited every comer.

There was no dearer spot to Senator Rollins than his farm at Rollinsford. It was his pride and joy, his only source of recreation. Whenever his public duties or his business interests permitted, he sought its seclu-sion. It was on this place that the freest and happiest hours of his life were spent. It had been the home of his childhood. Many of the neighbors were friends of his youth. All the associations of his early years clustered around this locality. There all cares were laid aside. After the strain of a long session of Congress, nothing did him so much good as his activities about this place. The house which his father had built he remodelled and improved. In April, 1881, all the buildings were destroyed by fire. When the news came to him of the conflagration, and he was assured that the family was safe, his only inquiry was regarding a stately old elm which stood in front of the house. When informed that this was uninjured, he said, "Then I shall rebuild on the old spot;" and rebuild he did, but on a larger scale.

Senator Rollins was a very ardent and genuine farmer. He loved the soil and had a very strong attachment for the place of his birth. Uniting his practical knowledge of agriculture, gleaned when a boy, with the information to be obtained from agricultural publications, he sought to bring this farm of his ancestors to the highest state of cultivation. In this he succeeded, for in productiveness his farm excelled any in that section of the State. With William A. Russell, of Lawrence, Massachusetts, he was a pioneer in the introduction of the Holstein breed of cattle into New England, importing them from Holland. At the time of his death, he had a handsome herd of Holsteins, of which he was very proud. They were all registered, and were a source of attraction to the farmers of the

State, for they were then comparatively new to this country.

The haying season Mr. Rollins particularly enjoyed. There was something about it that strongly appealed to him. It was the beginning of the harvest, and he took especial pride in cutting and curing the grass without injury from rainfall. He always drove the mowing-machine when at home. His dress, when at work in the field, consisted of high top boots with his trousers tucked into them, a flannel shirt, an ordinary coat, and a broad sombrero hat. On such occasions he hardly looked the well-dressed business man, in which character he generally appeared, but he thoroughly enjoyed himself. Amusing stories are told about the mistakes of strangers coming to the farm to see him on business or politics, who took him for the superintendent rather than the owner of the farm, a mistake which he was inclined to encourage, generally leading the caller to commit himself before he revealed his own identity. Mr. Rollins was a man of great quickness of motion, wiry and strong, and he could easily tire out men of larger physique who were accustomed to outdoor labor. As a boy, " he held the belt," as the phrase used to run, both as a mower and as cradler of rye and barley for the town of Rollinsford. Sparing not himself, he insisted that everybody under his eye should do a full day's work. His sons did not always take as much interest in the labor of the hay-field as he did, but, so long as the haying lasted, they were obliged to work. After the haying was over, they had to pick the stones out of the stubble in those parts of the fields which had been recently seeded down. Then they were free for the rest of the summer.

Mr. Rollins was very fond of horses and of driving. He always kept a pair of small Morgan horses, and they were invariably bought for him by one man, William Putnam, of Concord, familiarly known as " Old Put," a man of unerring judgment of horse flesh. When the family was in Concord, the horses were brought to the door directly after dinner Sunday afternoons, and, driving himself, Mr. Rollins took as many of the family as could be stowed into a two-seated carriage for a ride over the " dark plains," around Penacook or over the Dunbarton Road. To drive across from Concord to the farm at Rollinsford, a distance of forty miles, was a very common occurrence. This trip was made by an early start in the morning, breakfast being eaten on the way. The old tavern at Northwood was generally reached by noon, and here they dined.

Whenever Mr. Rollins was at the farm, it became the rendezvous for all the politicians and prominent men in the southeastern part of the State. Among the men frequently seen there were: Chief Justice Charles Doe, a neighbor at Rollinsford; Alfred F. Howard, Elbridge Pierce, Aaron Young, and J. Horace Kent, of Portsmouth; Edward Ashton and Daniel Rollins, of Somersworth; Daniel Hall, Andrew H. Young, J. F. Seavey, Reverend George A. Spaulding, Charles H. Sawyer, and Rev. Dr. Alonzo H. Quint, of Dover; Warren Brown, of Hampton Falls; Jacob

Young, of Barrington; Charles S. Whitehouse, of Rochester; Charles W. Talpey and Alonzo Nute, of Farmington, and Gilman Marston, of Eeter. Any pleasant afternoon in the summer was a time when some of these men were sure to be gathered at the Rollins homestead. It was their custom to repair to the pasture where was located a boiling spring. From this spring the water bubbled out of the ground cold and clear as crystal. The great pines towered overhead, and, seated around this spring on the soft pine needles, many a good story was told, and many a political campaign discussed.

During his early manhood Mr. Rollins was very active in masonry, and for many years devoted much time to its work. He passed through all the chairs in the Blue Lodge, and was master of Blazing Star Lodge, of Concord. Also Knight Templar, he became commander of Mount Horeb Commandery at the capital. In after life he frequently referred to the benefit he derived from his work in masonic bodies, placing special stress upon the training it gave him for public life. Accustomed to presiding in a masonic lodge, he surprised the members of the New Hampshire legislature by the familiarity he showed with parliamentary proceedings and the ease with which he discharged the duties of Speaker when first elected to that position. After his death a paper was found in the archives of the commandery requesting that he be buried with masonic honors.

At one time Mr. Rollins took a special interest in

military affairs. He was one of the charter members of the Horse Guards, a famous New Hampshire military organization. Elected first as a lieutenant, he subsequently became captain of one of the companies of this battalion. The membership of this organization embraced many prominent men of the State. Its uniform was that of the French Hussars, and, when mounted, the command made a most striking appearance. Each man supplied his own uniform and equipment, and all expenses were borne out of the battalion treasury. The Horse Guards gave an annual ball, which was a social feature of the capital. They performed escort duty at the inauguration of the governor, and sometimes appeared on other important occasions. They offered their services to the government at the very beginning of the Civil War, but the offer was declined, it was said, on the ground that the war would be so brief there would be no use for cavalry. A number of its officers and men, however, enlisted, and went to the front. Mr. Rollins would doubtless have been among the number had he not just been elected to Congress and continued there throughout the war. While not obliged to do so, he furnished at his own expense two recruits who served until the close of hostilities.

In keeping with the memory of Mr. Rollins, mention should be made of Julius Cone, an eccentric genius, well known to politicians of the State, and particularly well remembered by the older inhabitants of Concord. As a young man, Cone entered Mr. Rol-

lins's drug store as a temporary substitute for some
absent clerk. This temporary employment became permanent, and, until his death, Cone was as much a
fixture of that store as its furnishings. He slept in it,
or in a room directly overhead, and never went anywhere except for long walks in the woods. He was a
well-read man and quite a naturalist. A deep student
of human nature, Cone had a bitter hatred of all
pretence and fraud. His disposition was kindly,
and his sympathies broad. He had a handsome face,
and was loved by all who knew him. Mr. Rollins's
confidence in him was unbounded, and he never returned to Concord without calling upon Julius Cone.

Another character identified with Mr. Rollins's life
was his farm superintendent, William H. Prescott.
While a reliable man, Prescott's methods were not
always satisfactory to Mr. Rollins. The latter had a
quick and somewhat fiery temper, and when aroused
was apt to make his wishes known in a very peremp-
tory way. He was liable to be especially exasperated
when suffering from violent headaches, to which he was
subject whenever his nervous system was taxed by the
strenuous life he led. Then he would pace the floor
for hours, his head bound with a wet towel, in excruci-
ating pain. At such times and others he would be irri-
tated by some failure of his superintendent to meet his
expectations, or by some fancied shortcoming, and discharge him. He would say:

" Prescott, I am done with you. Come to the house
Saturday night and get your pay."

Prescott would reply, " All right, sir." When Saturday night came, Mr. Rollins would make out his time, pay him, and take his receipt in full. Then he would say, " Now we are square, and I am through with you." Prescott would reply, " Yes, sir?" and leave the room. Early Monday morning he would be at work again. Mr. Rollins would see him, but make no comment. Prescott would go on as if nothing had happened until the next disagreement, when the formality of dismissal would be repeated. This happened so many times that it became a standing joke in the family. Prescott, who is now employed by Mr. Rollins's sons, recounts with great gusto the number of times he was discharged but did not go. Sometimes after a discharge the boys would ask Prescott if he intended to go. He would reply, " Why, bless yer, no. Mr. Rollins don't mean it. He couldn't run the farm without me."

When Mr. Rollins was Senator, Governor Natt Head, of New Hampshire, came to Washington to secure the appointment of a friend to the position of keeper of the Whalesback lighthouse at Portsmouth, then vacant. Admiral Dewey was at that time at the head of the lighthouse board, with the rank of captain. Both Senator Rollins and Governor Head knew Dewey intimately, as the latter's first wife was the daughter of Governor Goodwin, of Portsmouth, and Dewey spent much time in that city. Calling at Captain Dewey's office, Rollins said: " Dewey, there is a vacancy, as you know, at the Whalesback lighthouse, and we want Governor Head's friend appointed

keeper." Captain Dewey appeared embarrassed, hesitated a little, and then said, "I am very sorry, Mr.
Rollins, but we have changed our custom. We don't
appoint any more. We promote." Rollins glared at
Dewey for a few seconds, his eyes snapping fire, and
then said, in his most sarcastic tone, " Oh, you promote,
do you, Dewey? That's the new thing. You promote.
We'll see about that. Come on, Head." Grabbing his
hat, he rushed out of the office, and over to the Secretary
of the Treasury, who is the president of the lighthouse
board. In less than ten minutes, he was back to
Dewey's office out of breath, but with a triumphant
smile lighting up his countenance. Throwing down
on Dewey's desk an order from the Secretary of the
Treasury to appoint Governor Head's friend, he exclaimed, " There, Dewey, we won't have any promotion
to-day."

It is, perhaps, needless to say that this incident occurred before the passage of the civil service law. In
common with other leaders of that time, Rollins believed
that those who helped to fight the battles of the party,
and contributed to the maintenance of its principles
were entitled to the rewards of office when the victory was won. This was also the belief of practically
all his constituents in New Hampshire, Democrats as
well as Republicans. In carrying out their wishes, Mr.
Rollins was just as persistent whether the request that
came to him was for an office or for the performance
of some legislative duty in Congress. Although he
was in sympathy with the political spirit of his time,

he had no patience with incompetent employees, whether in private or public life. Inefficient government clerks failed to enlist his interest to prevent their discharge. He made it a rule never to recommend any but competent men for office. So long as they maintained their efficiency, he stood by them, but, if they proved unworthy, he made no effort to secure their retention.

About nine years of Mr. Rollins's active life were spent as secretary and treasurer of the Union Pacific Railroad. His service with this road began right after the close of his third term in Congress. It was at a time when the building of the road was in progress and the corporation was having a hard struggle to maintain itself. The treasurer's position was an onerous one, for the road met with many reverses. Executive ability and financial skill were necessary to keep it from bankruptcy. Mr. Rollins's duties brought him in contact with some of the ablest financiers and railroad men of the country. They all bore testimony to his shrewdness and sagacity in meeting emergencies as they arose. He was present at the laying of the last rail and the driving of the golden spike of the Union Pacific Railroad, the completion of which was to connect by rail the Atlantic Coast with the Pacific. In memory of the event, Mr. Rollins wore on his watch chain a small spike made from the gold one used on this occasion.

While not a communicant of any church, Mr. Rollins was a regular attendant at service on Sunday.

When in Concord, out of deference to his wife, he went to St. Paul's Episcopal Church, and in its faith his children were reared. At Rollinsford, he attended the church of his youth, the First Congregational, of Dover. One of his most intimate friends was its pastor, the Reverend Dr. George A. Spaulding. Not strictly speaking a sectarian, he was nevertheless an earnest supporter and constant contributor to church work. In his observance of the Sabbath as well as in his daily conduct there was to be seen the strong impress of his mother's teaching and example. Of the strictest integrity, his word was never questioned in business or politics. He forgot no promise and disappointed no friend. In public life, he was scrupulously honest. He never sought by indirection to obtain that which could not be secured by open dealing. Throughout his long career, there was no reflection ever made upon his character. This is the more remarkable, considering the many political contests in which he was engaged. Even when his defeat for reëlection to the Senate was sought by fellow Republicans, envious of his success, there was not even a whisper that he had been other than a diligent, efficient, and upright public servant. Opportunities he had, both in financial life and as treasurer of the Union Pacific Railroad, to acquire wealth if guided only by the technical restraints of law, but he carefully avoided them all. He died leaving only a moderate fortune for his day, accumulated by industry, thrift, and careful investment.

CHAPTER XXVIII.

SUMMARY

To estimate justly the life of Edward H. Rollins and the part he played in an important epoch of our history, it is necessary to take into account the period of his activity and the influence of New Hampshire on the politics of the country. Rollins stood out preeminent as a party organizer and manager of political campaigns at a time when the success or defeat of the Republican party meant the destruction or perpetuation of slavery, the preservation or dissolution of the Union, and, after the close of the war, the reaping of its fruits or the failure of the harvest. He was at the head of the Republican organization in a doubtful State, whose influence in national affairs was all out of proportion to the size of the State. The New Hampshire election was the first in the year, and, being a debatable State, the election was regarded as the keynote of subsequent elections of the year. Both political parties sought to strike this note for the influence it would have upon other States. The State had been wrested from Democratic control during President Pierce's administration by the Know-Nothing coalition under Rollins's leadership. Being the home of the

504

President, the loss of New Hampshire to the Democratic party in 1855 brought the State into national prominence, and it retained that prominence until 1878, when its elections were changed from March to November. The Know-Nothing coalition was succeeded in power by the Republican party in 1856. The enrolment of the State in the Republican column that year was significant of the political transition going on throughout the country. Again in 1860, the March election foreshadowed the national triumph of the Republican party in the fall of that year. Throughout the Civil War, when the vital question was the upholding of President Lincoln's administration, New Hampshire Republicans never wavered. Other and larger Republican States were turned from their party allegiance, electing Democratic governors and legislatures, thus discouraging enlistments, but the vote of New Hampshire was always for the vigorous prosecution of the war. Later, during Grant's two administrations, when Republican supremacy in the nation was frequently threatened, New Hampshire Republicans stood true to their party and its principles. Often an October and November tidal wave of Democratic success was turned back at the following March election in New Hampshire. New York, Ohio, and Indiana were pivotal States because of their size. New Hampshire was pivotal because of the date of its election.

To Rollins was committed year after year the charge of keeping New Hampshire in line for the Republican party. He built up and perfected a party organization never equalled in any State of the Union in any period of our history. Party feeling was intense. The issues of the war and the reconstruction period which followed overshadowed all other questions. With elections occurring annually, there was little cessation of politics throughout the year. The margin by which the Republican party held the State was narrow. Any small defection imperilled the party ascendency. There was no place for experiments in politics. Party lines were tightly drawn. There was no room for third parties, and, when they sprang up, their existence was short-lived. The dissatisfied or independent voters were forced into one camp or the other. Men were either Republicans or Democrats. The Mugwump did not flourish on New Hampshire soil. Both Republicans and Democrats were taught that their own party was radically right and the other party radically wrong. The open ballot prevailed, and there were few voters of the State who were not proud to display their party allegiance. As exacting as that of an army in the field was the discipline in political campaigns. Men might not like personally their leaders, but they obeyed their orders. Individual interests and feelings had to be subordinated to the success of the party in the face of the enemy.

Yet there were personal differences to reconcile, party mistakes to excuse, conflicting ambitions to adjust, and disappointments to placate, that every Republican might be rallied to the polls to support the ticket. This is always more difficult to do in a small State than in a large one, for the reason that, in a small State, there is closer touch of individuals, and better knowledge of details. Men like John P. Hale, Amos Tuck, Daniel Clark, and George G. Fogg were in the forefront giving force to the principles of the Republican party, meeting the arguments of its opponents, shaping its policies, and appealing in the forum and the press to the voters. At a later date other strong and able men battled in the legislature, on the stump, and in the newspapers for the maintenance of the principles of the Republican party. But the work of holding the party intact for political campaigns devolved upon Rollins. He organized the local clubs, inspired the local leaders, secured the canvasses of the voters, marshalled the forces, and directed the contests in the strenuous political battles that were fought year after year. Detracting nothing from the services of other distinguished Republicans of the State, the situation of the Republican party in New Hampshire called for just such a leader as Rollins to direct and manage its political campaigns. The party could not have continued to hold power for so long a period in so many adverse circumstances without just such a general of its forces. It is not too much to say that, in several crises, Rollins's genius as a party manager saved the State to the Republican party.

It was the confidence of the rank and file of the party that kept Rollins so long at the head of the Republican State committee. There were times when his rivals for political honors would have gladly set him aside.

His aspirations were known. The chairmanship of the State committee, and his repeated successes in that position, gave him prestige and a strong following, but there was a feeling among those who sought preferment that Rollins had an undue advantage in being at the head of the Republican organization. Yet no one was ready to assume the responsibility of the position, and no disinterested individual appeared to take command. The place was not without its disadvantages. It was quite as easy to incur hostility in the discharge of its duties as to make friendships. The emergencies of the campaigns called for quick decisions, and Rollins's manner sometimes gave offence. He had a directness of speech not always pleasing. Clearly seeing himself what a crisis demanded, he was impatient when others did not quickly grasp the situation. His sharp and sometimes severe speech provoked personal hostility, but his outbursts of indignation had in them no resentment. After forcibly expressing himself, he dismissed from his mind the incident, and was surprised that others remembered it. He held sway at a time when almost military discipline was necessary to win political battles. Yet he was sagacious in his dealings with men, and there was method in the discipline he enforced. To the party at large in the State he was the successful leader. They saw little of the frictions and annoyances at headquarters. They were infused with his courage, and were sanguine of victory when he planned the campaign. They also shared his pride in keeping New Hampshire constantly in support of Republican policies. His appeals invoked their enthusiastic support, and they held him in affectionate regard.

Rollins's public service was the outgrowth of his identification with the politics of New Hampshire. He was ambitious. In the furtherance of his ambition he fully qualified himself for public position. The glamour of official life had little charm for him, but he enjoyed the struggle to attain position, and the labor and responsibility it entailed. He was a man of action, and the severe tension of political struggles appealed to him. In addition to this, he was a man of strong convictions, and the issues of his day enlisted his heartiest sympathies. He believed that the rewards of political contests should be bestowed upon those who were instrumental in winning those contests. This view was shared by a large majority of the people of the State. Neither party in the State had use for an individual who was not ready at all times to put on the political harness and work for the success of the cause with which he was identified. Some excelled as speakers, others as writers, and still others as organizers. The labors of all were essential to success. Therefore, all classes were entitled to recognition. The people of New Hampshire agreed with the late Thomas B. Reed that " statesmen are politicians who are dead." Every male citizen of New Hampshire was a politician in the broadest sense of the term, in that he had definite political principles, was ready to defend them, knew whom he desired to represent him in public position, and was not indifferent to holding office himself. There were many aspirants for political honors, and but few positions. These honors did not come without a contest and personal effort. In this struggle for party favor, Rollins had his part, tasting the bitterness of defeat as well as the pleasures of victory.

His service as a member of the legislature and Speaker of the House, a member of Congress and United States Senator, covered a period of fifteen years, or about half the time that he was active in politics. The twelve years he spent in both branches of Congress were years of unremitting toil. In his legislative career he never attempted to appear other than he was, a diligent, painstaking legislator, loyal to his State, and true to his convictions. He mastered the details of all subjects coming within the province of his assignments, and, if he had occasion to express his views, his speeches showed an intelligent grasp of the question under consideration. He made very few set speeches during his Congressional career, and none for home consumption. For all demagogical displays he had no feeling but contempt. It would have been to his credit if he had participated more frequently in debate, for he had that happy faculty of clear and direct statement which enlists the attention and appeals to the understanding. Rollins, however, comprehended as fully as any man in legislative life the value of silence when a measure is successfully running the gauntlet of its several parliamentary stages. Many a worthy measure has been imperilled or defeated by the ardor of its friends to go on record in its favor. Rollins's whole training in life had been to subordinate the individual to the triumph of the cause. His legislative service, therefore, while not conspicuous, was eminently creditable and successful. None of his associates in the Senate showed greater skill in piloting measures through that body.

New Hampshire interests especially appealed to Rollins. While he was a member of the House and the Senate, requests from home for assistance came directly to him in preference to his colleagues from the State. This preference oftentimes became so marked that Rollins was compelled to ask constituents to take the initiative through some colleague more directly interested, that his relations with his associates from New Hampshire might remain cordial. His attention to the wants of his constituents would have made him a busy man if he had done nothing else while in Washington. No call from New Hampshire was too trivial to be ignored. The reputation he acquired for bringing about results constantly increased these demands. Some were deserving attention, while others were not, but Rollins made no distinction if the requests were reasonable, and there was even a remote possibility of their being granted. Such work as this entailed contributed little or nothing to his public reputation, nor was it always justly appreciated by the beneficiaries. Oftentimes a request involving days or weeks of persistent effort to attain it was indifferently received. Yet the appreciation and gratitude of some humble claimant seemed to compensate Rollins for the ingratitude of others.

Rollins had earned and was entitled to a reëlection to the Senate. Had his service been at a later period, he undoubtedly would have secured it. He suffered defeat partly because of the belief of the Republican party of New Hampshire in the principle of rotation in office, a principle which Rollins himself had long advocated. The Republicans of New Hampshire at that time had more concern in holding the State than in the influence her representatives exerted in Washington. If members of Congress and Senators were given long periods of service, the door of opportunity seemed to be closed to the active and ambitious Republicans of the State. Valuable as Rollins's service was to the party and to the State, there were others who believed that they could do equally well or better in the Senate. The younger generation coming upon the stage of action had more intimate association with other leaders. Rollins made the mistake so frequent with men long in leadership of not recognizing the passing influence of older men. Loyal to his friends, he stood by them long after they ceased to be of service to him or to the party, and not infrequently when they were unworthy of his confidence. The revolt against caucus action which had been effective in changing Senatorial successions in other States made its appearance in New Hampshire at a time when Rollins was seeking a reëlection to the Senate. The bolt of the Republican Senatorial caucus of 1881 in the State on the ground that the question was constitutional rather than political made it easier to bolt in 1883, and really paved the way for setting aside party custom that year.

When the blow came, Rollins was not prepared for it. He had abided caucus action with good grace when it brought disappointment to him. That the first bolt of a Republican Senatorial caucus should be visited upon him after his long service for the party savored to his mind of base ingratitude. For a time he was not without hope that the prevailing sentiment of the party would triumph and his election follow. Yet when it was apparent that he could not be reëlected, he withdrew from the contest that some other Republican might be chosen. Intense as was his disappointment, his loyalty to the party would not permit him to favor a course which would prevent a choice of Senator by the legislature, leaving New Hampshire partially unrepresented, and the Republicans without a vote in the Senate which they especially needed at that time.

Had Rollins been in his prime, it is not impossible that he would have controlled the situation and ultimately triumphed. The action of the bolters met with no popular approval. The rank and file of the party in the State believed Rollins entitled to an election and to have been fairly renominated. His withdrawal left the party in a quandary. The leaders of the bolt preferred Rollins quite as much as they preferred one another. A cheerful acceptance of the situation on his part would have softened much of the antagonism to him then existing. Age and the tremendous strain he

had been under for years robbed Rollins of his usual
buoyancy and confidence. The sympathy of friends
intensified his feelings, and his defeat was for a time
uppermost in his mind. Gradually his thoughts were
diverted to other matters, and he found pleasure in
both active business pursuits and the domestic life of
the fireside. In 1885, when Blair's term in the Senate
expired, and again in 1887, when a vacancy occurred
in the Senate by the death of Senator Pike, Rollins's
friends urged his return to the Senate. He, however,
made no effort to secure votes or put himself forward
as a candidate, and the result of these elections brought
him no disappointment.

To the old guard now living the thought of Rollins
brings to memory interesting recollections of the intense political contests waged in New Hampshire under
his leadership. Reviewing his career, they are free to
give praise to his ability, his integrity, and his fidelity
to the party, the State, and the nation. Few there are
who would not now say that his defeat for reëlection
to the Senate was a mistake. The causes contributing
to it are well-nigh forgotten, but the ardent devotion
of Rollins to the principles of the Republican party,
his untiring labors to promote the success of those
principles, and his valuable service as a public servant
are still held in appreciative remembrance by those
whom he so often led to victory.

Measured with the men of his time, he stands out
conspicuous and successful. Those of his contemporaries who were rivals for political honor approached

a public career from other environments than his, and they became prominent in the development of other talents. Yet in what Rollins made of his opportunities, in the part he took in public affairs and in his service to the people, he was in his sphere of action their peer. In the era of his activity, his work was as essential to the triumph of the great cause for which all battled as the labors of those whose deeds are more conspicuously of record.

In his efforts to make his life a success, Mr. Rollins wronged no man, dealt justly by all, and assisted others to rise above their environments. He was intensely patriotic, and his public spirit was pronounced. As a citizen he was loyal to the community. To his neighbors he was considerate, kind, and helpful. In the family circle he was dearly beloved. Whatever the obligation resting upon him, he performed well his part, turning aside from no responsibility and avoiding no duty.

THE END.

APPENDIX

DESCENDANTS OF EDWARD H. ROLLINS

EDWARD WARREN ROLLINS, eldest son, born November 25, 1850. Twice married, first to Jessie Witter, of Denver, Colorado, by whom he had one son, Ashton Rollins; and second, to Clara Sherwood, St. Louis, Mo., by whom he also had a son, Sherwood Rollins.

Helen Mary Rollins, only daughter, born September 4, 1853, married Henry Robinson, of Concord, New Hampshire. Their children are, Ethel Rollins,[1] Marjorie Sawyer, Rupert West, Ruth Cora, Helen Natalie, Rollins, and Barbara Robinson.

Charles Montgomery, second son, born February 27, 1856; died June 25, 1861.

Frank West Rollins, third son, born February 24, 1860, married Katharine Wallace Pecker, of Concord, New Hampshire. They have one son, Douglas Rollins.

Montgomery Rollins, fourth son, born August 25, 1867, married Grace Webster Seavey, of Dover, New Hampshire. They have two children, Ellen West Rollins and Sarah Webster Rollins.

[1] Married William A. Foster, of Concord, New Hampshire. They have one child, Helen Foster.

517

OFFICERS OF THE REPUBLICAN AND DEMOCRATIC STATE COMMITTEES FROM 1856 TO 1905

An attempt has been made to compile a list of the principal officers of the Republican and Democratic State committees from 1856 to the present time. Unfortunately, the records of the committees for the greater part of this period cannot be found, and have probably been destroyed. The data has been obtained almost wholly from newspapers. While these contain full information of the membership of the committees as a part of the proceedings of State conventions, the organization of the committees and their election of officers for some reason was not always reported. Especially is this true of the organization of the Democratic State committee. Nearly all of the chairmen, secretaries, and treasurers of both committees for the first half of this period are dead. Inquiries of living contemporaries have given some information which it was possible to verify, but, in the main, there is only a vague tradition of the time when these men served who played so important a part in the strenuous campaigns of New Hampshire.

The list of officers of the Republican State committee is complete, unless the committee had a treasurer in the years 1856 and 1857, of which there is no record. The chairman may have acted as treasurer during these two campaigns, as the Republican party was then in its infancy. The list herewith given is, therefore, nearly or quite accurate.

Until early in the seventies there is no record in newspapers at the capital of the organization of the Democratic State committee. About the only information presented by these newspapers that bears upon this subject is what is contained in the proceedings of the State conventions. This body was almost invariably called to order by the chairman of the State committee. It is, therefore, a safe assumption to consider this individual as the chairman during the previous campaign. Occasionally a call for the various conventions is signed by the chairman and secretary of the Democratic State committee, but usually by the chairman alone. No record of the election of a treasurer of the Democratic State committee is found prior to 1876, though it is probable that John M. Hill held this position at a much earlier date. It is likely that Lewis W. Clark was secretary for more than one year, and may have held this position in 1859, when Joseph Robinson was chairman. Owing to the intimacy of John H. George, John M. Hill, and Lewis W. Clark, it is very probable that one of them was secretary when George was chairman. In the early years the chairman may have selected his own secretary without the formality of an election by the State committee. Francis B. Peabody, chairman in 1856, who is still living, is unable to recall after this lapse of time who served with him as secretary, and he is inclined to the opinion that John H. George selected some law student in his office to act in this capacity in the campaigns he conducted. It is regretted that the records are lacking to make this list as complete as that of the Republican State committee.

REPUBLICAN STATE COMMITTEE

1856
Edward H. Rollins, Concord, chairman.
Sylvester Dana, Concord, secretary.

1857
Edward H. Rollins, Concord, chairman.
Sylvester Dana, Concord, secretary.

1858
Edward H. Rollins, Concord, chairman.
William E. Chandler, Concord, secretary.
Frederick Smyth, Manchester, treasurer.

1859
Edward H. Rollins, Concord, chairman.
William E. Chandler, Concord, secretary.
Thomas L. Tullock, Portsmouth, treasurer.

1860
Edward H. Rollins, Concord, chairman.
Benjamin F. Prescott, Epping, secretary.
Thomas L. Tullock, Portsmouth, treasurer.

1861

Edward H. Rollins, Concord, chairman.
Benjamin F. Prescott, Epping, secretary.
Thomas L. Tullock, Portsmouth, treasurer.

1862

Anthony Colby, New London, chairman.
Benjamin F. Prescott, Epping, secretary.
Thomas L. Tullock, Portsmouth, treasurer.

1863

Nehemiah G. Ordway, Concord, chairman.
Benjamin F. Prescott, Epping, secretary.
Thomas L. Tullock, Portsmouth, treasurer.

1864

William E. Chandler, Concord, chairman.
Benjamin F. Prescott, Epping, secretary.
Thomas L. Tullock, Portsmouth, treasurer.

1865

William E. Chandler, Concord, chairman.
Benjamin F. Prescott, Epping, secretary.
John Kimball, Concord, treasurer.

1866

Austin F. Pike, Franklin, chairman.
Benjamin F. Prescott, Epping, secretary.
John Kimball, Concord, treasurer.

1867
Austin F. Pike, Franklin, chairman.
Benjamin Gerrish, Jr., Concord, secretary.
John Kimball, Concord, treasurer.

1868
Edward H. Rollins, Concord, chairman.
Benjamin Gerrish, Jr., Concord, secretary.
John Kimball, Concord, treasurer.

1869
Edward H. Rollins, Concord, chairman.
Wyman Pattee, Enfield, secretary.
John Kimball, Concord, treasurer.

1870
Edward H. Rollins, Concord, chairman.
Charles H. Roberts, Concord, secretary.
John Kimball, Concord, treasurer.

1871
Edward H. Rollins, Concord, chairman.
Benjamin F. Prescott, Epping, secretary.
John Kimball, Concord, treasurer.

1872 (Spring Campaign)
Edward H. Rollins, Concord, chairman.
Benjamin F. Prescott, Epping, secretary.
Asa Fowler, Concord, treasurer.

1872 (Fall Campaign)

Orrin C. Moore, Nashua, chairman.
Benjamin F. Prescott, Epping, secretary.
Asa Fowler, Concord, treasurer.

1873

Orrin C. Moore, Nashua, chairman.
Benjamin F. Prescott, Epping, secretary.
Carlos G. Pressey, Concord, treasurer.

1874

Daniel Hall, Dover, chairman.
Benjamin F. Prescott, Epping, secretary.
Charles H. Roberts, Concord, treasurer.

1875

Daniel Hall, Dover, chairman.
Benjamin F. Prescott, Epping, secretary.
John Kimball, Concord, treasurer.

1876

Daniel Hall, Dover, chairman.
Benjamin F. Prescott, Epping, secretary.
John Kimball, Concord, treasurer.

1877

Elijah M. Topliff, Manchester, chairman.
George E. Jenks, Concord, secretary.
John Kimball, Concord, treasurer.

1878 (Spring Campaign)

Eliijah M. Topliff, Manchester, chairman.
George E. Jenks, Concord, secretary.
John Kimball, Concord, treasurer.

1878 (Fall Campaign)

Henry H. Huse, Manchester, chairman.
George E. Jenks, Concord, secretary.
John Kimball, Concord, treasurer.

1880

Henry H. Huse, Manchester, chairman.
George E. Jenks, Concord, secretary.
John Kimball, Concord, treasurer.

1882

Jacob H. Gallinger, Concord, chairman.
Frank D. Currier, Canaan, secretary.
John Kimball, Concord, treasurer.

1884

Jacob H. Gallinger, Concord, chairman.
Frank D. Currier, Canaan, secretary.
John Kimball, Concord, treasurer.

1886

Jacob H. Gallinger, Concord, chairman.
Frank D. Currier, Canaan, secretary.
John Kimball, Concord, treasurer.

1888

Jacob H. Gallinger, Concord, chairman.
Frank D. Currier, Canaan, secretary.
John Kimball, Concord, treasurer.

1890

Frank C. Churchill, Lebanon, chairman.
Stephen S. Jewett, Laconia, secretary.
Edgar H. Woodman, Concord, treasurer.

1892

Stephen S. Jewett, Laconia, chairman.
William Tutherly, Concord, secretary.
William F. Thayer, Concord, treasurer.

1894

Stephen S. Jewett, Laconia, chairman.
William Tutherly, Concord, secretary.
William F. Thayer, Concord, treasurer.

1896

John A. Spalding, Nashua, chairman.
James O. Lyford, Concord, secretary.
William F. Thayer, Concord, treasurer.

1898

Jacob H. Gallinger, Concord, chairman.
Louis G. Hoyt, Kingston, secretary.
William F. Thayer, Concord, treasurer.

1900

Jacob H. Gallinger, Concord, chairman.
Thomas F. Clifford, Franklin, secretary.
William F. Thayer, Concord, treasurer.

1902

Jacob H. Gallinger, Concord, chairman.
Thomas F. Clifford, Franklin, secretary.
William F. Thayer, Concord, treasurer.

1904

Jacob H. Gallinger, Concord, chairman.
Thomas F. Clifford, Franklin, secretary.
William F. Thayer, Concord, treasurer.

DEMOCRATIC STATE COMMITTEE

1856 (Spring Campaign)

Francis B. Peabody, Concord, chairman.

1856 (Fall Campapign)

John H. George, Concord, chairman.

1857

John H. George, Concord, chairman.

1858

John M. Hill, Concord, chairman.
Lewis W. Clark, Manchester, secretary.

1859
Joseph Robinson, Concord, chairman.

1860
Josiah Minot, Concord, chairman.
John M. Hill, Concord, secretary.

1861
Josiah Minot, Concord, chairman.
John M. Hill, Concord, secretary.

1862
Aaron P. Hughes, Nashua, chairman.
John M. Hill, Concord, secretary.

1863
Josiah Minot, Concord, chairman.
John M. Hill, Concord, secretary.

1864
Lewis W. Clark, Manchester, chairman.
John M. Hill, Concord, secretary.

1865
Lewis W. Clark, Manchester, chairman.
John M. Hill, Concord, secretary.

1866
John M. Hill, Concord, chairman.

1867
John M. Hill, Concord, chairman.

1868
Anson S. Marshall, Concord, chairman.

1869
Samuel B. Page, Haverhill, chairman.
Henry H. Metcalf, Concord, secretary.

1870
Samuel B. Page, Haverhill, chairman.
Henry H. Metcalf, Concord, secretary.

1871
Lewis W. Clark, Manchester, chairman.
William M. Thayer, Portsmouth, secretary.

1872
John G. Sinclair, Littleton, chairman.
Henry H. Huse, Manchester, secretary.

1873
George F. Putnam, Haverhill, chairman.
Charles B. Griswold, Lebanon, secretary.

1874
George F. Putnam, Haverhill, chairman.
Charles B. Griswold, Lebanon, secretary.

1875

George F. Putnam, Haverhill, chairman.
Charles H. Smith, Newmarket, secretary.

1876

Isaac N. Blodgett, Franklin, chairman.
William Butterfield, Concord, secretary.
John M. Hill, Concord, treasurer.

1877

Isaac N. Blodgett, Franklin, chairman.
William Butterfield, Concord, secretary.
John M. Hill, Concord, treasurer.

1878 (Spring Campaign)

George F. Putnam, Haverhill, chairman.
Herbert F. Norris, Epping, secretary.
John M. Hill, Concord, treasurer.

1878 (Fall Campaign)

George F. Putnam, Haverhill, chairman.
Isaac N. Andrews, Nashua, secretary.
John M. Hill, Concord, treasurer.

1880

George F. Putnam, Haverhill, chairman.
Herbert F. Norris, Epping, secretary.
John M. Hill, Concord, treasurer.

1882

Charles F. Stone, Laconia, chairman.
Herbert F. Norris, Epping, secretary.
John M. Hill, Concord, treasurer.

1884

Charles F. Stone, Laconia, chairman.
Nathaniel E. Martin, Concord, secretary.
John M. Hill, Concord, treasurer.

1886

Charles F. Stone, Laconia, chairman.
Nathaniel E. Martin, Concord, secretary.
John M. Hill, Concord, treasurer.

1888

Charles F. Stone, Laconia, chairman.
Frank M. Rollins, Laconia, secretary.
John M. Hill, Concord, treasurer.

1890

John P. Bartlett, Manchester, chairman.
James R. Jackson, Littleton, secretary.
John M. Hill, Concord, treasurer.

1892

John P. Bartlett, Manchester, chairman.
James R. Jackson, Littleton, secretary.
John M. Hill, Concord, treasurer.

1894

John T. Amey, Lancaster, chairman.
Daniel M. White, Peterboro, secretary.
Howard F. Hill, Concord, treasurer.

1896

John T. Amey, Lancaster, chairman.
Daniel M. White, Peterboro, secretary.
Eliphalet S. Nutter, Concord, treasurer.

1898

John T. Amey, Lancaster, chairman.
Henry W. George, Barnstead, secretary.
John M. Mitchell, Concord, treasurer.

1900

John T. Amey, Lancaster, chairman.
Thomas H. Madigan, Jr., Concord, secretary.
William J. Ahern, Concord, treasurer.

1902

Nathaniel E. Martin, Concord, chairman.
Thomas H. Madigan, Jr., Concord, secretary.
John P. Goggin, Nashua, treasurer.

1904

Thomas Madigan, Jr., Concord, chairman.
John P. Bartlett, Manchester, secretary.
Franklin P. Kellom, Winchester, treasurer.

ADDENDA

On page 41, there should be added to list of residents of Ward 4, who have held State offices, Solon A. Carter, State Treasurer, and Irving A. Watson, Secretary of the State Board of Health.

On page 52, " John J. Prentiss of Keene " should read " John J. Prentiss of Claremont."

On page 182 " A. P. Stackpole " should read " P. A. Stackpole."

On page 373, " Edward K. Mann " should read " Edward F. Mann."

On page 407, " McMillan of Michigan " should read " McMillan of Minnesota."

On page 497, " Gilman Marston of Eeter " should read " Gilman Marston of Exeter."

INDEX

Lightning Source UK Ltd.
Milton Keynes UK
UKHW031204240620
365514UK00009B/1023